Dynamic Competition and Public Policy

Technology, Innovation, and Antitrust Issues

During the 1990s, U.S. antitrust policy began to take greater account of economic theories that emphasize the critical role of innovation and change in the competitive process. Several high-profile antitrust cases have focused on dynamic innovation issues as much as or more than static economic efficiency. But does dynamic competition furnish a new rationale for activist antitrust or a new reason for government to leave markets alone? In this volume, leading scholars with extensive antitrust experience explore this question in the context of the Microsoft case, merger policy, and intellectual property law.

Jerry Ellig is a senior research fellow at the Mercatus Center and the Institute for Humane Studies at George Mason University. He is also a research fellow at Citizens for a Sound Economy Foundation in Washington, DC. Dr. Ellig has previously served as senior economist for the Joint Economic Committee of the U.S. Congress, assistant professor of economics at George Mason University, and consultant to the President's Commission on Privatization. He has published numerous articles on government regulation of business and business management in books, academic journals, and the popular press. Dr. Ellig has also coauthored *Economic Deregulation and Customer Choice: Lessons for the Electric Industry, Municipal Entrepreneurship and Energy Policy*, and *Introduction to Market-Based Management*, and he coedited *New Horizons in Natural Gas Deregulation*.

Dynamic Competition and Public Policy

Technology, Innovation, and Antitrust Issues

Edited by

JERRY ELLIG

Mercatus Center
George Mason University

CAMBRIDGE
UNIVERSITY PRESS

CAMBRIDGE UNIVERSITY PRESS
Cambridge, New York, Melbourne, Madrid, Cape Town, Singapore, São Paulo

Cambridge University Press
The Edinburgh Building, Cambridge CB2 2RU, UK

Published in the United States of America by Cambridge University Press, New York

www.cambridge.org
Information on this title: www.cambridge.org/9780521782500

First published 2001
This digitally printed first paperback version 2005

A catalogue record for this publication is available from the British Library

Library of Congress Cataloguing in Publication data

Dynamic competition and public policy : technology, innovation, and antitrust issues /
edited by Jerry Ellig.
    p. cm.
A collection of papers by the editor and other researchers.
Includes bibliographical references.
ISBN 0-521-78250-3
1. Industrial policy – United States.   2. Antitrust law – United States.
3. Competition – Government policy – United States.   4. Restraint of trade –
Government policy – United States.   5. Technological innovations – Government
policy – United States.   6. Information technology – Government policy –
United States.   7. Computer software industry – Government policy – United States.
8. Microsoft Corporation.   I. Ellig, Jerome, 1962–

HD2795.D95   2001
338.973 – dc21   00-041419

ISBN-13 978-0-521-78250-0 hardback
ISBN-10 0-521-78250-3 hardback

ISBN-13 978-0-521-02181-4 paperback
ISBN-10 0-521-02181-2 paperback

Contents

v

Figures and Tables

Acknowledgments

In addition to the contributors who authored chapters, a number of other individuals played a key role in making this volume a reality. Authors received helpful feedback from the many individuals who commented on papers at the conference where they were first presented: Manus Cooney, Michael Etchison, Harold Furtchgott-Roth, Michael Klass, William Kovacic, Robert Raben, Erik Sirri, Greg Vistnes, and Greg Werden. Mike Etchison also deserves special thanks for asking some probing questions about practical applications of dynamic competition theories that eventually prompted us to explore the idea of holding the conference in the first place.

At the Mercatus Center, Tom Reardon and Rob McCutcheon did yeoman's work in organizing our first ever symposium held specifically for economists and attorneys in federal antitrust and economic regulatory agencies. LaTrease Williams stepped in at the last minute to provide the extra help we needed to make the conference work. Graham Barron provided some last-minute editorial assistance in preparing the manuscript for publication, and Chris Grengs, Kirstin Lindsey, Colleen Morretta, and Felipe Ward rectified some significant eleventh-hour problems.

Thanks also go to the Mercatus Center and the James Buchanan Center at George Mason University for financial support. I am especially indebted to the president of the Institute for Humane Studies, David Nott, for understanding and supporting this project at a time when it was still vaguely formed in my own mind.

Contributors

Jay B. Barney is a professor and Bank One Chair of Strategy at the Fisher College of Business at Ohio State University.

Michelle M. Burtis is a director at LECG, Inc., an international economic and financial consulting firm.

Jerry Ellig is a senior research fellow at the Mercatus Center and Institute for Humane Studies at George Mason University. He is also a research fellow at Citizens for a Sound Economy Foundation in Washington, DC.

Franklin M. Fisher, the author of fifteen books and well over one hundred articles, is the Jane Berkowitz Carlton and Dennis Carlton Professor of Economics at MIT, where he has taught for forty years. He has had an extensive career as an expert witness in antitrust cases, most notably as the chief economics witness for IBM in its long-lasting antitrust case of the 1970s and for the Antitrust Division in the recent Microsoft case.

John Hoven is an economist in the Antitrust Division of the U.S. Department of Justice. He has worked on several recent investigations where innovation issues were prominent, including the merger of Halliburton Company and Dresser Industries, Inc., and the proposed merger of Lockheed Martin and Northrop Grumman.

Bruce H. Kobayashi is an associate professor of law at the George Mason University School of Law.

Richard N. Langlois is a professor of economics at the University of Connecticut.

Stan Liebowitz is associate dean and professor of managerial economics in the School of Business at the University of Texas at Dallas.

Daniel Lin is a research associate at the Mercatus Center at George Mason University.

Stephen E. Margolis is professor of economics and head of the Department of Economics at North Carolina State University.

Christopher Pleatsikas is a principal at LECG, Inc., an international economic and financial consulting firm. He serves as an expert witness and expert consultant in antitrust and intellectual property litigation.

Daniel L. Rubinfeld is Robert L. Bridges Professor of Law and Professor of Economics at the University of California at Berkeley. He recently completed a term as deputy assistant attorney general in the Antitrust Division of the U.S. Department of Justice. He has received fellowships from the National Bureau of Economic Research, the Center for Advanced Studies in the Behavioral Sciences, and the John M. Guggenheim Foundation.

David Teece is a founder and director of LECG, Inc., an international economic and financial consulting firm. He is Mitsubishi Bank Professor at the Haas School of Business and director of the Institute of Management, Innovation and Organization at the University of California at Berkeley.

Introduction

When sweeping economic change occurs, new technologies and business methods rapidly replace old ones. Previously unheard-of firms dominate their markets by successfully pioneering new ways of doing things. But a dominant firm also raises fears of monopoly. At what point does a successful competitor cross the line separating proconsumer innovation from anticonsumer monopolization?

During the past decade, scholars and government officials have asked that question more frequently as a "postindustrial" revolution, fueled by information technology and globalization, produces new winners and losers. Conceptually, the answer is simple and stated succinctly in U.S. antitrust law. A firm is engaged in monopolization if it employs "exclusionary" practices, but not if it dominates its market due to "superior skill, foresight, and industry," or "as a consequence of a superior product, business acumen, or historical accident" (*United States v. Alcoa, United States v. Grinnell*). Congressional debate surrounding the Sherman Act reveals that the legislation's sponsors never intended antitrust enforcement to apply to a company that "merely by superior skill and intelligence get the whole business because nobody could do it as well" (*Congressional Record* 1890: 3146–52). This kind of distinction attempts to categorize firms with market power into those which succeed by harming consumers, and those which acquire their market power innocently through superior service to consumers or perhaps dumb luck. Surely, one would think, a highly innovative firm belongs in the second category.

ANALYSIS IN A DYNAMIC ECONOMY

In actual cases, it is much harder to categorize firms. Does Microsoft help or harm consumers when it combines a computer operating system and an Internet browser that were formerly separate products? Does Intel promote or stunt innovation by withholding advance product

1

information from firms with which it has intellectual property disputes? When banks join both the Visa and Mastercard systems, are they expanding competition by offering multiple credit cards or stifling competition by allowing the same member companies to control both card networks? When Pfizer charges a premium price for Viagra, is it exploiting monopoly power or reaping a well-deserved reward on a risky investment in intellectual property?

Market Power

If a firm lacks market power and has no prospect of obtaining it, then its conduct is of little antitrust concern. Competition from numerous other substitutes ensures that seemingly "exclusionary" practices survive only if they allow the firm to produce greater value or reduce costs. Value-destroying business practices are self-penalizing, because they harm the firm's bottom line as well as harming consumers.

But how do we know whether a firm in an innovative industry faces competition? In textbook economic theory, numerous competitors with access to the same technology and resources compete on price. In a growing number of real industries, competitors with different technologies and resources compete on the basis of product attributes and performance as well as price. Indeed, product performance may be much more important to many customers than price. In the medical marketplace, for example, the prices of human, animal, and man-made replacements for arteries and veins are much less important than the performance of the material in a specific application (Pleatsikas and Teece, Chapter 4, in this volume). Declaring that a firm has market power if it can sustain a "significant but nontransitory price increase" completely misses the performance dimension of competition.

Potential competition can curb market power, but its impact is also more difficult to assess in a dynamic economy. Contestable market theory demonstrates that potential entrants can make even a monopolist behave as if it faces competition – as long as entrants have access to the same technology and there are no barriers to entry in the form of sunk costs (Baumol, Panzar, and Willig 1982). However, dynamism changes the nature of potential competition.[1] Intellectual property laws,

---

[1] As two of the developers of contestable market theory (Baumol and Ordover 1992: 85) note, "By entailing the complete absence of barriers to entry, perfect contestability, again like perfect competition, threatens to rule out entirely the reward mechanism that elicits the Schumpeterian innovative process. This mechanism, as we have seen, rests on the innovator's supernormal profits, which are permitted by the temporary possession of monopoly power flowing from priority in innovation. Since perfect contestability rules out all market power ... the market mechanism's main reward for innovation is destroyed by that market form."

trade secrets, and tacit knowledge all combine to make it difficult for potential entrants to possess the same technology as the incumbent. Developing capabilities equivalent to the incumbent's may involve substantial sunk costs. These factors suggest that potential competition may operate less effectively in a dynamic economy.

At the same time, potential competition could be a much more vigorous force in a dynamic economy. Contestable market theory postulates a world in which technology and resources are fixed and given, not a world in which technology continually changes and new resources can be discovered. When innovation and discovery are possible, potential entrants can leapfrog an incumbent by offering superior products and services. Sunk costs depreciate more rapidly – and more unpredictably – because of ceaseless change. Potential competition, in the form of Schumpeterian "creative destruction," could be much more vigorous in spite of sunk costs.

How these two opposing effects net out can vary from case to case. But even this brief discussion illustrates how a seemingly simple task like identifying market power becomes much more complicated in a rapidly advancing economy.

Exclusionary Practices

Thirty years ago, Ronald Coase (1972: 67) complained that "if an economist finds something – a business practice of one sort or another – that he does not understand, he looks for a monopoly explanation." Since then, the economics profession has come a long way in improving its understanding of restrictive business practices. Nevertheless, courts still sometimes condemn as exclusionary dominant-firm business practices that are later revealed to be efficient. A principal reason is that competition and exclusionary conduct can be hard to distinguish:

Aggressive, competitive conduct by a monopolist is highly beneficial to consumers. Courts should prize and encourage it under the antitrust laws. Aggressive, exclusionary conduct by a monopolist is deleterious to consumers. Courts should condemn it under the antitrust laws. There is only one problem. Competitive and exclusionary conduct look alike. The dominant firm is an aggressor and expands its market share at the expense of its smaller rival. The rival yelps and sues. (Easterbrook 1986: 982)

Dynamism makes the analysis of exclusionary practices even more complicated. When an exclusionary practice creates both consumer benefits and consumer harms, the benefits should be weighed against the harms to determine whether the firm is engaged in monopolization. The logic of this tradeoff was rigorously expounded by Williamson (1968) and subsequently incorporated into the U.S. government's *Horizontal Merger*

Guidelines (United States 1997, sec. 4). The most common application occurs when a merger creates market power but also produces economies of scale or scope. The merger is economically efficient if the cost savings outweigh the loss to consumers created by the market power. Similar logic can be applied to various types of exclusionary business practices.

There is, however, a critical difference between the nature of such tradeoffs in a dynamic and a static world. The classic tradeoff analysis assesses the effect of corporate conduct *given* the products, sources of supply, production technologies, marketing practices, and management methods that are currently possible. But innovative competition by its very nature involves a continuous stream of new products, sources of supply, production technologies, marketing practices, and management methods. The critical antitrust issue is not just whether a particular exclusionary practice produces some identifiable consumer benefit in the present, but also how that practice will affect the path of innovation in the future. Firm strategies and public policies determine which companies will have superior incentives to produce which types of innovations.

The Microsoft case provides a good example. Standard tradeoff analysis proceeds something like this. If Microsoft is permitted to integrate its Internet browser with the Windows operating system, there might be harms to competition as well as benefits to consumers. Microsoft could acquire market power in the browser market, but it could also offer consumers a superior product at a lower price. Integration should be prohibited if the harms associated with the extension of market power exceed the consumer benefits of integration. Integration should be permitted if the consumer benefits of integration outweigh the harms.

Dynamic analysis suggests a different set of cost and benefits, based on different paths that innovation might take. If Microsoft is permitted to integrate the browser with Windows, it has greater incentives to proceed with similar types of innovations in the future. Such integration may reinforce the position of Windows as the dominant computer operating system, and so firms that want to compete with Microsoft might have to develop an operating system that can displace Windows. If Microsoft is not permitted to integrate the browser with Windows, then browsers and other software applications will compete as freestanding products. Microsoft's competitors will have much stronger incentives to develop software applications on the Windows platform.[2]

---

[2] For an argument that focuses on the importance of multiple sources of innovation in the context of intellectual property, see Merges and Nelson (1992).

Clearly, the direction of innovation is different under the two scenarios. The first scenario is more likely to produce competition among operating systems and suites of associated applications, whereas the second creates more competition among individual software applications within the Windows standard. Simply stating the tradeoff reveals the difficulty of determining the efficient answer. The answer requires not just an evaluation of the immediate consequences of Microsoft's business practices but also accurate predictions of alternative futures.

A rule-based approach lessens the burden on courts in individual cases. Perhaps the court need not assess whether consumers will be better off if Microsoft or its competitors receive superior incentives to innovate. All that is necessary is a more general understanding of typical results in cases of this type. If market dominance fostered by product bundling tends to produce superior innovations, then Microsoft should be left alone. If superior innovations come from markets where there is more competition in the production of individual components, then Microsoft should be prosecuted. Or perhaps bundled systems and unbundled, more open systems each tend to produce better results under different, objectively identifiable circumstances.

Although such an approach makes court decisions easier, it offers no shortcuts for academic researchers. If courts are to develop general rules, how are they to know which rules tend to produce the best results, if not by accessing research on past situations where different approaches were tried?

In a dynamic economy, antitrust policy implicitly involves a choice among alternative innovative paths. Implicitly or explicitly, enforcers are betting that their intervention will give consumers a better stream of price, product, and service improvements in the future.

RESEARCH ON DYNAMIC COMPETITION

To understand competition and monopolization in this environment, we need additional theoretical tools and empirical research. Fortunately, multiple and eclectic groups of scholars in economics and business strategy are now developing theories of competition that place innovation and change at the heart of the competitive process.[3] This volume brings together a heterogeneous group of dynamic approaches and associated implications for antitrust and regulatory policy.

---

[3] In addition to Chapter 1 of this book, extensive discussions of dynamic competition theories, along with extensive lists of references, can be found in Hunt (2000) and Machovec (1995).

The first chapter, by Jerry Ellig and Daniel Lin, sets the stage by outlining different theories of dynamic competition. It describes four key aspects of each theory: the theory's assumptions, the fundamental nature of competition, indicators of competition, and policy implications. Principal strands of dynamic competition scholarship include:

- Schumpeterian. Firms compete not on the margins of price and output, but by offering new products, new technologies, new sources of supply, and new forms of organization. Possession of market power is consistent with vigorous competition, and many seemingly anticompetitive practices actually facilitate innovation.
- Evolutionary. Firms develop different "routines" for doing things, and competition among firms selects for survival the bundles of routines that best allow the firm to grow and prosper in its environment. Policy interventions should focus on improving the ability of the competitive process to produce and reward innovation, rather than penalizing seemingly anticompetitive market structures.
- Austrian. The future is unknowable, information about production methods and consumer desires is seriously incomplete, and much economically relevant knowledge is highly specific and difficult to communicate. In this kind of world, competition is a process by which firms discover new resources and better ways of satisfying consumers. Especially alert innovators may acquire market power, but the resulting profits are a reward for discovering things that would otherwise go undiscovered.
- Path dependence. Increasing returns and network effects magnify the results of small, seemingly unimportant events that give one competitor an advantage over others. "Winner take all" competition can produce monopoly. Consumers could get "locked in" to a product or technology that turns out to be inferior in the long run, or a market with "insufficient friction" could generate costly and suboptimal changes among technologies.
- Resource-based. Firms compete by assembling heterogeneous combinations of resources to meet consumer desires. Key determinants of a firm's competitiveness are its capabilities to transform resources into valuable outputs. Capabilities that are rare and difficult to imitate lead to superior profitability. Empirical research suggests that firms' unique capabilities, rather than market power, account for most of the supranormal profits that firms earn.

There is, of course, considerable overlap among the dynamic literatures. For example, most dynamic theories include some notion of path dependence, but not all reach the same conclusions about market efficiency as does "the" path dependence theory. Similarly, Schumpeterian

Table I.1. Dynamic Theories Employed in Subsequent Chapters

Chapter	Author(s)	Dynamic Theory(ies)
2	Jay Barney	Resource-based
3	Daniel Rubinfeld and John Hoven	Schumpeterian, path dependence, resource-based, evolutionary
4	Chris Pleatsikas and David Teece	Schumpeterian, resource-based
5	Franklin Fisher	Path dependence
6	Stan Liebowitz and Stephen Margolis	Path dependence, Austrian, Schumpeterian
7	Richard Langlois	Evolutionary, path dependence
8	Michele Burtis and Bruce Kobayashi	Schumpeterian, Austrian

themes can be found also in evolutionary and Austrian competition theories. Resource-based theory can be viewed as the application of Schumpeterian, evolutionary, and Austrian insights to strategic management, just as Porter's (1985) work developed management strategy implications from structure-conduct-performance microeconomics. Perhaps the greatest similarity shared by all of the theories is their focus on innovation, broadly defined, as a key component of the competitive process.

Contributors to this volume were invited to write chapters that reflected one or more of these dynamic approaches. Table I.1 illustrates the principal dynamic approaches illustrated in each chapter.

Chapter 2, by Jay Barney, provides a more detailed exposition of strategic management theories that offer unconventional insights on competition issues. Mainstream research in strategic management views corporate capabilities as a principal source of economic profit. Successful firms possess capabilities to use their resources to create value for customers. Different firms possess different packages of tangible and intangible assets, and many of these assets (particularly intangible ones) are difficult to imitate or transfer across firms. As a result, even firms with access to the same physical resources may have large differences in marketplace success. Although capabilities theory was largely developed to aid strategic management, Barney suggests a number of policy implications:

- A seemingly competitive product market may in fact be hampered by firms' anticompetitive activities not just in physical resource markets but also in markets where firms acquire intangible capabilities. Conversely, a highly competitive market for intangible capabilities can significantly constrain anticompetitive activity in product markets.

- Mergers can create significant value by bringing together complementary corporate capabilities that are difficult to duplicate or sell across firms. Such intangibles are harder to document than traditional economies of scale and scope, but they are no less real, and so policy makers ignore them at their peril.
- A firm's resources and capabilities are often path dependent, causally ambiguous, and socially complex. In such situations, patent protection is likely to be superfluous, because the firm's profits are already protected by advantages that are difficult or impossible for rivals to imitate. Patents take on greater importance in industries like chemicals and pharmaceuticals, where innovation stems from objectively observable changes in chemical formulas.
- When new competitors enter an industry where entry was previously barred, they will have advantages over the incumbent firms if the incumbents did not themselves compete, but will likely suffer disadvantages if competition within the regulated industry was already vigorous.

Both the economic and the management theories have influenced the way economists think about antitrust enforcement at the U.S. Department of Justice (DoJ). In Chapter 3, Daniel Rubinfeld and John Hoven offer insider accounts of the rationales behind several recent and prominent antitrust cases. Schumpeterian and evolutionary competition, network effects, and heterogeneous corporate capabilities have all played a role in the department's approach:

- DoJ filed a complaint against Visa and Mastercard, because the two credit card systems are owned by substantially the same banks. This common ownership is alleged to diminish either network's incentives to introduce innovations, and DoJ maintains that entry by new competitors is extremely costly due to network effects.
- Conditions attached to the Halliburton-Dresser merger reflected the department's conclusion that difficult-to-duplicate know-how is a significant barrier that prevents new competitors from developing cutting-edge innovations in certain types of oil drilling tools. Thus, heterogeneous capabilities can become barriers to entry.
- The *Microsoft* case is heavily influenced by the theory of network effects, along with concerns that suppression of competing Internet browsers will suppress innovation that could lead to the development of different and better software. This latter factor reflects an

evolutionary focus on maintaining multiple sources of variation and innovation.

- The federal challenge to the Lockheed-Northup merger was based on a large number of concerns rooted in theories of corporate capabilities, including the importance of difficult-to-duplicate capabilities, the value of information interchange among diverse firms, and the contribution that firm diversity and outside challengers make when the path of innovation is difficult to predict.

Of course, as several subsequent chapters dealing with the *Microsoft* case demonstrate, reasonable people employing dynamic reasoning could also conclude that federal antitrust action is unwarranted in some or all of these cases. Nevertheless, Rubinfeld and Hoven's chapter illustrates how the world's leading antitrust enforcement agency has grappled with the economics of innovation.

How will policy makers know dynamic competition when they see it? Chris Pleatsikas and David Teece take up this foundational issue in Chapter 4. In their view, the type of analysis presented in the Department of Justice *Horizontal Merger Guidelines* and courtroom antitrust practices systematically overestimates the threat of market power in high-technology industries. In such industries, much competition takes place along nonprice dimensions, and new breakthroughs continually threaten the position of dominant firms. Static analysis that focuses on market-share measures and the effects of price changes over one or two years overstates the danger of monopoly because it defines markets too narrowly and tends to find market power where none exists.

Pleatsikas and Teece offer several insights that could improve the way enforcement officials define markets and test for the existence of market power:

- If related technologies that could be used in similar applications are advancing, the market is broad and competition is vigorous.
- Examining customer perceptions of and responses to product innovation may aid in defining the relevant market.
- Repeated changes in market share are a good sign that a market is competitive, and such shifts should be examined over a period of four to five years to take product life cycles into account.
- A high level of innovation, perhaps measured as a high ratio of research and development (R&D) spending to sales, is a good sign that a market is competitive, because it shows that firms are competing on performance.

- Even if a firm earns high profits on some products, it lacks market power if it is earning a competitive rate of return on its entire R&D portfolio.

The leveraging of monopoly is a perennial hotbed of contention, and dynamic concerns introduce new wrinkles. In Chapter 5, Franklin Fisher examines how innovation affects monopoly leveraging, and how monopoly leveraging affects innovation. A firm with monopoly power may seek to bundle another product with a monopolized product for three reasons: to increase the monopoly rents from the monopolized product, to extend monopoly power into a second market, or to shut off avenues for innovation that may threaten the original monopoly. The last two explanations are most relevant to the three cases Fisher analyzes: airline computerized reservation systems, the *IBM* case, and the *Microsoft* case.

- In the airline industry, American and United developed computerized reservation systems for use by travel agents. Several other airlines followed suit, but most did not develop their own systems. Until regulators outlawed the practice, the displays on these systems were biased so that agents were more prone to select flights offered by the airlines owning the systems. Hence, Fisher argues, the airlines used their market power in reservation systems to create opportunities to charge higher prices in the market for airplane tickets.
- The *IBM* case was alleged to involve extension of IBM's monopoly power into new markets, but the facts of the case show that IBM lacked market power to begin with. IBM faced competition from other firms offering their own bundles of products and services, as well as firms offering stand-alone products and services. With no monopoly to exploit or defend, IBM's bundling could not constrain competition. Customers would only buy its bundles if they offered a better value than competitive alternatives.
- Microsoft, on the other hand, possesses market power in computer operating systems due to economies of scale and network effects in the software market. Most of the costs of writing software are fixed. There is also a tendency for one operating system to dominate the market, because most buyers want to use the system for which the most software applications are available. In Fisher's view, Microsoft's bundling of its Internet browser with the Windows operating system is a predatory attempt to protect its operating system monopoly. Competitors' Internet browsers could undermine this monopoly because the availability of Internet-based computing applications would eliminate the network effects that have made Windows the dominant operating system.

Even if alleged leveraging strategies of the airlines and Microsoft create monopoly power, they might ultimately benefit consumers if the resulting profits serve as a reward that spurs greater innovation. This is the nature of the Schumpeterian tradeoff; a greater degree of monopoly power may be worth tolerating if it generates greater cost reductions or a larger stream of new products and services. Fisher considers this trade-off but believes that it is not sufficient to spare these firms from antitrust prosecution, because their leveraging actions were accompanied by additional alleged anticompetitive initiatives. For example, in the currently most controversial case – *Microsoft* – he argues that product bundling was accompanied by the predatory act of pricing the browser below cost (and in some cases even paying customers to adopt it). He suggests that a less restrictive means of making the bundle available would have been for Microsoft to offer Windows and the browser separately or bundled, with the stand-alone browser sold at a positive price. If the bundle really is more valuable to customers, then they would voluntarily choose it.

Stan Liebowitz and Stephen Margolis offer a different perspective on the *Microsoft* case in their empirical examination of network effects in Chapter 6. Network effects occur when a particular product or service becomes more attractive to consumers if more people are already using it. Some network effect theories predict that consumers will be locked into using inferior products as a result of small, even random, events that give one product a larger market share in the early stages of competition between different versions of substitutable products.

This theory has frequently been discussed in the context of the *Microsoft* case, because many observers have suggested that network effects in computer software give rise to path dependence and lock-in. Liebowitz and Margolis's research, however, suggests that such broad claims are mistaken. Data on product quality (as measured by product reviews) and market share show that the software companies offering the best products consistently earn large market shares – even at the expense of an established firm that already dominates the market. Moreover, Microsoft's dominance of various software markets has often been accompanied by price reductions, whereas network effects theory predicts that such dominance should lead to price increases as growth in the user base raises the value of the software to individual customers. Liebowitz and Margolis conclude that Microsoft achieved its market position by offering superior products at attractive prices.

Their analysis does suggest that software markets are often "winner-take-all"; the leading firm captures most of the market share. However, network effects do not seem to pose a significant barrier to entry. There is no inefficient lock-in. A firm offering an identifiably better product quickly captures market share from the previous leader.

These findings could be read to imply that software markets are highly contestable, and any market power is short-lived. But Liebowitz and Margolis tell a richer empirical story than that. Recall that the introduction of new and improved products is a form of dynamic efficiency that contestable market theory does not predict, because the theory assumes that all firms have access to the same capabilities and technology (Baumol and Ordover 1992). When Microsoft offered a better spreadsheet than Lotus 1-2-3, and when Quicken offered better personal finance software than Microsoft, they were engaged in prototypical acts of entrepreneurship that both Joseph Schumpeter (1942) and Israel Kirzner (1973, 1997) would recognize as the essence of the competitive process. Viewed in this light, the Liebowitz and Margolis research illustrates how alert and creative entrepreneurs can overcome lock-in problems by offering products sufficiently better to make switching worthwhile.

Richard Langlois joins the network effects discussion in Chapter 7. Langlois suggests that technological standards and specifications can be analogous to essential facilities, like the only bridge over a river or the only pipeline leading to a particular location. Not all standards have this characteristic, but if one standard dominates due to network effects, the owner of the standard can find itself a monopolist. By this reasoning, a company like Microsoft or Intel could have an obligation to make standards for its software or hardware available to competitors who want to design complementary products.

Although Langlois suggests applying something like antitrust's "essential facilities" doctrine to technological standards, his reasoning is somewhat different from the reasoning that justifies application of this doctrine to bridges or utility wires. The essential facilities doctrine traditionally sought to prevent the static exercise of market power by forcing the owner of the facility to offer nondiscriminatory access at a reasonable charge. Langlois is concerned not with monopoly pricing but with other, dynamic problems inherent in technological standards.

Whoever controls the standard has the ability to foreclose future avenues of innovation proposed by producers of complementary products by controlling access to the standard. This creates problems in a dynamically competitive market because firms possess heterogeneous knowledge and visions of future innovative possibilities. When multiple competitors have access to the information underlying a standard, then multiple knowledge sets and innovative visions can build on the same platform. A standard owner who denies access to others implicitly ensures that only his set of knowledge and vision of the future will be tried. For this reason, antitrust or regulation might enhance economic welfare by compelling access to the standard, even if the price of such access remains unregulated.

When should government compel access to technological standards? Langlois suggests that the decision should depend on the extent of the system the standard affects. The more components of a system the standard affects, the greater is the potential for the owner to close off others' innovation. Therefore, standards with a broader scope provide a potentially greater justification for government intervention.

A final discussion of dynamic competition and software markets occurs in Chapter 8. Michelle Burtis and Bruce Kobayashi take up time-tested Schumpeterian and Austrian themes in analyzing the role of copyrights and contracts in the protection of intellectual property. Different constraints impair enforcement of contracts for intellectual property, including uncertainty surrounding the intellectual property laws themselves, general contract principles, and antitrust laws. Advocates of restrictions on freedom of contract argue that existing law embodies an optimal tradeoff between providing incentives for creation of intellectual property and securing the benefits of widespread use. Burtis and Kobayashi challenge this notion by distinguishing between the economic effects of copyright and contract.

Copyright laws generate incentives for the creation of new software by penalizing imitators, but they also raise the cost of creating original software by reducing the stock of ideas in the public domain on which original software developers can draw. Contracts, on the other hand, typically prevent imitators from copying software without constraining original creation. The analysis presented by Burtis and Kobayashi suggests that economic welfare is maximized when a moderate degree of copyright protection is combined with the opportunity to write strong contracts. Contracting allows software developers to protect themselves against copying without raising the cost of developing new software.

Contracting is especially important in a world where lawmakers lack detailed knowledge of circumstances faced by different software developers in different markets. Unlike legislation, contracts can adjust in case-by-case fashion to knowledge of "specific circumstances of time and place," which Hayek (1945) emphasized was so important to making sound economic decisions.

These conclusions, Burtis and Kobayashi argue, are at odds with a great deal of current policy and legal doctrine, under which contracts protecting intellectual property are often ruled invalid because they are viewed as an attempt to gain more protection than the law allows. The received view holds that copyright laws already reflect an optimal trade-off between incentives for creation and the benefits of use. The law itself already provides adequate incentive for the efficient level of innovation. From this perspective, contracts that further limit a licensee's use of copyrighted material are akin to attempts to extend a monopoly. Burtis and Kobayashi charge that enforcement actions often ignore the potential for free riding on intellectual property entirely, simply assuming that the property at issue would have come into existence even if antitrust enforcement seriously attenuated the incentives for its creation.

Perhaps most novel, however, is the application of their reasoning to the federal government's complaints against Microsoft. They view the government's 1994 complaint against Microsoft's contractual provisions with licensees as a threat to incentives for innovation. More intriguing is their analysis of the current antitrust suit. The current case involves a claim that Microsoft practiced predation against Netscape's Internet browser in order to spread a version of the Java programming platform that could not function without Microsoft's operating system. By spreading a Microsoft-dependent version of Java, the company allegedly attempted to prevent "pure" Java from turning into a rival for Microsoft's operating system. Sun Microsystems, Java's inventor, claims that Microsoft's version of Java violated its licensing agreement with Sun. If contractual restrictions on intellectual property were defended more vigorously, this licensing agreement may have been sufficient to prevent any alleged predatory behavior by Microsoft.

These chapters represent a variety of different approaches to dynamic competition, but all demonstrate a similar point: if policy makers want to take innovation, creativity, and change seriously, they need new analytical approaches that treat these phenomena as the main act rather than a sideshow.[4] This book offers a step in that direction.

---

[4] Most of these chapters were originally written for a two-day symposium on Dynamic Competition and Public Policy, sponsored by George Mason University's Mercatus Center and James Buchanan Center for Political Economy. The symposium was held on December 16 and 17, 1998. All but two of the chapters were the subject of a round table discussion by scholars and antitrust and regulatory officials. The survey chapter on dynamic competition was not discussed because of its focus on metatheory rather than specific policy applications. Franklin Fisher's chapter on leveraging was originally on the program but was not discussed due to his involvement as the Department of Justice's economist witness in the Microsoft trial, which was ongoing at the time of the conference.

The interpretation of individual chapters as exemplars of specific theories of dynamic competition represents the judgment of the editor of this volume; individual authors may or may not agree with the way their chapters have been classified in this introduction.

REFERENCES

Baumol, William J., and Janusz A. Ordover. 1992. Antitrust: Source of Dynamic and Static Inefficiencies? In Thomas M. Jorde and David J. Teece, eds., *Antitrust, Innovation, and Competitiveness*, 82–97. New York: Oxford University Press.

Baumol, William J., John Panzar, and Robert Willig. 1982. *Contestable Markets and the Theory of Industry Structure.* New York: Harcourt Brace Jovanovich.

Coase, Ronald H. 1972. Industrial Organization: A Proposal for Research. In V. R. Fuchs, ed., *Policy Issues and Research Opportunities in Industrial Organization*, 59–73. New York: National Bureau of Economic Research.

Congressional Record. 1890. Vol. 21.

Easterbrook, Frank H. 1986. On Identifying Exclusionary Conduct. *Notre Dame Law Review* 61: 972–80.

Hayek, Friedrich A. 1945. The Use of Knowledge in Society. *American Economic Review* 35: 519–30.

Hunt, Shelby. 2000. *A General Theory of Competition.* New York: Sage.

Kirzner, Israel M. 1973. *Competition and Entrepreneurship.* Chicago: University of Chicago Press.

  1997. Entrepreneurial Discovery and the Competitive Market Process: An Austrian Approach. *Journal of Economic Literature* 35: 65–80.

Machovec, Frank M. 1995. *Perfect Competition and the Transformation of Economics.* London: Routledge.

Merges, Robert P., and Richard R. Nelson. 1992. Market Structure and Technical Advance: The Role of Patent Scope Decisions. In Thomas M. Jorde and David J. Teece, eds., *Antitrust, Innovation, and Competitiveness*, 185–232. New York: Oxford University Press.

Porter, Michael. 1985. *Competitive Advantage.* New York: Free Press.

Schumpeter, Joseph. 1942. *Capitalism, Socialism, and Democracy.* New York: Harper & Row.

United States, Department of Justice and Federal Trade Commission. 1997. *Horizontal Merger Guidelines.* Revised April 8. Washington, DC.

United States v. Aluminum Company of America, 148 F.2d 416 (2nd Cir. 1945).

United States v. Grinnell Corp., 384 U.S. 563 (1966).

Williamson, Oliver. 1968. Economies as an Antitrust Defense: The Welfare Tradeoffs. *American Economic Review* 58: 18–36.

1

A Taxonomy of Dynamic Competition Theories

Jerry Ellig and Daniel Lin

Exactly what *is* dynamic competition, anyway?

Scholars offer a number of answers to that question, and there is no consensus on which theory of dynamic competition is the most accurate or useful. To underscore the diverse intellectual currents that flow through this volume, our initial chapter offers short synopses of the principal dynamic theories of competition.

By far the most prominent dynamic theory of competition is associated with Joseph Schumpeter. Although Schumpeter did not deny that real-world markets can resemble the perfectly competitive model, he argued that the most significant advances in human well-being come from forms of competition that involve new products, new technologies, new sources of supply, and new forms of business organization.

In addition to Schumpeter, other scholars have also developed dynamic theories of competition. "Evolutionary" competition theorists are perhaps Schumpeter's best-known modern descendants. Some of Schumpeter's fellow Austrian economists developed complementary theories that emphasize competition as a process for the discovery of new knowledge.[1] More recently, the interaction of competition and technological change has prompted interest in theories of path dependence, in which small variations in initial conditions can lead to large and unpre-

---

[1] Although Schumpeter was born in Austria and studied under prominent Austrian economists, he is not always considered an economist from the "Austrian" school of thought. Instead, his theories reflect many influences. With the Austrians, he shares an interest in the role of the entrepreneur and in dynamic qualities of competition. However, he parts with them by accepting the usefulness of general equilibrium analysis and by emphasizing disequilibrating change. As an indication of Schumpeter's modern-day influence, two schools of thought – evolutionary economists and a subset of neoclassicals – both describe themselves as "Neo-Schumpeterians" for their emphasis on innovation in competition. For the evolutionary perspective, see Nelson and Winter (1982a). For the neoclassical perspective, see Futia (1980), Dasgupta and Stiglitz (1980), and Loury (1979).

dictable changes in the market's evolution. Finally – and less well known in the economics profession – are strategic management theories that explicitly view competition as a dynamic process.

SCHUMPETERIAN COMPETITION

The fundamental neoclassical economic problem is the allocation of scarce resources among unlimited desires. Consumers maximize utility, constrained by their budgets and preferences. Firms maximize profit, constrained by production technologies. After all maximizing calculations are made, no one can be better off without making someone else worse off, so no further exchanges are made – the economy has settled into a general equilibrium.

Schumpeter focused on changes that upset an existing equilibrium, because he believed capitalist economies were rife with such shocks. He argued that allocation in static environments was an unimportant phenomenon compared with the enormous innovations that capitalist economies produced.

Assumptions

In order to analyze significant change, Schumpeter made the following assumptions:

- Initially, a general equilibrium. The plans of all households and firms start out in sync. All markets have cleared, all demands are satisfied at equilibrium prices, and there is no incentive for any individual to alter his behavior. Without any exogenous disturbance, the economy continues this circular flow with the same prices, quantities, qualities, resources, and knowledge (Schumpeter 1939: 41–43).
- Endogenous creation of innovations. Innovation is created within the system by individual entrepreneurs or firms' R&D departments (Schumpeter 1908).
- Innovation is disequilibrating. Innovation jars the economy out of its equilibrium. Quick implementers earn greater profits than reluctant firms. The actions that yielded the old equilibrium will not yield equilibrium in this new environment (Schumpeter 1942: 131–32).
- Imitation is equilibrating. When an economy is bombarded with innovation, the result is not chaos. Instead, firms see that certain innovations lead to superior performance, so they incorporate them into their "familiar practices" (Schumpeter 1939: 47). As more firms copy an innovation, its attendant supranormal profits fall. Eventually, all supranormal profits are competed away, and the economy settles into a new equilibrium.

The Nature of Competition

Schumpeterian competition is primarily about active, risk-taking decision makers who seek to change their parameters (Schumpeter 1942: ch. 7). Schumpeterian competition can attack on many fronts. Businesses face "competition from the new commodity, the new technology, the new source of supply, the new type of organization – competition which commands a decisive cost or quality advantage and which strikes not at the margins of the profits and the output of existing firms, but at their foundations and their very lives" (Schumpeter 1942: 84).

By breaking with established routines and conventional wisdom, the entrepreneur searches for new ways of doing things. He is motivated by more than profit maximization, such as "the joy of creating, of getting things done, or simply of exercising one's energy and ingenuity" (Schumpeter 1911: 93). He may have expertise in discovering innovations or in implementing them.

Because such skills are not common, innovations are not costlessly discovered, understood, and implemented. As a result, a firm's managers cannot know the profit-maximizing strategy before facing a market test in which they must form different opinions on the desirability of different innovations. Some firms will aggressively implement innovations; others will take half steps or abstain. Competition reveals which firms are closest to following the profit-maximizing strategy by yielding winners and losers. Over time, this process results in different-sized firms that have expertise in different areas (Nelson 1991).

As entrepreneurs repeatedly inject novelty into the economy, survival is no longer guaranteed to the firm that produces with an unchanged set of processes. Innovations constantly shake the economy out of equilibrium and render old technologies, knowledge, skills, and practices obsolete. Firms that refuse to change wither away. Firms that innovate or imitate with greater success become relatively more profitable. Eventually, as innovations are fully incorporated, the economy settles into a new equilibrium – until the process begins anew with more innovations.[2]

Schumpeterian competition is not squeezing the price down to marginal cost but creating a lower cost curve. It is not bringing more inputs to the same production function but discovering a new production function altogether. It creates vastly more long-run benefits than mere price

---

[2] Note that Schumpeter's entrepreneur shares many similarities with Kirzner's entrepreneur. There is one important difference, however; the former is a disequilibrating force, the latter is an *equilibrating* force. This difference may not have serious implications for policy, because neither economist views equilibrium as the appropriate focus of competition. Kirzner (1973: 73; 1999: 5–18).

competition. It is about continually destroying the old economic structure *from within* and replacing it with a new one – what Schumpeter called "creative destruction" (Schumpeter 1942: 83).

The type of firm that thrives in creative destruction is different from the appropriate one for perfect competition. Developing innovations is costly, so the most innovative firms should have a large stream of resources for R&D. The incentive to innovate is greatest where there is little threat of imitation, so the most innovative firms should have few competitors. In addition, successful innovation may itself lead to market power and supranormal profits. This reading of Schumpeter implies three hypotheses: large firms are more innovative than small firms, monopolistic industries are more innovative than competitive ones, and firms will be more innovative when they anticipate that they will be allowed to exploit the market power created by their innovations. Attempts to test the first two hypotheses generate the second-largest empirical literature in the field of industrial organization. Some studies found mild confirmation, whereas others appear to reject the Schumpeterian hypotheses (Kamien and Schwartz 1975; Scherer 1970). We are unaware of any attempts to test the third.

Schumpeterian competition is a dynamic vision. Because change requires time, the benefits of competition may not arrive immediately. Market participants may have to tolerate short-run inefficiencies in order to gain long-run efficiencies.[3] In addition, any acknowledgment of endogenous innovation prohibits discussion of predictable equilibria. Due to the continuous and unpredictable nature of the process, equilibrium describes only the state of affairs after the process ceases.

Telltale signs of competition include:

- Heterogeneous firms. Because no single profit-maximizing strategy is obvious to all firms before facing the market test, firms choose different innovation strategies.
- Monopolies or market power. From the perspective of allocative efficiency, monopoly and market power are undesirable. From the perspective of Schumpeterian competition, however, they encourage development. Firms with these qualities are better able to finance R&D expenses, to spread innovation risks, to attract more qualified human capital, and to exploit innovations. In addition, market power arising from innovation is itself an incentive for innovation.

---

[3] "A system – any system, economic or other – that at *every* given point in time fully utilizes its possibilities to the best advantage may yet in the long run be inferior to a system that does so at *no* given point in time, because the latter's failure to do so may be a condition for the level or speed of long-run performance." Schumpeter (1942: 83).

- Changing leaders in a market. Disruptions occur within industries as well as across industries. As better forms of organization and production are discovered, the contours of an industry change. Because old firms tend to be the most reluctant to adopt innovations (due to past investments and business strategies), they are the most vulnerable to losing their leadership position.
- Discontinuous change. Schumpeterian competition yields dramatic departures from previous practices, products, and technologies.
- Supranormal profits. Because entrepreneurial skills are scarce, the innovations discovered by entrepreneurs are valuable. Firms that are quick to adopt innovations will capture this value in the form of supranormal profits. Over time, as imitators learn about the innovation, the profit is bid away.
- Continual innovation in dominant firms. Dominant firms are still vulnerable to competition. Innovations that threaten to make their products less desirable or obsolete arise every day, so they research ways to maintain their dominance.

Policy Implications

A series of policy recommendations emerges from the Schumpeterian approach.

Aim for long-run efficiency. Competition is a process that takes time to reveal "its true features and ultimate effects." What may appear inefficient today (market power, monopoly, fluctuations) may actually be a vital step toward achieving efficiency tomorrow. Because there is no way of knowing the ultimate effects of this process beforehand, caution is required.

Allow rewards to entrepreneurship. Entrepreneurship drives competition, but it is not a riskless activity. The high likelihood of failure means that entrepreneurs need to be rewarded heavily for their successes. Rewards usually come in the form of supranormal profits. They serve as an encouragement for firms to implement current innovations and for entrepreneurs to seek more innovations.

Market power is not per se anticompetitive. Firms with market power have potentially more resources to channel into discovering or implementing innovations. In addition, a firm possessing market power today may have earned it through past innovation.[4]

---

[4] While Schumpeter does not explicitly address the link between concentration and innovation, some economists have used Schumpeterian ideas to suggest that a link exists, where greater innovativeness leads to faster growth and greater concentration. Nelson and Winter (1978); and see Nelson and Winter (1982b).

Do not subsidize dying firms. Firms that refuse to implement new production techniques, to adopt new types of organization, or to provide new products should feel the consequences of their actions.

Allow for dynamic considerations in regulation. Traditional monopoly regulation focuses on maintaining a predetermined rate of return in an effort to approximate the allocative efficiency of perfect competition. Schumpeterian competition, however, reveals a greater source of efficiency from the potential for new combinations and new processes. Rate-of-return regulation and territorial monopoly privileges impede the pressures of creative destruction.

EVOLUTIONARY COMPETITION

In real-world markets, novelty constantly arises, innovations can be endogenous, firms are heterogeneous, and decision makers have information-processing limitations. Understanding such markets requires dynamic models where competition is an open-ended process of innovation, experimentation, and feedback (Nelson 1986). Evolutionary economics attempts to provide such models by using evolutionary metaphors to flesh out Schumpeter's belief that innovation is the primary engine of progressive change.[5]

An evolutionary approach to economics is not new. Alfred Marshall used both biological and mechanical metaphors to describe economic activity. He considered equilibrium models to be a useful development in the progress of economic science, but suggested that biological descriptions should prevail once economics had matured (Marshall [1890] 1982, 1898). In an influential article, Armen Alchian showed that evolutionary reasoning could guide neoclassical analysis (1950). There have been many other applications of evolutionary analogies to economic phenomena, but one of the most detailed and influential expositions of evolutionary competition theory comes from Nelson and Winter (1982a). Our discussion draws heavily from their work.

Assumptions

The evolutionary model entails the following assumptions:

- Bounded rationality. Individuals have limitations on their ability to receive, process, and communicate information. These limitations go beyond problems due to imperfect information. Even when all relevant information is known, the relationship of one datum to other data may be so complex that individuals cannot process all of the implications (e.g., the decision tree in a chess game). In an

---

[5] For an early form of such a model, see Nelson, Winter, and Schuette (1976).

ever-changing and uncertain environment, it is so difficult to plan for all contingencies that timely calculations of optima are unlikely. Maximizing behavior is no longer an appropriate guide to action (Simon 1955).

- Behavioral view of the firm. When facing a world of complexity and change, decision makers cannot calculate the single best strategy and continually reoptimize as conditions change. Instead, they cope with uncertainty by following decision rules. Decision rules can change, but such changes are slow since they are learned behaviors (Cyert and March 1963; Baumol and Stewart 1971).

- Endogenous change. Past choices influence how firms are affected by change, and consequently, how they will likely react. In addition, evolutionary economics allows a decision maker to actively change market conditions (Nelson 1991).

- Real time. Evolutionary economics functions in "real time." There is no discernible end point. Many actions are irreversible, and the sequence of events is important. One implication of real time is that path dependence is possible.[6]

The Nature of Competition

The basic unit of evolutionary economics is the "routine," just as the basic unit of biology is the gene. A routine is the decision rule that shapes the firm's response to different market stimuli. In evolutionary economics, firms cannot plan for every possible contingency or calculate the optimal action at all times. As a result, they must rely on routines to guide their responses to unforeseen market conditions.

Routines can exist for every activity of the firm: production, R&D outlays, inventory management, hiring and firing, and marketing. However, they are costly to develop and are learned behaviors. For effective utilization, routines require practice and concentration (Dosi, Teece, and Winter 1992). In other words, the routines that currently exist in a firm depend on the firm's past decisions and experiences (Winter 1964). For this reason, routines cannot be costlessly transplanted from one firm to another. Because firms are likely to have unique histories, we should expect different firms to have different routines – and thus, different reactions to the same stimuli. Even when two firms have the same rou-

---

[6] The path dependence literature sees lock-in as the result of increasing returns and network externalities. Alternatively, evolutionary economics sees lock-in as the consequence of operating in real time. Without perfect knowledge and the ability to "rewind" time once errors are detected, firms are inevitably constrained by their past decisions. Unlike the path dependence literature, evolutionary economics does not consider this phenomenon to be a market failure; it is simply an unavoidable consequence of real-world action. Langlois and Everett (1994).

tines, they may have different reactions if one firm has superior complementarities among its routines.

Routines determine the limits of a firm's expertise. For a given combination of routines, some activities a firm can perform profitably but others it should avoid. The decision maker's role is to steer the firm into activities it can best perform, while preparing for changing market conditions by developing new complementarities among old routines – or by developing new routines altogether. To gain these new routines, it must choose between innovation and imitation.

In a world of change and uncertainty, however, the optimal routines are not immediately obvious. The firm needs an environment for conducting and evaluating experiments on desirable courses of action. It also needs a mechanism for identifying successful routines in rival firms. The competitive market provides both.

A firm searches for better routines by experimenting with new ways of doing things, such as new production processes, new organizational cultures, and new products. A firm can cast up several innovations that appear equally useful, but not all will be well suited for the current market environment. Only when the market "selects" the better innovations (via increased profitability) can the firm identify the better routines. The firm can also imitate the routines that were cultivated by rivals. Unusually high profits are signals that some or all of a rival's routines are well suited for the current environment. Over time, firms tend to imitate the appropriate routines and discard the inappropriate ones. The competitive market selects superior routines, with profitability as the criterion for survival.

To test the plausibility of the evolutionary approach, several economists constructed computer simulations in which firms followed regular and predictable decision rules that were subject to imitation. They found that the rules that were well suited for the environment came to dominate the industry through the growth of firms following those rules.[7] Nelson and Winter (1974) performed a similar test that generated results consistent with actual U.S. aggregate time-series data. They concluded that evolutionary models could predict well and had the added benefits of greater realism and more explanatory power.

Telltale signs of competition include:

- Heterogeneous firms. If firms were only different combinations of a fixed and known number of routines, then eventually all firms would converge to a single cluster of routines. However, new routines are constantly introduced. In addition, not all firms can utilize

---

[7] For a survey of such models, see Silverberg (1988).

routines in the same way. The accumulated routines in one firm may be incompatible with those that are well suited for the current environment; the accumulated routines at another may provide a good fit. As a result, we should expect firms to take different actions, have different sizes, and earn different profits in a competitive market. Because it is nonsensical to speak of "optimal" adaptation to an environment, different bundles of routines can profitably coexist in the same market.

- Constant trial-and-error. The process of determining profitable strategies is continual, because uncertainty is never eliminated and novelty is continually introduced into the system (often by the participants in the system). One firm's actions send ripple effects to other firms, leading them to respond, which, in turn, affects other firms. When there is an absence of competition, this trial and error ceases, and the market settles into an equilibrium.
- Short-run adjustments. The process of discovering profitable strategies takes time. At any given moment, there will be short-run adjustments that appear inefficient, but are necessary in the long run for the proper discovery of profitable strategies.
- Positive profits, not maximum profits. Because the economy is dynamic and uncertain, firm decision-making cannot be represented as maximizing a static and certain function. Instead, firms aim for survival through positive profits.

Policy Implications

The evolutionary approach to economies results in a range of policy implications.

Deemphasize market concentration. Market structure endogenously emerges out of the process of innovation and adaptation. Thus, the ability of a large firm to exhibit market power is not due to its size but to its success in innovating or adapting. It is not relevant whether this market structure is more or less efficient than another – this structure just *is*, given the parameters of the competitive environment.

Deemphasize interventions on outcomes. Progress occurs when firms discover what satisfies consumers in the current environment. The benefits of competition flow from this process of innovation, selection, and adaptation. If regulatory authorities are troubled by certain outcomes of this process (profit rates, market share, industry structure), they should not aim their interventions at the outcomes. They should also refrain from trying to achieve the "perfect" outcome since such outcomes are too difficult to calculate and continually change.

Emphasize interventions on processes. There is still room for intervention, but the approach is different. If regulators want to change certain outcomes, they should understand the processes that generate them. For example, if they want to expand output or improve product quality, they should look for ways to encourage discovery, innovation, adaptation, and feedback in the market.

Allow failure. Failure is a necessary outcome of the selection process. Without failure, there is no way to distinguish profitable strategies from unprofitable ones. Firms lose the incentive to innovate, and valuable strategies remain undiscovered.

AUSTRIAN COMPETITION AND ENTREPRENEURSHIP

In Austrian analysis, individuals operate in a world of uncertainty.[8] They make mistakes and learn from them. They try to change the world around them, rather than passively accepting market variables as fixed. Their actions cause other people to revise their plans of action, sending successive ripples of change through the market.

When we acknowledge that uncertainty is a normal part of life, the focus of inquiry should no longer be on the reaction of individuals to "given" economic variables. Instead, it should be on the process that creates and transmits those variables (Hayek 1948b). Recast in these terms, economics becomes the study of how individuals cope with uncertainty over time.[9]

Assumptions

To analyze change, the Austrian approach makes the following assumptions:

- Methodological individualism. A society can only be understood from the motivations and actions of its individuals, not from a systemwide or marketwide perspective that masks the interactions of its participants (Mises 1966: ch. 2).
- Uncertainty. There are two forms of uncertainty. First, there is ignorance, which occurs when a person is aware of the existence of all relevant knowledge but does not have all of it because not all knowledge is worth acquiring. The second form, which Austrians emphasize, is *sheer ignorance*. This describes knowledge of which an

---

[8] The roots of the Austrian school go back to Carl Menger, Friedrich von Wieser, and Eugen von Bohm-Bawerk, subjective value theorists of the late nineteenth and early twentieth centuries.

[9] For an introduction to this approach, see O'Driscoll and Rizzo (1985).

individual does not know he is ignorant, knowledge that he cannot imagine to exist. In this view, knowledge is an unbounded set and can never be complete (Kirzner 1997). The Austrian conception of uncertainty is akin to Knightian uncertainty and different from the "imperfect information" of most economic models. In imperfect information models, individuals do not know all prices. However, they *do* know the probability distribution of prices, which is assumed to exist in an objective sense. As they engage in costly search, they learn the shape of the distribution until it is no longer valuable to do so.[10] From the Austrian viewpoint, this search contradicts the subjective nature of knowledge. In addition, it does not accommodate sheer ignorance – you cannot search for what you do not know to exist; you cannot assign a probability to an outcome that you cannot imagine.

- Radical subjectivism. Most economists assume that utility is subjective, but most other factors are effectively objective. Austrians broaden the subjective category to include knowledge, expectations, and understandings of the relationship between means and ends. Because economic decision making depends on human understanding, the subjective nature of the latter leads to the subjective nature of the former (Hayek 1948a).[11] It also deepens the category by asserting that this information does not exist outside of the mind, like books in an enormous library, so it cannot be centralized or known in the same way to all people. Finally, much economically significant information is difficult or impossible to verbalize.
- Real time. Austrian economists view time as an irreversible and path-dependent flow of events. Individuals are constantly influenced by new knowledge and new experiences, which affect future plans. Because there is never a point when events cease to influence individuals, there is never an end point.[12]

Removing the assumption of perfect information multiplies the complexity of the economic problem. A world of subjective knowledge and ignorance does not lend itself to equilibrium modeling, so Austrians propose a different way to view the market. In addition, a satisfactory explanation of action in the face of uncertainty must include a theory of learning, discovery, and communication. It must also explain why uncertainty leads to order instead of chaos.

---

[10] For an introduction to this literature, see Lippman and McCall (1976) and Rothschild (1973).

[11] For radical subjectivism, see Lachmann (1986) and Shackle (1979).

[12] This concept is based on the writings of the philosopher Henri Bergson. See Bergson (1911).

The Nature of Competition

In a world of uncertainty, subjective knowledge, and real time, change and surprise are inevitable. To facilitate interaction with others, individuals must make plans. Due to change and surprise, however, different people's plans will not mesh perfectly. Incompatibilities arise, causing people to revise their plans and to discover new incompatibilities. Change and surprise prevent this process from ever settling down into something resembling a static equilibrium (O'Driscoll and Rizzo 1985: ch. 5).

With individuals engulfed in so much uncertainty, how does anything get done? Human action does not require perfect information. Buyers can decide to buy without knowing the absolute lowest price available; sellers can operate their businesses without knowing the most efficient production process available. In addition, individuals are not passive agents. They respond to the inevitable incompleteness of knowledge by searching for palliatives. They experiment with different ways to reduce their sheer ignorance and to cope with their limitations (O'Driscoll 1976). Market exchange arose through this search for palliatives.

In this sense, Austrians reverse the conventional relationship between markets and uncertainty. Most economic analysis treats uncertainty as a factor that prevents the creation or diminishes the efficiency of markets. Austrian analysis treats markets as one response to uncertainty. Markets permit individuals to act on their limited information, to receive feedback, and to discover and communicate knowledge to others (Hayek 1978). The market price system is a way to summarize and transmit information in a swift and flexible way to the people who would be most interested (Hayek 1945).

Information conveyed by the price system is often incomplete, creating profit opportunities that most people do not notice. Entrepreneurs are alert to such opportunities. They seek new products, new production methods, and new technologies that would be more valuable than the resources exhausted in implementing them. By exploiting these profit opportunities, entrepreneurs uncover previously hidden knowledge, and their actions unintentionally increase coordination in the market (Kirzner 1985).

The innovations that arise from entrepreneurial discovery need not be limited to technical improvements. They can also include improvements in management methods, corporate culture, arbitrage opportunities, and organizational learning. Entrepreneurs capitalize on both "high-tech" and "low-tech" knowledge, and so analysis focused solely on measurables like R&D will likely miss a great deal of entrepreneurial

innovation.[13] When relevant information about technologies, preferences, and other data is not known, competition becomes a *dynamic
process* for discovering this information.

Austrians are reluctant to believe that monopolies exist for long
periods of time in an unhampered market. The lure of supracompetitive
profit often motivates a seller to bring its product to market in the first
place. Were it not for this potential profit, the product may never have
been offered. If the choice is between a product supplied at a high price,
and no product at all, even a monopoly may increase consumer welfare
(Littlechild 1981). Where market power exists, there is much to gain from
wresting away a piece of a monopolist's business. The larger the monopoly profit, the more intense the entrepreneurial effort. The advantages
of a dominant company (efficient production processes, highly skilled
workers, strong brand names) raise the costs of entrepreneurial activity
for rivals, but they do not eliminate the possibility of entry altogether,
and the advantages will eventually be worn away. When a company is
the exclusive owner of a resource with no substitutes, however, then
some Austrians are willing to concede that entrepreneurial activity is
impossible and government intervention may be necessary (Kirzner
1973).

Austrians are also reluctant to associate a specific market structure
with competitive intensity. It is the inherent nature of the unhampered
market process to be competitive – even for processes that lead to
monopolies (because these same processes wear away monopolies).
Efforts at finding the "competitive" level of concentration or allowing
only "competitive" business practices are misguided. Competition exists
as long as free markets exist. Only when they fail to operate will there
be no competition (Kirzner 1991).

Telltale signs of competition include:

- Unexpected events. Due to sheer ignorance and the passage of time,
  knowledge is inevitably incomplete and changing. Regardless of
  how hard a buyer or seller looks, he will never operate with full
  information. His plans will inevitably be incompatible with other
  people's plans and, as a result, he will commit errors and receive
  surprises (O'Driscoll 1977). Such unanticipated events are not signs
  of inefficiency or waste but a normal part of real-world action that
  spurs the discovery of new knowledge.

---

[13] There is disagreement among Austrians as to whether any real-world markets tend
toward equilibrium – or whether equilibrium is a useful theoretical construct. Kirzner
describes entrepreneurship as strictly equilibrating, but Ludwig Lachmann also sees
endogenous disequilibrating forces in the market process. Ultimately, this difference in
theory does not affect the Austrian view of competition. See Lachmann (1976).

- Brand names and advertising. Without perfect information, individuals must rely on institutions and devices that economize on knowledge, such as brand names and advertising. These are not barriers to entry but necessary components of operating without complete information. The traditional distinction between informative advertising (benign) and persuasive advertising (harmful) is meaningless because sheer ignorance creates an opportunity for people to discover products and desires that they previously did not know existed. The "meaningless" hype and glitz associated with much advertising serves the crucial economic function of getting the consumer's attention in a world crowded with alternatives. Even if buyers are already aware of a product, they may be ignorant of new and desirable uses.
- Innovation. The benefits of the market process do not necessarily come in the form of another producer offering an identical product to drive price closer to marginal cost. Instead, the benefits come from the producer who enters the market with an entirely different cost structure, or who offers a new product for which there was previously no demand expressed in the marketplace. Greater discovery and innovation are the bench marks of dynamic competition, not the driving down of price to marginal cost.
- Product differentiation. As entrepreneurs push back the boundaries of sheer ignorance, better ways to satisfy consumer needs will come to light. Coordination between buyer and seller improves, and sellers tailor their products to satisfy the variety of preferences among their buyers.
- Entrepreneurial profits. Some entrepreneurs will develop product or service ideas that are highly desirable to consumers, or greatly increase coordination within a market. The high value of these ideas will lead to large entrepreneurial profits – profits that arise from beneficial alertness and implementation rather than from "overcharge" or inefficiency.
- Rivalrous behavior. In a perfectly competitive equilibrium, there is little behavior that noneconomists associate with competition. In real life, rivalry is omnipresent. Buyers bid against other buyers for products. Sellers undercut other sellers for customers. Such battles are not limited to price competition; market participants can use durability, selection, service, support, and other valued qualities to outdo their rivals.

Policy Implications

Followers of the Austrian approach make specific recommendations on how policy makers should operate in a world of uncertainty.

Intervene sparingly if at all. Policy makers should not use static efficiency as a guide to policy. Laws and regulations based on static efficiency risk blocking the types of market dynamics that bring forth new products and ideas, wear down monopolies, and increase efficiency and human welfare in the long run. Policy makers who accept the concept of dynamic competition should resist the temptation to "improve" it through regulations that tend to impair the discovery process in unforeseen ways. The benefits of dynamic competition are only available when alert entrepreneurs are free to enter markets and to exploit unseized opportunities (Kirzner 1978).

Allow brand names, advertising, and product differentiation. Brand names and advertising reduce customer information costs and make customers aware of new opportunities. Product differentiation allows producers to more precisely satisfy consumer desires.

Allow supranormal profits. A price exceeding marginal cost is not a sign of inefficiency or anticompetitive behavior, unless it is due to government intervention. Instead, the profits show that the seller has made a substantial contribution to consumer welfare and increased coordination where less existed before. The profit is the reward for taking advantage of opportunities that were previously ignored or not perceived, and it encourages others to be alert to new opportunities.

Deemphasize market concentration. In the absence of government-imposed barriers to entry, high concentration can be a sign that the sellers have been especially successful in satisfying consumer desires. Concentration indices convey no information about the intensity of competition within an industry. To break up firms or to prohibit mergers in order to reduce concentration in an industry is not likely to increase efficiency. On the contrary, it is more likely in the short run to force firms to operate at inefficient scale and in the long run to discourage firms from noticing and exploiting opportunities to reduce costs or to introduce new products.

Analyze barriers to entry over longer time frame. Barriers created by superior firm performance are not inimical to consumer welfare if they reflect superior efficiency. Indeed, they may reflect a firm's ability to create value for consumers in ways that are difficult for competitors to duplicate. The search for unique advantages over time is precisely what drives new discoveries. Therefore, the efficiency of a privately created barrier depends largely on the analyst's time frame. If regulators gain a greater appreciation of the market process, they will likely find that privately created barriers to entry provide long-run benefits that offset the short-term inefficiencies.

Deemphasize market power. In dynamic competition, most sellers possess some degree of market power as they translate their unique capabilities into advantages over other sellers (lower costs, more highly valued products, etc.). Eliminating market power may penalize the sellers who most successfully satisfy consumer desires.

PATH DEPENDENCE

The classification of path dependence as a static or dynamic theory is a complicated issue. There are static elements in that it compares starting and end points, and many path dependence models assume that industries, once tipped in a particular direction, inevitably continue in that direction. There are also dynamic elements, because the outcomes are unpredictable. In addition, some scholars dispute the claim that there is an end point to competition in path dependence theory. Even if an industry is "locked in" to a particular standard, companies can still compete *within* that standard on conventional economic dimensions of price and quality (Besen and Farrell 1994). Most scholars prefer to avoid the static-dynamic distinction altogether. Instead, they describe path dependence as the study of "nonergodic" processes (where outcomes are shaped by the sequence of small events), as opposed to "ergodic" processes (where the effects of small events are averaged away).

Assumptions

Path dependence theory assumes:

- Increasing returns technology. As output increases, average costs of production can decrease. Often, this occurs when a large initial outlay is required, but incremental production is relatively cheap (e.g., software production). It can also occur when workers become more familiar with the production process, more confident about its efficacy, discover new efficiencies, or improve their skills as they produce more.[14]
- Network effects. Network effects describe a different phenomenon: average consumer benefit rises as output increases. This trend occurs when a product has little value in isolation but larger value as part of a growing network. Average consumer benefit rises because an additional user of the product raises the value for *all* consumers of the product. For example, as more people buy telephones, current users are able to call more people.[15]
- Uncertainty. Market participants do not have enough information to identify dominant products or standards, ex ante. There is also

---

[14] For an overview of the implications of increasing returns, see Arthur (1990).
[15] For an early model of competition in the presence of network externalities, see Katz and Shapiro (1985).

enough uncertainty about production technologies that firms can learn as they use the technology more.[16]

- No persuasion. Brand names, reputations, trade publications, and product experts have no ability to influence the choices that consumers make.
- Irreversible investments. Individuals cannot costlessly dispose of one product or technology in the course of adopting another. Some investments are relationship- or technology-specific and have no value when applied to other uses.

The Nature of Competition

Traditionally, neoclassical economic theory has assumed that industries exhibit decreasing returns. This pattern simplifies the analysis – as a product's demand rises, its price also rises, so individuals have an incentive to switch to other products. The decreasing returns assumption acts as a counterweight, allowing the industry to settle into a single, predictable equilibrium where resources are allocated efficiently. Equilibrium is inevitable, preordained by resources, tastes, technology, and preferences. The timing of economic choices is irrelevant, and small events that occur along the way are averaged out in the long run.

If an industry exhibits increasing returns and network effects, however, then there is no built-in stabilizing process. Instead, a product that gains more users will become cheaper to manufacture and more valuable to the consumer. Lower production costs allow the seller to reap larger profits on each unit. The higher consumer value allows the seller to raise prices without losing sales to rivals. Rival sellers are unable to survive against such cost and pricing advantages. As a result, products with an early foothold in the marketplace gain an ever-growing advantage over their rivals.

In this scenario, competition acts as a magnifier rather than a counterweight. If all firms begin with equal market shares, there is no inevitable equilibrium. Instead, the market rests precariously on the edge of many possible equilibria, awaiting the influence of small events to "tip" the industry toward an outcome where one firm's product dominates.[17] Once tipped, the industry accelerates in that direction as the newly created cost and pricing advantages beget even larger cost and

---

[16] Even if uncertainty about future events can be modeled as random "white noise" that, on average, does not affect our long-run expectations, path dependence postulates that the *timing* of these random events can have a large influence on long-run outcomes. Arthur (1989).

[17] For examples of "tipping" in different industries, see Besen and Johnson (1986), Farrell and Shapiro (1992), and Cusumano, Mylondadis, and Rosenbloom (1990).

pricing advantages.[18] Factors previously considered irrelevant (the number of early purchasers, the timing of product introductions) become important determinants of the outcome.

The primary innovation of path dependence theory is describing why competition might not select the most efficient winner. Assume two identical firms in an industry with increasing returns and network effects. For whatever reason (directed effort, luck, managerial whim, sunspots), one firm gains market share. Its average costs fall, and its customers are willing to pay a higher price. The firm uses the advantages from its early gains to pull further ahead of its rival. As the firm's market share grows, its rival becomes increasingly unable to compete until the growing firm dominates the market. In effect, the market becomes "locked in" to one firm.[19] The dominant firm does not succeed because it offers a superior product but because it is the beneficiary of small events unrelated to product cost or quality.

Critics have suggested that lock-in is an artifact of the theory's strong assumptions. However, path dependence theorists relax a few assumptions and find that the results are not dramatically different. For example, Arthur and Lane (1994) relax the assumption of "no persuasion" by allowing consumers to seek advice from current and previous users of the product in question. In this setting, lock-in can still occur because products that, by chance, gain early footholds will have a larger pool of current and previous users, creating an information advantage.

Path dependence theory has also been criticized for assuming market participants are only concerned about immediate benefits rather than looking toward the long term. Arthur also relaxes this assumption. Consumers can now see that a product which is inferior today would be superior in the future, *if it were the dominant product in the future.* If consumers have rational expectations, they realize that the market will lock in to those products with an early market-share lead. Even if they can see the long-run superiority of the less popular product, they will still refuse to buy it. Lock-in remains.

There is currently no consensus about the applicability of path dependence theory to public policy.[20] For empirical support of the inefficiency claim, advocates of path dependence offer several historical examples.

---

[18] These self-reinforcing elements of path dependence are often called "positive feedback mechanisms." Arthur (1988).

[19] Path dependence may also explain the geographic clustering of industries. See Arthur (1986) and Rockoff (1994).

[20] Katz and Shapiro write that economists "are far from having a general theory of when government intervention is preferable to the unregulated market outcome" (Katz and Shapiro 1994: 113). On the other hand, Arthur and Saloner contributed to a white paper on the lack of competition in the software industry (Reback et al. n.d.).

Some claim that, despite the superior picture quality of the Beta video format, the early market-share gains of VHS secured its inevitable success (Katz and Shapiro 1986). The alleged superiority of the Dvorak typewriter keyboard was not enough to displace the long-established QWERTY keyboard (David 1985). Information about the Beta and Dvorak standards was public, yet consumers chose to remain with VHS and QWERTY. Some scholars believe these examples prove that decentralized decision making can lead markets to prematurely lock in inefficient products and technologies. Not all researchers accept this conclusion. The Beta videocassette actually reached the market two years before VHS, and tests performed at the time of the standards battle revealed neither format as superior to the other in picture quality. Similarly in the keyboard struggle, the only study identifying the Dvorak keyboard as superior was overseen by the keyboard's inventor. Other, widely publicized studies concluded that the QWERTY keyboard was faster (Liebowitz and Margolis 1990, 1995).

Lock-in to inferior standards is an attention-grabbing notion, yet some scholars have stressed that there is no theoretical reason for path dependence to be biased toward inefficiency. On the contrary, private institutions may arise to increase coordination and internalize network effects, thereby ensuring that the industry remains on the efficient path (Katz and Shapiro 1994).[21] Alternatively, firms may try to lock in the industry to paths that are advantageous and seek to destroy paths that are disadvantageous.[22] Competition to *create* standards may be just as efficient as traditional competition within standards.

In addition, the existence of multiple equilibria opens the possibility that industries may exhibit "insufficient friction" rather than lock-in. Markets may be biased in favor of new, superior, but incompatible technology since the buyers of the new technology do not bear the cost of incompatibility that falls on users of the old technology (Katz and Shapiro 1994: 108). Despite the emphasis in the literature on too little change, theory also allows markets to exhibit *too much* change.

Telltale signs of competition include:

- Long-standing market dominance. In markets with strong increasing returns and network effects, firms that race to an early lead will remain in the lead.
- Concentrated markets. Eventually, lock-in causes one firm to dominate the entire market. If firms have been able to build large market

[21] For a related discussion of "institutional entrepreneurs" who help these institutions to arise, see Rao and Singh (1997).

[22] For a sample of the growing literature concerning "path destruction" and "path creation," see Garud, Nayyar, and Shapira (1997).

shares and broad familiarity with their products, then opening their markets to competition may not have any effect on their dominance. Consumers may already be locked in.

- Profit opportunities left unseized. When consumers avoid switching to a superior product or technology, a profit opportunity exists. However, entrepreneurs who recognize this opportunity are unable to exploit it since consumers are locked in to their past choices.
- No assurance of efficiency. Consumers will lock in to products based on the timing of small events, not efficiency considerations. Dominance in a free market is not necessarily socially optimal.

Policy Implications

In path dependence research, policy implications concern intervention and deconcentration.

Intervention has a role. If consumers are ignoring an obviously superior alternative, government intervention (e.g., standardization) may be socially optimal. It is less clear what form such intervention should take.

Intervene in young markets. Intervention is futile in markets that have existed for a long time, and thus are close to being locked in.

Employ an efficiency rationale for deconcentration. Because there is no assurance that a free market will result in the most efficient outcome, the government should prevent any one firm from gaining too much market share.

Deregulate and deconcentrate together. Deregulation, without aggressive deconcentration, may not be efficiency-enhancing. The socially desirable aspects of competition do not arise simply by removing barriers to entry.

RESOURCE-BASED COMPETITION

Most of the work on the resource-based theory of competition has occurred in business schools, where scholars have focused more on strategic management than issues of competition policy. Business scholars wanted a theory that was as rigorous as price theory yet explained the heterogeneity and rivalry found in real-world markets. While neoclassical methodology asserts that accurate predictions can justify a theory's unrealistic assumptions, business scholars wanted strong predictive power *and* realistic assumptions. The first step toward this new theory came with the creation of the resource-based view of the firm.

Assumptions

Resource-based competition assumes the following:

- Broad definition of resources. Resource-based theory defines resources as tangible and *intangible* items that enable a firm to better produce a valuable product.[23] Examples of intangible resources include human items (skills and knowledge of individual employees), legal items (trademarks, patents), organizational items (corporate culture), and relational items (brand names, reputation, relationships with suppliers) (Hofer and Schendal 1978: 144–53).
- Resources are heterogeneous. Resources are heterogeneous and scarce, creating the potential for a firm to earn rents from them (Barney 1991).
- Resources are imperfectly mobile. Resources are imperfectly mobile because they may be less valuable away from their current owners (Williamson 1979; Teece 1986), too costly to move (Rumelt 1987), or impossible to trade due to a lack of property rights (Dierickx and Cool 1989). As a result, certain resources may be bound to a firm for a long time. Different levels of resources will accumulate in different firms, resulting in different profit rates.
- Costly information. Information on discovering and developing valuable resources is costly for a firm to obtain. Otherwise, all firms would simultaneously perceive the advantage to using a resource and bid up the cost of creating it until anticipated rents are dissipated. The existence of rents proves that information is costly (Barney 1986). In addition, attempts by rival firms to imitate a resource will be unsuccessful if the source of value and the process of extracting it are difficult to explain.[24] Thus, costly and hard-to-communicate information leads firms to discover new resources and to shield them from imitation.

The Nature of Competition

Resource-based theory suggests that the roots of competition are in the firm, specifically, in the efforts of managers. The manager's task is to create a framework that fosters the discovery, development, and dissemination of resources within his firm (Penrose 1990). The significance of frameworks increases when we acknowledge that valuable resources can arise from tacit knowledge – knowledge that is gained and most easily communicated through experience. By altering the organization of a firm, the manager can influence which workers will participate in the

---

[23] "Better" can be defined as producing something more efficiently (the same good at lower cost) or more effectively (a good with higher quality or new characteristics that are valued by consumers). Barney (1991).

[24] Rumelt (1984) describes this phenomenon as "causal ambiguity."

development of such knowledge, which ultimately affects the resources at a firm's disposal (Teece 1982).

Firms do not value the resource itself but the services that flow from the resource, and this flow depends on the way in which the resource is used. Therefore, creating new resources is not the only option available to managers; they can also find new ways to combine old resources. Because resources are heterogeneous and imperfectly mobile, the resource bundle in one firm is likely to be different from bundles in other firms, even for long periods of time. Due to this variety of options, there is no single "optimal" pattern of resource use that applies to all firms.

The diversity of resource bundles that can exist at any moment suggests that different firms will be better suited for different types of work; firms will have distinct "competencies" (Chandler 1962). The manager is responsible for matching the firm's particular competencies with opportunities in the product markets. If he selects a product market (or market niche) that is a good fit, the firm will successfully compete and grow. If he leads the firm into an area where rivals have superior competencies, the firm will languish (Andrews 1980). The lesson is that superior performance requires managerial attention to the cultivation of resources within the firm *and* to the choice of product market for the firm.

In resource-based theory, firms not only compete in product markets, but they also compete to acquire resources from each other. When a firm has a superior resource, rival firms will attempt to purchase it, imitate it, or find a substitute that is equivalent or superior. However, this is difficult. Without experiencing the learning process that created the resource, rival firms may be unable to imitate it – or, once successfully imitated, to extract the same flow of services from it. Plus, a resource may be valuable due to complementarities with other resources in a firm. (For example, the effectiveness of a trademark may be intertwined with a certain corporate culture.) Therefore, taking a resource out of the environment in which it was created may reduce its usefulness (Peteraf 1993).

All of these factors contribute to the imperfect mobility of a resource. When a firm utilizes its unique superior resource, it can produce a valuable product with lower costs or higher quality than rivals. This firm is said to have a "comparative advantage" in resources, and to the extent this superior resource remains limited in supply, the comparative advantage will be sustainable. As a result, a *comparative advantage* in resources translates into a *competitive advantage* in the marketplace. Even if all firms are price takers in the product market, the firm with the superior resource will earn more profits than rivals (Wernerfelt 1984).

Note that the superior returns are not a result of market power, restriction of output, or inefficiency. Instead, they are due to the scarcity of the superior resource, despite the best efforts of rivals to acquire, imitate, or substitute for it (Conner 1991). Persistent differences among firm organization and profit rates can be easily explained by resource-based theory as part of the competitive process.

To summarize, competition is the struggle among heterogeneous firms for a comparative advantage in resources that will yield a competitive advantage in the marketplace. If one firm achieves a comparative advantage in resources, rivals will attempt to neutralize or leapfrog the firm through resource acquisition, imitation, or substitution. There is no equilibrium end point that acts as a gravitational center to this process; hence it is a dynamic theory of competition (Hunt and Morgan 1995).

Resource-based theory suggests that analysis of competition should make the firm, not the industry, the primary focus. Recent studies have found in many cases, firm strategy has a much *larger* effect than industry characteristics on firm profitability (Rumelt 1991).[25] This supports the resource-based theory's position that environmental factors influence, but do not determine, firm performance. Strategic managerial decisions matter.

Telltale signs of competition include:

- Disequilibrium. All firms want to have superior financial performance. However, by definition, not all firms can be superior; some must be (temporarily) inferior. The fact that there will always be inferior firms means there will always be pressure to neutralize or leapfrog the superior firms. Disequilibrium is the normal and healthy state of affairs (Dickson 1992).
- Heterogeneous firms. Heterogeneity of resources results in the heterogeneity of firms. Some firms may have better resources for satisfying a niche market. Some may have superior relational resources with suppliers so that vertical integration is unnecessary. Some may have excess resources that cannot be sold to others, leading them to diversify into other product lines or markets (Teece 1980). Different bundles of resources lead firms to target different market segments. The size and scope of firms should reflect this diversity.
- Above-normal profits. As resources are more heterogeneous and immobile, they become more scarce. Firms earn sustained economic rents from their superior resources as long as rivals are unable to acquire, imitate, or substitute them. However, this is not a sign of inefficiency. The resource raises the quality of the good or lowers its cost; above-normal returns are the efficient outcome from these effects.

---

[25] Rumelt estimated that industry and firm effects accounted for 8% and 46%, respectively, of a firm's profit variability. Also see Roquebert, Phillips, and Westfall. Roquebert et al. (n.d.) used a much larger data set, sampling from more industries and firm sizes, and found industry and firm effects to be 10% and 57%, respectively.

Policy Implications

Proponents of a resource-based theory of competition provide a range of policy recommendations.

Deemphasize market structure. Concern with market structure comes from the belief that market structure determines firm conduct, with con-centrated markets being dangerous per se. However, resource-based theory presents theoretical and empirical arguments that firm strategies affect profitability to a much greater degree than market structure.

Allow firms to experiment with strategies. Because firm strategies play such a large role, they should be the focus of any measurement of com-petitive intensity. Because firms operate in a world of heterogeneity, immobility, and imperfect information, there is no single "best" strategy for all firms to have. Each firm has a unique history, which has nurtured unique resources, so we should expect different firms to have different strategies. Actions that have been traditionally considered anticompeti-tive (product differentiation, advertising) can be procompetitive in this environment.

Examine interactions between markets. Firms compete by acquiring or developing resources that are scarce, valuable, and difficult to imitate. For this reason, the state of competition in resource markets can have significant effects on competition in downstream markets.

Deregulation may benefit incumbents or new entrants. In deregulated industries that formerly enjoyed government-enforced entry barriers, the likely success of new entrants depends on the state of competition under regulation. If competition existed under regulation, incumbent firms may have developed unique advantages that will take time for entrants to replicate. If regulation protected monopolies, incumbents may be at a disadvantage because they acquired capabilities that are liabilities in a deregulated environment.

Deemphasize profit rates. Some firms will have higher rates of return than other firms. However, this is not due to market power or restriction of output, but to superior resources and the increased efficiency that flows from them. The potential for these higher profit rates is the reason why firms develop new resources and search for new complementarities among existing resources. Equalizing profit rates through regulation would reduce the intensity of competition.

CONCLUSIONS

Competition theory has come a long way since the "structuralist vs. Chicago" debates of the 1960s and 1970s. At that time, the principal issue was whether outcomes in real-world markets look more or less like the perfect market ideal. Structuralists argued that genuine markets must be rife with imperfections, because significant concentration and high barriers to entry are inconsistent with perfect markets. Chicagoans tended to overlook the real world's failure to conform to the models' assumptions, presenting empirical evidence that market outcomes often conform to the predictions of the perfect market models. Combined with a burgeoning analysis of government failure, such research was sufficient to tip Chicago's scales against activist antitrust and regulatory policy. But despite intense disagreements, both sides believed their point of view was in some way grounded in the perfect market model.

Since that time, the scholarly playing field has shifted. Dynamic theories of competition are based on assumptions fundamentally different from those of the perfect market models, and they offer different predictions about likely market outcomes as well. Widespread application of these theories could dramatically alter antitrust and regulatory analysis and policies. Schumpeterian and Austrian theories of competition, for example, have fueled economists' and public utility regulators' disillusionment with rate-of-return regulation and pointed the way toward various types of "incentive" plans that allow firms with supranormal efficiency to capture supranormal returns. Path dependence theories have played a role in the U.S. government's prosecution of Microsoft. In the debate over retail electricity competition, the nature of the market as a discovery process was cited as a reason to avoid forcing all consumers to buy power through a centralized pool.

Such policy initiatives, however, have largely been adjuncts grafted onto a paradigm that still regards the outcomes of perfect market models as the welfare ideal. If, as Schumpeter argued, human innovation and creativity account for the lion's share of material progress, then a more extensive application of dynamic competition theories is in order.

REFERENCES

Alchian, Armen A. 1950. Uncertainty, Evolution, and Economic Theory. *Journal of Political Economy* 58: 211–22.
Andrews, Kenneth. 1980. *The Concept of Corporate Strategy*. Homewood, IL: Richard D. Irwin.
Arthur, W. Brian. 1986. Industry Location Patterns and the Importance of History. Center for Economic Policy Research, Publication No. 84. Palo Alto, CA: Stanford University.
    1988. Self-Reinforcing Mechanisms in Economics. In Anderson K. Arrow and D. Pines, eds., *The Economy as an Evolving Complex System*, 111–32. Redwood City, CA: Addison-Wesley.
    1989. Competing Technologies, Increasing Returns, and Lock-In by Historical Events. *Economic Journal* 99: 116–31.
    1990. Positive Feedbacks in the Economy. *Scientific American* 262 (February): 92–99.

Arthur, W. Brian, and David A. Lane. 1994. *"Information Contagion," Increasing Returns and Path Dependence in the Economy.* Ann Arbor: University of Michigan Press.

Barney, Jay. 1986. Strategic Factor Markets: Expectations, Luck, and Business Strategy. *Management Science* 32: 1231–41.

———. 1991. Firm, Resources, and Sustained Competitive Advantage. *Journal of Management* 17: 99–120.

Baumol, William J., and M. Stewart. 1971. On the Behavioral Theory of the Firm. In R. Marris and A. Wood, eds., *The Corporate Economy: Growth, Competition, and Innovative Potential,* 118–43. Cambridge, MA: Harvard University Press.

Bergson, Henri. 1911. *Time and Free Will: An Essay on the Immediate Data of Consciousness.* Trans. F. L. Pogson. London: George and Allen Unwin.

Besen, Stanley, and Joseph Farrell. 1994. Choosing How to Compete: Strategies and Tactics in Standardization. *Journal of Economic Perspectives* 8: 117–31.

Besen, Stanley, and Leland Johnson. 1986. *Compatibility Standards, Competition, and Innovation in the Broadcasting Industry.* Santa Monica, CA: Rand Corporation.

Chandler, Alfred. 1962. *Strategy and Structure.* Cambridge, MA: MIT Press.

Conner, Kathleen. 1991. A Historical Comparison of Resource-Based Theory and Five Schools of Thought within Industrial Organization Economics: Do We Have a New Theory of the Firm? *Journal of Management* 17: 121–54.

Cusumano, Michael, Yiorgos Mylondadis, and Richard Rosenbloom. 1990. Strategic Maneuvering and Mass Market Dynamics: The Triumph of VHS over BETA. CCC Working Paper No. 90-5. Center for Research in Management, Haas School of Business, University of California, Berkeley.

Cyert, R. M., and J. G. March. 1963. *A Behavioral Theory of the Firm.* Englewood Cliffs, NJ: Prentice-Hall.

Dasgupta, Partha, and Joseph Stiglitz. 1980. Uncertainty, Industrial Structure, and the Speed of R&D. *Bell Journal of Economics* 11: 1–28.

David, Paul A. 1985. Clio and the Economics of QWERTY. *American Economic Review* 75: 332–37.

Dickson, Peter R. 1992. Toward a General Theory of Competitive Rationality. *Journal of Marketing* 53: 3–15.

Dierickx, Ingemar, and Karel Cool. 1989. Asset Stock Accumulation and Sustainability of Competitive Advantage. *Management Science* 35: 1504–11.

Dosi, Giovanni, David J. Teece, and Sidney G. Winter. 1992. Towards a Theory of Corporate Coherence. In Giovanni Dosi, Roberto Giannetti, and Pier-Angelo Toninelli, eds., *Technology and Enterprise in a Historical Perspective,* 185–211. Oxford: Clarendon Press.

Farrell, Joseph, and Carl Shapiro. 1992. Standard Setting in High Definition Television. *Brookings Paper on Economic Activity: Microeconomics*: 1–93.

Futia, Carl A. 1980. Schumpeterian Competition. *Quarterly Journal of Economics* 94: 675–95.

Garud, R., P. Nayyar, and Z. Shapira. 1997. Beating the Odds: Toward a Theory of Technological Innovation. In R. Garud, P. Nayyar, and Z. Shapira, eds.,

Technological Innovation: Oversights and Foresights, 345–54. Cambridge: Cambridge University Press.

Hayek, Friedrich A. 1945. The Use of Knowledge in Society. *American Economic Review* 35: 519–30.

1948a. The Facts of the Social Sciences. In F. A. Hayek, *Individualism and Economic Order*, 57–76. Chicago: University of Chicago Press.

1948b. The Meaning of Competition. In F. A. Hayek, *Individualism and Economic Order*, 92–106. Chicago: University of Chicago Press.

1978. Competition as a Discovery Procedure. In F. A. Hayek, *New Studies in Philosophy, Politics, and Economics*, 179–90. Chicago: University of Chicago Press.

Hofer, C. W., and D. Schendel. 1978. *Strategy Formulation: Analytical Concepts*. St. Paul, MN: West Publishing.

Hunt, Shelby D., and Robert M. Morgan. 1995. The Comparative Advantage Theory of Competition. *Journal of Marketing* 59: 1–15.

Kamien, Morton, and Nancy Schwartz. 1975. Market Structure and Innovation: A Survey. *Journal of Economic Literature* 8: 1–37.

Katz, Michael L., and Carl Shapiro. 1985. Network Externalities, Competition, and Compatibility. *American Economic Review* 75: 93–116.

1986. Technology Adoption in the Presence of Network Externalities. *Journal of Political Economy* 1986: 822–41.

1994. Systems Competition and Network Effects. *Journal of Economic Perspectives* 8: 93–116.

Kirzner, Israel M. 1973. *Competition and Entrepreneurship*. Chicago: University of Chicago Press.

1978. The Perils of Regulation: A Market-Process Approach. Occasional paper, Law and Economics Center, University of Miami.

1985. *Discovery and the Capitalist Process*. Chicago: University of Chicago Press.

1991. The Driving Force of the Market: The Idea of "Competition" in Contemporary Economic Theory and in the Austrian Theory of the Market Process. In Richard Ebeling, ed., *Champions of Freedom: Austrian Economics: Perspectives on the Past and Prospects for the Future*, 139–60. Hillsdale, MI: Hillsdale College Press.

1997. Entrepreneurial Discovery and the Competitive Market Process: An Austrian Approach. *Journal of Economic Literature* 35: 65–80.

1999. Creativity and/or Alertness: A Reconsideration of the Schumpeterian Entrepreneur. *Review of Austrian Economics* 11: 5–18.

Lachmann, Ludwig M. 1976. On the Central Concept of Austrian Economics: Market Process. In Laurence Moss, ed., *Foundations of Modern Austrian Economics*, 126–32. Kansas City, MO: Sheed and Ward.

1986. *The Market as an Economic Process*. Oxford: Basil Blackwell.

Langlois, Richard, and Michael Everett. 1994. What Is Evolutionary Economics? In Lars Magnusson, ed., *Evolutionary and Neo-Schumpeterian Approaches to Economics*, 11–47. Boston: Kluwer Publishers.

Liebowitz, Stan, and Stephen E. Margolis. 1990. The Fable of the Keys. *Journal of Law and Economics* 33: 1–26.

1995. Path Dependence, Lock-In and History. *Journal of Law, Economics and Organization* 11: 205–26.

Lippman, Steven A., and John J. McCall. 1976. The Economics of Job Search: A Survey. *Economic Inquiry* 14: 155–89.

Littlechild, Stephen S. 1981. Misleading Calculations of the Social Costs of Monopoly Power. *Economic Journal* 91: 350–60.

Loury, Glenn. 1979. Market Structure and Innovation. *Quarterly Journal of Economics* 93: 395–410.

Marshall, Alfred. [1890] 1982. *Principles of Economics.* 8th ed. Philadelphia: Porcupine Press.

1898. Distribution and Exchange. *Economic Journal* 8: 37–59.

Mises, Ludwig. 1966. *Human Action.* 3rd ed. Chicago: Henry Regnery.

Nelson, Richard R. 1991. Why Do Firms Differ, and How Does It Matter? *Strategic Management Journal* 14: 61–74.

1986. The Tension between Process Stories and Equilibrium Models: Analyzing the Productivity-Growth Slowdown of the 1970s. In Richard N. Langlois, ed., *Economics as a Process: Essays in the New Institutional Economics*, 135–51. Cambridge: Cambridge University Press.

Nelson, Richard R., and Sidney G. Winter. 1974. Neoclassical versus Evolutionary Theories of Growth. *Economic Journal* 84: 886–905.

1978. Forces Generating and Limiting Concentration under Schumpeterian Competition. *Bell Journal of Economics* 9: 524–48.

1982a. *An Evolutionary Theory of Economic Change.* Cambridge, MA: Harvard University Press.

1982b. The Schumpeterian Tradeoff Revisited. *American Economic Review* 72: 114–32.

Nelson, Richard R., Sidney G. Winter, and Herbert L. Schuette. 1976. Technical Change in an Evolutionary Model. *Quarterly Journal of Economics* 90: 90–118.

O'Driscoll, Gerald. 1976. Spontaneous Order and Coordination of Economic Activities. In E. Dolan, ed., *Foundations of Modern Austrian Economics*, 120–31. Kansas City, MO: Sheed and Ward.

1977. *Economics as a Coordination Problem: The Contributions of Friedrich A. Hayek.* Kansas City, MO: Sheed Andrews & McMeel.

O'Driscoll, Gerald, and Mario Rizzo. 1985. *The Economics of Time and Ignorance.* New York: Routledge.

Penrose, Edith. 1990. *The Theory of the Growth of the Firm.* Oxford: Basil Blackwell.

Peteraf, Margaret A. 1993. The Cornerstones of Competitive Advantage: A Resource-Based View. *Strategic Management Journal* 14: 179–91.

Rao, H., and J. Singh. 1997. Towards an Institutional Ecology of Speciation. Working Paper Prepared for Conference on Path Dependence and Path Creation, Copenhagen Business School.

Reback, Gary, Susan Creighton, David Killam, and Neil Nathanson, with assistance from Garth Saloner and W. Brian Arthur. N.d. *Technological, Economic and Legal Perspectives Regarding Microsoft's Business Strategy in Light of the Proposed Acquisition of Intuit, Inc.*

Rockoff, H. 1994. History and Economics. In E. Monkkonen, ed., *Engaging the Past: The Uses of History across the Social Sciences*, 48–76. Durham, NC: Duke University Press.

Roquebert, Jaime A., Robert L. Phillips, and Peter A. Westfall. N.d. Market versus Management: What "Drives" Profitability. Working Paper, Texas Tech University.

Rothschild, Michael. 1973. Models of Market Organization with Imperfect Information: A Survey. *Journal of Political Economy*. 81: 1283–308.

Rumelt, Richard. 1984. Toward a Strategic Theory of the Firm. In R. B. Lamb, ed., *Competitive Strategy Management*, 556–70. Englewood Cliffs, NJ: Prentice-Hall.

    1987. Theory, Strategy, and Entrepreneurship. In David Teece, ed., *The Competitive Challenge*, 138–58. Cambridge, MA: Ballinger.

    1991. How Much Does Industry Matter? *Strategic Management Journal* 12: 167–85.

Scherer, F. 1970. Market Structure and Technological Innovation. In F. Scherer, *Industrial Market Structure and Economic Performance*, 613–60. Chicago: Rand McNally.

Schumpeter, Joseph A. 1908. *The Nature and Essence of Theoretical Economics*. Munich and Leipzig: Duncker & Humblot.

    1911. *The Theory of Economic Development: An Inquiry into Capital, Credit, Interest, and the Business Cycle*. Cambridge, MA: Harvard University Press.

    1939. *Business Cycles: A Theoretical, Historical and Statistical Analysis of the Capitalist Process*. New York: McGraw Hill.

    1942. *Capitalism, Socialism and Democracy*. New York: Harper and Row.

Shackle, G. L. S. 1979. *Imagination and the Nature of Choice*. Edinburgh: Edinburgh University Press.

Silverberg, G. 1988. Modeling Economic Dynamics and Technical Change: Mathematical Approaches to Self-Organisation and Evolution. In Giovanni Dosi, ed., *Technical Change and Economic Theory*, 531–59. London: Frances Pinter.

Simon, Herbert A. 1955. A Behavioral Model of Rational Choice. *Quarterly Journal of Economics* 69: 99–118.

Teece, David. 1980. Economies of Scope and the Scope of the Firm. *Journal of Economic Behavior and Organization* 1: 223–33.

    1982. Toward an Economic Theory of the Multiproduct Firm. *Journal of Economic Behavior and Organization* 7: 39–63.

    1986. Firm Boundaries, Technological Innovation, and Strategic Management. In L. G. Thomas, ed., *The Economics of Strategic Planning*, 187–99. Lexington, MA: Lexington.

Wernerfelt, Birger. 1984. A Resource-Based View of the Firm. *Strategic Management Journal* 5: 171–80.

Williamson, Oliver. 1979. Transaction-Cost Economics: The Governance of Contractual Relations. *Journal of Law and Economics* 22: 233–61.

Winter, Sidney G. 1964. Economic "Natural Selection" and the Theory of the Firm. *Yale Economic Essays* 4: 225–72.

2

Competence Explanations of Economic Profits in Strategic Management

Some Policy Implications

Jay B. Barney

Economics offers at least two classes of explanations of the existence of economic profits (Demsetz 1973). The first, which can be described as a *monopoly theory of economic profits*, suggests that economic profits emerge as a result of firms acting to reduce output below and increase prices above the competitive level. Several large theoretical and empirical literatures on topics such as tacit and explicit collusion, industry concentration, oligopolies, and vertical and horizontal exclusive agreements (to name just a few) all fall within this broad category of monopolistic theories of economic profit (Scherer 1980).

The second class of explanations, which can be called the *capability theory of economic profits* (Rumelt 1984; Barney 1986a), suggests that economic profits emerge because some firms are more capable than others. If the cost of developing these capabilities is less than the value they create, they can be a source of economic profit. Though not having spawned as extensive an empirical and theoretical literature as monopolistic theories of economic profits, capability explanations of these profits have received some attention – for example, from evolutionary economists (Nelson and Winter 1982) and some information economists (e.g., Demsetz 1973).

There is little doubt that both these explanations of economic profits are valid in at least some circumstances. Some firms gain economic profits by engaging in monopolistic activities, others by exploiting their superior capabilities. Indeed, a single firm's economic profits might reflect both monopolistic actions and superior capabilities. Moreover, a more capable firm may, because of its capability advantage, be able to create a situation

I appreciate comments from Barry Baysinger, Steve Mangum, and Abby McWilliams. Any errors are mine.

where it can behave monopolistically.[1] In a similar way, a firm operating in a monopolistic situation may be able to gain capability advantages that further extend its ability to earn economic profits.[2]

These different explanations of the existence of economic profits are not just the source of interesting debates among scholars but have important policy implications as well. In particular, as Demsetz (1973) has noted, the source of a firm's economic profits largely determines whether a firm's actions are consistent or inconsistent with consumer welfare. In general, economic profits that are derived primarily from a firm's monopolistic activities reduce consumer welfare, whereas economic profits that are derived primarily from a firm's taking advantage of its superior capabilities increase consumer welfare. Or, if a firm's economic profits depend both on its monopolistic activities and its superior capabilities, the adverse impact of a firm's monopolistic actions must be carefully weighed against the benefits to consumers derived from its capability advantages before the impact of that firm's actions on consumer welfare can be determined.

Although both monopoly and capability explanations of economic profits have potentially important policy implications, the policy implications of monopoly explanations have received substantially more attention in the literature (Demsetz 1973). One reason for this differential level of intellectual investment may be that much economic theory has only a limited vocabulary for describing the kind of interfirm differences that are critical in studying capability explanations of economic profits (Porter 1981). Differences in the ability of firms to learn, to create, to·innovate, to cooperate – all capabilities that are likely to be important in any capability explanation of economic profits – are difficult to incorporate into models of economic profits, where what goes on inside of firms is characterized as a "black box."[3]

---

[1] This is one characterization of actions taken by Microsoft in the personal computer operating system and applications software markets (Meese 1999). In this version of the Microsoft story, Microsoft used its ability to develop operating systems to create a competitive advantage that it then used to gain monopolistic advantages in applications. Of course, these facts are in dispute.

[2] This was one of the major concerns in the breakup of AT&T – that the regional operating companies would be able to take profits earned from their monopoly position in the local telephone market to subsidize their entry into different markets. If that subsidy involved the regional operating companies developing unique capabilities that could be used in these new markets, then they would have used their initial monopoly position to develop capability-based competitive advantages (Brennan 1987).

[3] I do not mean to imply here that no economic theories have been developed that investigate what goes on within the "black box" of the firm. Certainly, this is not the case. For example, agency theory (Jensen and Meckling 1976), transactions cost economics

Indeed, even the field of strategic management was dominated, for many years, by conceptual tools that focused primarily on industry structure as a source of economic profits and had only a limited vocabulary for describing interfirm capability differences. Found in the work of Porter (1980, 1985) and his associates, this explanation of economic profits is derived from the structure-conduct-performance (SCP) paradigm in economics (Bain 1956) and describes the conditions under which firms in an industry will be able to exercise market power, tacitly collude, and erect barriers to entry in order to create and sustain economic profits.

Over the past ten years or so, however, this industry structure approach to understanding sources of economic profits in the field of strategic management has been largely displaced by capability explanations (Rumelt, Teece, and Schendel 1991). While manifesting itself in a series of specific theoretical and empirical traditions, including the resource-based view of the firm (Wernerfelt 1984; Barney 1986a, 1991), the dynamic capabilities model (Teece, Pisano, and Shuen 1997), and models of the core competence of the organization (Prahalad and Hamel 1990), these capability explanations of economic profits all focus on precisely the kinds of heterogeneous firm capabilities – including organizational culture (Barney 1986b), tacit knowledge (Itami 1987), the ability to learn (Cohen and Levinthal 1990), and the ability to cooperate (Henderson and Cockburn 1994) – that are difficult to analyze in economic models with limited vocabularies for describing interfirm differences.

Unfortunately, there has been virtually no effort among strategic management scholars to understand the antitrust and other policy implications of the capability explanations of economic profits they have developed. Such an effort is simply not within the range of the strategic management research question as it has been traditionally posed. Thus, the present chapter has two purposes: to briefly describe the capability explanation of economic profits that has developed within the field of strategic management, and to begin to explore some of the antitrust and other policy implications of this explanation of economic profits.

(Williamson 1985), and work on research and development has all begun to investigate intrafirm phenomena. The difference between the literature discussed in this chapter (e.g., the resource-based view) and these other economic models is a matter of degree. Resource-based logic suggests that intrafirm capabilities are the most important efficiency determinants of economic profits. It also focuses on path-dependent, socially complex capabilities that are usually not featured as prominently in other kinds of analysis.

CAPABILITY EXPLANATIONS OF ECONOMIC PROFITS IN STRATEGIC MANAGEMENT

Capability explanations of economic profits in strategic management adopt, as a primary unit of analysis, a firm's resources and capabilities. In this context, a firm's resources and capabilities are the tangible and intangible assets a firm uses to choose and implement its strategies. Firm strategies, on the other hand, are the set of actions a firm takes in an attempt to gain competitive advantages.

Two assumptions about resources and capabilities are central to capability explanations of economic profits: the assumption of *resource heterogeneity* and the assumption of *resource immobility* (Barney 1991). The former asserts that some resources and capabilities may be heterogeneously distributed across competing firms, thus making some firms more capable than others, whereas the latter asserts that these capability differences can be long-lasting. Contrary to much received microeconomics, this explanation of economic profits suggests that differences in the competitive performance of different firms are not always quickly competed away through imitation and substitution. Rather, in some circumstances, stable differences in firm capabilities can lead to stable differences in the strategies firms pursue and the economic profits they realize (Lipman and Rumelt 1982).

There are several reasons why resources and capabilities may be heterogeneously distributed across a set of competing firms and why it may be costly for a firm without a particular resource or capability to imitate it. Three of the most important of these reasons are the role of history and path dependence, the role of causal ambiguity, and the role of socially complex resources and capabilities (Barney 1991; Dierickx and Cool 1989).

History and Path Dependence

Many of a firm's resources and capabilities are path-dependent, in the sense that only those firms with a particular set of experiences, over a particular time in history, can have obtained low-cost access to these resources and capabilities (Arthur 1989). Firms that were unable to obtain access to resources and capabilities during these special historical conditions may be able to obtain access later on. Once the full value of these resources and capabilities in generating competitive advantages is revealed, however, it will usually no longer be possible for firms to obtain access to them in a low-cost manner. Any economic profits these resources and capabilities could have generated will be reflected in the cost of obtaining access to them (Barney 1986a).

Consider, for example, Caterpillar, the heavy-duty construction equipment firm (Rukstad and Horn 1989). Before the Second World War, Caterpillar was one of several moderate-sized firms in the heavy construction industry in the United States. None of these firms had a global presence. None even had global aspirations.

During the years before the entry of the United States into the war, the federal government decided that it would need a primary worldwide supplier of much of the heavy duty construction equipment needed to build and maintain military bases, landing fields, and other military projects throughout the world. After a brief competition, Caterpillar was chosen as this primary supplier. The government agreed to pay Caterpillar prices for its equipment high enough to enable Caterpillar to develop a worldwide service and support network that could be used to help supply Allied forces. Caterpillar gladly accepted this opportunity and went about building such a network. Upon commencement of hostilities, Caterpillar's network was a vital part of the Allied war machine.

After the war, Caterpillar was the only firm with a worldwide service and support network. Domestic competitors did not have the opportunity to build such an extensive network during the war, and whatever networks had been built by foreign competitors before the war were destroyed. Clearly, having such a worldwide service and support network gave Caterpillar a significant competitive advantage.

Now, consider the position of a firm trying to compete with Caterpillar by duplicating its worldwide service and support network. In order to develop this network at the same low cost as Caterpillar, this competing firm would have to receive the same kind of subsidies – from the government or elsewhere – that Caterpillar received, support that was not likely to have been forthcoming. A competing firm might decide that in order to build this network at the same low cost as Caterpillar, it must simply recreate the Second World War – a very difficult thing to do.

If a firm has a competitive advantage because it gained access to capabilities at a low cost through its unique historical situation and path through time, those capabilities can be a source of economic profits, competing firms will find it costly to imitate those capabilities, and they can be a source of sustained competitive advantage.[4]

---

[4] The concept of sustained competitive advantage suggests that a firm's competitive advantage will not be competed away through imitation. However, a firm's competitive advantage can be lost through mismanagement or significant and unanticipated changes in demand, technology, or other attributes of the markets within which a firm operates. These significant and unanticipated changes are Schumpeterian shocks and, by definition, cannot be anticipated by firms.

Causal Ambiguity

Sometimes, it is not exactly clear what a firm is doing to gain competitive advantages and economic profits. As long as competing firms have multiple hypotheses about another firm's sources of competitive advantage, and as long as it is too costly to test these hypotheses to see which of these resources and capabilities – alone or in combination – are the source of this competitive advantage, causal ambiguity exists. Under conditions of causal ambiguity, competing firms may not know which of a firm's resources and capabilities they should imitate and which strategies they should pursue using those resources and capabilities. Lippman and Rumelt (1982) have shown that, under these conditions, firms with a competitive advantage can earn economic profits in equilibrium.

At first it seems unlikely that causal ambiguity about the sources of competitive advantage for a firm would ever exist. After all, managers in a firm should understand the sources of their own competitive advantage, and if managers in one firm understand these sources of advantage, it seems likely that managers in other firms would be able to learn about them as well. As this information is diffused throughout a set of competing firms, any causal ambiguity should be eliminated (Reed and DeFillippi 1990).

Managers in successful firms, however, may not be completely aware of their sources of competitive advantage. For example, if one asks entrepreneurs what enabled them to be successful, they are likely to reply with several common hypotheses, including "hard work, a willingness to take risks, and a high-quality management team." If one asks unsuccessful entrepreneurs what happened, however, they will often reply that they do not know, for they too "worked hard, were willing to take risks, and had a high-quality management team." If both successful and unsuccessful entrepreneurs are telling the truth, then "working hard, taking risks, and having a high-quality management team" does not differentiate between successful and unsuccessful entrepreneurial firms.

Indeed, two of the most powerful indicators of the existence of causal ambiguity in business are the failure rates of new businesses and new products. If the steps needed to gain competitive advantage were known, fewer firms would fail, and fewer products would have to be withdrawn from the market. When it is not clear what needs to be done to be successful, firms that are successful can earn economic profits, and their competitive advantages can be sustained.

Socially Complex Resources

Sometimes, the resources and capabilities that enable a firm to have a competitive advantage are socially complex. Examples of these kinds of capabilities include the interpersonal relations among a firm's top management team (Hambrick 1987), a firm's culture (Barney 1986b), and a firm's reputation among suppliers (Porter 1980) and customers (Klein, Crawford, and Alchian 1978; Klein and Lefler 1981). Firms that possess these resources and capabilities are able to conceive of and implement value-creating strategies that firms without these resources and capabilities are either unable to conceive of or implement. In most of these cases, it is possible to specify how these socially complex resources add value to a firm. Thus, there is little or no causal ambiguity surrounding the link between many socially complex resources and capabilities and competitive advantage.

But understanding that an organization's culture or high-quality relations among a firm's top management team can improve a firm's efficiency and effectiveness does not imply that a firm lacking these attributes can engage in low-cost activities to develop them (Porras and Berg 1978). For the time being, such social engineering may be beyond the abilities of most firms. At the very least, it is likely to be much more costly than it would be if socially complex resources evolved naturally within a firm.

The Attributes of Firm Resources and Economic Profits

In general, capability explanations of economic profits in strategic management predict that when a firm controls valuable, rare, and costly-to-imitate resources and capabilities, that firm can gain a sustained competitive advantage and earn economic profits. Such sustained competitive advantages are not competed away through imitation, although they may disappear when the basis for competitive advantage is changed, for example, through the development of new technologies or a change in consumer tastes.

If a firm controls valuable and rare resources and capabilities, but those resources and capabilities are not costly to imitate, a firm will gain only a temporary competitive advantage. Such a firm will earn economic profits while it enjoys a competitive advantage, but those profits will be competed away through imitation.

If a firm controls valuable resources and capabilities, but they are neither rare nor costly to imitate, it will enjoy only competitive parity and will earn zero economic profits.

Finally, if a firm controls resources and capabilities that are not valuable, the use of these resources in conceiving of and implementing strategies will lead to competitive disadvantages and negative economic profits (Barney 1991, 1997).

Tests of Capability Explanations of Economic Profits

Many of the general implications of this capability explanation of economic profits have been subject to empirical test. For example, Rumelt

(1991) and others have shown that firm level variables explain a greater percentage of the variance in firm profitability than do industry level variables, a result that is consistent with capability explanations of economic profits.[5]

Many of the more specific implications of this explanation of economic profits have also been subjected to empirical test. For example, Barnett, Greve, and Park (1994) have shown that a firm's history in surviving a difficult economic climate has a significant impact on explaining that firm's performance in a difficult economic climate several decades later. Mancke (1977) and other authors have shown how luck and causal ambiguity can be parsimonious explanations of observed performance differences between firms.[6] Henderson and Cockburn (1994) and Zaheer and Venkatraman (1995) have shown that socially complex capabilities, such as the level of teamwork in a firm and a firm's trustworthiness, can be important predictors of a firm's level of economic profitability.

ANTITRUST AND OTHER POLICY IMPLICATIONS OF CAPABILITY EXPLANATIONS OF ECONOMIC PROFITS

Factor Market Competition

Most antitrust enforcement activities focus on the actions that firms take to dominate specific product markets. For example, the General Motors and Toyota joint venture was subject to regulatory concern because of the possibility that these two giant firms could cooperate to create domination in the automobile market in the United States. Microsoft is currently under antitrust scrutiny because of its domination of the personal computer operating systems product market, and its potential domination of the personal computer software applications product market.

However, antitrust enforcement also recognizes the importance of competition in what might be called "strategic factor markets," or the markets within which firms compete to acquire the resources and capabilities they need to implement their product market strategies (Barney

---

[5] This finding contradicts earlier findings by Schmalensee (1985) and Wernerfelt and Montgomery (1988) who found that industry effects explain more variance in firm profitability than firm effects. Rumelt (1991) explains the differences between these sets of findings by observing that the earlier investigators used a single year of data for their analysis, while he used three years of data. Rumelt's (1991) findings suggest that there is little market power inherent in a market economy, that regulators' actions have the effect of limiting market power, or both.

[6] This interpretation has been hotly contested by Caves, Gale, and Porter (1977), among others.

1986a). Thus, for example, when baseball owners colluded to restrict competition for free-agent players – one of the critical resources that baseball teams need to compete in the sports entertainment market – the antitrust implications of such actions led to a finding against baseball owners (Bernstein 1990).

Capability explanations of economic profits also focus attention on strategic factor market competition, for this is where the competition that often determines which firms will or will not earn economic profits actually takes place. However, capability explanations go beyond traditional antitrust analyses of strategic factor markets in at least three ways.

First, where the range of strategic factor markets analyzed in many current antitrust approaches is limited to land, labor, and capital, capability explanations of economic profits suggest that the competitiveness of a broad range of strategic factor markets needs to be considered. These strategic factor markets include those markets where firms compete to acquire such resources and capabilities as the ability to produce high-quality products, to develop new technologies, and to co-operate with suppliers and customers. These path-dependent, causally ambiguous, and socially complex resources and capabilities are often as important, if not more important, in determining a firm's competitive position in a product market than the more traditional resources of land, labor, and capital. More precisely, these are the capabilities that enable a firm to use uniquely the land, labor, and capital it may have acquired in relatively competitive factor markets. Failure to evaluate the competitiveness of the factor markets within which these resources and capabilities are acquired could lead to the conclusion that consumer welfare is being maximized when, in fact, it is not.

Second, just because a firm is operating in an apparently competitive product market does not mean that anticompetitive behavior has not occurred. Indeed, if anticompetitive actions have taken place in the strategic factor markets associated with a particular product market, those actions can hurt consumer welfare even though the product markets in which firms are operating are apparently competitive. Antitrust policy must consider not only the anticompetitive activities of firms in product markets but also the anticompetitive activities of firms in the markets for the resources needed to compete in product markets. Exclusive dealing, tacit collusion, and other per se antitrust violations can be just as important in strategic factor markets as they are in product markets. This is true for all the strategic factor markets where firms acquire the resources they need to compete in product markets – including the path-dependent, causally ambiguous, and socially complex resources and capabilities emphasized in capability explanations of economic profits.

For example, suppose firms in the consumer electronics industry collude in the acquisition of critical engineering talent (i.e., they agree among themselves to pay less than the market wage for engineering talent) and that the highest-valued use of this talent is in the consumer electronics industry. In the long run, the inability of engineers to obtain their full market value will lead individuals to seek alternative careers where the full value of their human capital can be realized (e.g., maybe they will become lawyers). The ability of consumer electronic firms to introduce innovative new products to meet consumer needs depends critically on gaining access to high-quality engineering talent. With fewer people becoming engineers, the level of innovation in the consumer electronics industry will fall, and this would reduce consumer welfare in the long run. Notice that consumer welfare is reduced even if the consumer electronics product market is highly competitive in terms of the products and services that are actually available in that market. Anticompetitive actions in strategic factor markets can create consumer welfare problems even if product markets are highly competitive.

Finally, the existence of competitive strategic factor markets can place a significant limitation on the ability of firms in imperfectly competitive product markets to adversely affect consumer welfare. If the value of a resource or capability in creating an imperfectly competitive product market is anticipated in a strategic factor market, that value will be reflected in the price a firm will have to pay to gain access to that resource or capability in the factor market. In this setting, the price of a resource or capability will rise to equal its value in implementing a strategy. Even if a firm is successful in creating an imperfectly competitive product market by, say, acquiring a dominant market share or by acquiring a unique technology, the cost of acquiring this product market position will rise to the point that a firm will not earn economic profits from doing so.

The existence of efficient strategic factor markets represents a market-based constraint on the anticompetitive behavior of firms. In general, profit-maximizing firms will not seek product market domination if the factor markets where the resources needed to create product market domination are very competitive. Governmental constraints on anticompetitive product market behavior could, in this situation, be redundant because a firm will not find it in its self-interest to pursue actions that would reduce consumer welfare.

For example, suppose there are five firms in a highly competitive industry, that each of these firms has 20 percent market share, and that in order to exercise market power in this industry, a firm must possess at least 40 percent market share. Also, suppose that one of these five firms (firm A) wants to acquire another (firm B, C, D, or E) in order to exercise market power in this industry. How much will it cost to acquire one of these firms? If we assume semistrong efficient capital markets, the price to acquire any one of these firms will rise to at least equal its value in creating opportunities for firm A to exercise market power (Barney 1988). Thus, even if firm A successfully buys another firm in the industry and has the opportunity to exercise market power, the price of acquiring such power will have been fully reflected in the cost of such an acquisition, and thus not be a source of economic profits. If firm A is a profit-maximizing firm, it will not seek to acquire one of its competitors, even though doing so would create the opportunity to exercise market power, because there is no profit opportunity in doing so.

Searching for Efficiency Gains in Evaluating Firm Behavior

In evaluating the anticompetitive implications of firm actions, the possible efficiency gains from such activities are very important. Sometimes, a reduction in consumer welfare created by, say, an industry becoming more concentrated through a merger can be more than offset by an increase in consumer welfare if industry concentration also increases efficiencies that are passed on to consumers.

Several sources of possible efficiencies have been identified in the traditional antitrust literature. Among these are the realization of economies of scale through shared activities, the realization of learning-curve efficiencies through the increased volume of production, and the reduction in overhead costs per unit of production. The realization of these kinds of efficiencies has often been cited as a reason for allowing what might otherwise be considered an anticompetitive activity to go forward.

Capability explanations of economic profit acknowledge that these kinds of efficiencies can be important and can create economic value. However, this approach to analyzing economic profits suggests that other sources of efficiency are likely to be even more important. In particular, whenever the combination of two or more firms brings together complementary capabilities that are path-dependent, causally ambiguous, or socially complex, the value created can be substantial. These efficiency gains may justify mergers and other actions that would otherwise not be allowable under antitrust guidelines.

These less tangible efficiencies are likely to be particularly important in information-intensive industries. In such industries, integrating the complementary knowledge of different firms may create enormous economic value and benefit consumers, even if no traditional economies of scale, learning-curve efficiencies, or overhead reduction efficiencies exist. A failure to appreciate the important value-added role of these nontraditional efficiencies could lead to decisions not to allow a merger or other form of consolidation to go forward, and thus a failure to realize fully the potential benefits to consumers of such actions.

In the strategic management literature, some empirical work speaks directly to the role of these less tangible efficiencies in motivating firms to diversify their operations, often through acquisitions. Traditional research on the relationship between the strategic relatedness of the businesses within which a diversified firm operates and that firm's overall performance has used measures of strategic relatedness based on the industries of the business units that a firm owns. Using standard industrial classification (SIC) codes, this approach to measurement assumes that industries that are more similar to each other, in terms of the product markets they serve, are more strategically related. Using the ideas developed here, firms that are operating in industries very similar to each other should be able to realize economies of scale and learning-curve efficiencies, and should be able to reduce overhead costs per unit of production. In general, there is a weak but significantly positive relationship between strategic relatedness measured this way and overall firm performance (Barney 1997).

Recently, Robbins and Wiersema (1995) adopted a different approach to measuring strategic relatedness. Instead of measuring efficiency gains by examining how similar the industries of different business units owned by the same firm are, these authors examined how complementary these business units are in terms of the underlying technologies they employ. Technological complementarity is closer to the kind of efficiency gain that capability explanations of economic profit expect to be important. Using economy-level technology input-output matrices, Robbins and Wiersema (1995) estimated the extent to which one business unit used the technology outputs of another business unit in its productive efforts, and vice versa. This measure of strategic relatedness has a much stronger positive and significant relationship to the overall profitability of a diversified firm than the traditional measure. Moreover, when the traditional measure of strategic relatedness is included in a multiple regression with this capability-based measure of strategic relatedness, the capability measure of relatedness remains important whereas the traditional measure is no longer significant. This research suggests that efficiency gains based on intangible resources and capabilities can be very important – and perhaps even more important than efficiency gains from any of the more tangible sources traditionally studied.

Of course, one of the great liabilities associated with searching for efficiencies created by complementary, path-dependent, causally ambiguous, and socially complex capabilities is that these less tangible efficiencies can be used to justify virtually any merger or other consolidation. Their very intangibility makes it easier to use them as a justification for inappropriate anticompetitive activities. In this context, it is very important to be able to apply the logic of the capability explanations of economic profits described earlier – do these capabilities add economic value, are they rare, are they costly to imitate, and so forth? – to distinguish between those firm actions that actually increase efficiency and those that only claim to increase efficiency.

However, simply because the efficiencies created through firm actions are not of the tangible variety cited in the traditional antitrust literature does not mean they are not real. Nor does it mean that these less tangible efficiencies do not have the potential for significantly enhancing consumer welfare. Capability explanations of economic profits, in the end, suggest that more capable firms are able to earn economic profits precisely because they are more able to meet consumer needs than less capable firms. The tangibility or intangibility of the bases of these consumer welfare gains per se should not have an impact on antitrust deliberations.

The Role of Patents in Generating Economic Profits

The role of patents continues to be an important issue in antitrust analysis. Clearly, patents play some role, in at least some industries, in creating incentives for firms and individuals to innovate, and thus should be encouraged by policy. Such innovation can be very beneficial to consumers. On the other hand, this need to encourage innovation is counterbalanced by the need to maximize consumer welfare by encouraging increased competition once an innovation is introduced.

The debate over the antitrust implications of patents has been overshadowed, in recent years, by empirical research that suggests that patents are not all that effective in discouraging competitive imitation, and thus not all that effective in enabling firms to gain and sustain competitive advantages. Levin (1986) found that firms in 130 lines of business felt that patents were the least important means of securing competitive advantages for new products. Mansfield (1986) studied firms in 12 industries and concluded that only 14 percent of their innovations would not have been developed without patent protection. Mansfield, Schwartz, and Wagner (1981) also found that 60 percent of all the patents issued in the United States each year are imitated within four years of being issued – without violating legal patent rights of innovators – and that the cost of imitating another firm's patents was only 65 percent of the cost of the original innovation.

Patents seem to serve their intended roles in only a few industries, including specialty chemicals and pharmaceuticals. In these industries, patents are not imitated quickly, and firms see patent protections as being extremely important in sustaining competitive advantages (Levin 1986).[7]

The conclusion that patents do not secure a firm's competitive advantages – with the exception of patents granted to firms in the specialty chemicals and pharmaceuticals industries – is quite consistent with capability explanations of economic profits. In this model, it is the path-dependent, causally ambiguous, and socially complex nature of a firm's resources and capabilities that make competitive imitation costly. Because patents make a firm's capabilities explicit and tangible, patenting can, in many circumstances, actually reduce the ability of firms to sustain competitive advantages.

Consider, for example, a firm like Sony. Sony introduces numerous products to the consumer electronics marketplace each year. Invariably, after Sony introduces a new product class (e.g., the Sony "Walkman," the Sony "Discman"), competitors rapidly introduce similar product categories. Clearly, product by product, Sony gains no sustained competitive advantages. However, Sony's source of sustained competitive advantage is not in each of its highly imitable products, but in its ability to constantly innovate and introduce new products. That capability is path-dependent, causally ambiguous, and socially complex, and thus is costly for other firms to imitate – all without explicit patent protection (Barney 1997; Henderson and Cockburn 1994).

Given the conclusion that patents are not a source of sustained competitive advantage in most industries, an important question becomes, Why do firms continue to engage in patenting behavior? One possible explanation of this behavior is that the act of patenting sends important signals to potential employees, to customers, and to competitors about a firm's innovative capabilities (Spence 1973). Moreover, these signals can be sent well before specific products or services are introduced into the market.

A firm's innovative capability is difficult to observe directly yet is an important organizational capability for many of a firm's stakeholders. Potential employees want to know that they will be working with a very innovative firm, customers want to know that a firm is able to provide the most advanced products and services available, and competitors want to know with which firms they might want to cooperate in strategic

---

[7] This may be the case because, in these industries, small changes in product attributes can lead to large changes in product performance (e.g., changing a few atoms in a molecule can radically change the performance attributes of that molecule). When firms obtain patents in these kinds of industries, competing firms are unable to introduce similar products that do not, in fact, violate these patents.

alliances to develop technologies further. Patents provide information about this organizational capability because it is more costly for firms without this capability to engage in patenting than firms with it. Moreover, patents provide this information without reducing a firm's competitive advantage, because that competitive advantage is usually a function of their innovative capability and not a function of the specific products they introduce into the market. In most industries, those specific products are not a source of sustained competitive advantage whether or not they are patented.

Using patents as signals of a firm's innovative capability may also have some anticompetitive implications – for example, if firms used their patents to indicate the kinds of innovative capabilities they were developing, and if firms in an industry tacitly colluded by not competing in the same areas of innovation.

Increasing Competition in an Industry and Consumer Welfare

One of the central objectives of much antitrust and other government actions is increasing the level of competition in an industry. This objective is based on the belief that increased competition in an industry enhances consumer welfare. Actions that increase the level of entry into an industry, through deregulation or the dismantling of other barriers to entry, or actions that have the effect of breaking up previously dominant firms in an industry, are both designed to increase the level of competition.

Capability explanations of economic profits acknowledge that increasing competition in an industry can enhance consumer welfare. However, given the idea of the costly imitation of resources and capabilities that is central to these explanations of economic profits, certain cautions are appropriate.

First, as Demsetz (1973) originally noted, sometimes the reason a firm (or set of firms) is dominant in a particular industry is that it is very capable. Large market share may not always be the result of anticompetitive actions by a firm but may sometimes be the result of a highly competitive process where a more capable firm has been able to use its capabilities to gain a dominant position. A decision to break such a dominant firm up into smaller firms in order to increase competition in an industry may actually reduce consumer welfare, if the capabilities developed in the dominant firm cannot be transferred to the smaller firms that such actions would create.

For example, in the pharmaceutical industry in the United States, there are a few large dominant firms that have been able, over the past several decades, to develop remarkable skills in developing, testing,

marketing, and distributing drugs. Research by Henderson and Cockburn (1994) and others has shown that many of these skills are highly
path-dependent, causally ambiguous, and socially complex. Moreover, it
is the ability of these firms to take the resources and capabilities developed in one part of their business and leverage them to create innovations in other parts of their business that is a particularly important
driver of innovation. Any effort to break these large successful firms up
into smaller firms in order to increase the level of competition in the
pharmaceutical industry would almost certainly have an adverse effect
on the level of innovation in this industry. And less innovation in this
industry could adversely affect consumer welfare.

Put differently, if one concludes that the size and profitability of large
pharmaceutical firms in the United States are a function of their anticompetitive actions, then an appropriate remedy would be to break
these firms into smaller entities, thereby increasing competition and lowering prices in this industry. On the other hand, if one concludes that
the size and profitability of large pharmaceutical firms in the United
States are a function of their high level of capability and their ability to
use that capability in a wide range of innovative efforts, then breaking
these firms into smaller entities would not necessarily enhance consumer
welfare.

Second, deregulation and the dismantling of other barriers to entry to
an industry are designed to increase the level of competition in an industry under the assumption that increased competition enhances consumer
welfare. However, increased competition enhances consumer welfare
only if new entrants are capable. If new entrants into an industry are less
capable, and if consumers find it difficult to distinguish between more
and less capable firms in the short term, increased competition can actually reduce consumer welfare.

Consider the savings and loan industry in the United States. For years,
this was a highly regulated segment of the financial services market.
Firms in this market segment operated a relatively simple business: they
collected deposits and made loans on private homes. As part of an effort
to broadly deregulate the financial services industry, however, many of
the regulatory constraints on savings and loan institutions were relaxed
in the early 1980s. Savings and loan institutions began investing in a much
wider range of real estate and other projects, shifted much of their investment out of their local geographic markets, and in general began behav-
ing more like banks than savings and loans. Unfortunately, many of these
savings and loans had not developed the resources and capabilities –
including knowledge about how to estimate and manage risk and the
ability to control their operations – necessary to compete successfully
in this newly deregulated, wide-open financial services market. The

outcome was predictable as an economic downturn forced many of these firms into bankruptcy. The cost of rescuing the savings and loan industry was incredibly high.

When the resources and capabilities that enable a firm to be success-ful in an industry are path-dependent, causally ambiguous, or socially complex, and firms not in this industry do not possess these resources and capabilities, government efforts to facilitate new entry into an indus-try will have one of two effects. Either new entry will not be forthcom-ing, because potential new entrants will realize they do not possess the skills they need to be successful, and incumbent firms will continue to dominate that industry; or new entry will occur and new entrants will not succeed, in which case incumbent firms will still continue to dominate that industry. Incumbent firms will continue to dominate a newly dereg-ulated industry as long as the resources and capabilities needed to compete successfully in that industry continue to be possessed only by firms that have extended experience in that industry.

In general, capability explanations of economic profits suggest that it can take a great deal of time, some luck, and enormous skill to develop the tacit and intangible resources and capabilities needed to succeed in an industry. A failure to recognize the nature of these resources and capabilities could lead to policies that break up extremely capable firms or that encourage the entry of less capable firms – both to the detriment of consumer welfare.

CONCLUSIONS

In 1973, Demsetz wrote that "Superior performance can be attributed to the combination of great uncertainty plus luck or atypical insight by the management of a firm. . . . None of this is necessarily monopolistic (although monopoly may play some role). Profit does not arise because the firm creates 'artificial scarcity' through a reduction of its output. Nor does it arise because of collusion." Two important theoretical traditions partially trace their intellectual roots back to this 1973 article. The first of these is research on the economics of antitrust. In this literature, Demsetz's article was among the first of what later became a torrent of work that questions the policy implications of the naive application of the structure-conduct-performance paradigm. One of the most impor-tant implications of Demsetz's argument is that industry concentration per se cannot be taken as prima facie evidence of anticompetitive behav-ior. Sometimes, the reason that a small set of firms may dominate a par-ticular industry is that these firms are simply more capable than their competition.

The second of these literatures is research on what has come to be known as the capabilities explanation of economic profits in the field of strategic management. Rather than focusing on government policy, the field of strategic management tries to develop explanations of why some firms outperform others. Demsetz (1973) suggests that there are at least two reasons why there may be heterogeneity in firm performance: some firms may be lucky and some firms may be more capable. Rather than focusing on the policy implications of these conclusions, however, strategic management work has focused on their managerial implications in an attempt to suggest ways that managers may be able to create and sustain competitive advantages for their firms.

Although research on the economics of antitrust and research on competitive advantage in strategic management have common intellectual roots, there has been little or no interaction between these literatures over the past twenty-five years. This chapter begins to address this lack of interaction by summarizing how capability explanations of economic profits have evolved, how these capability explanations have been examined empirically, and some of the policy implications of these explanations. Among the policy implications of capability explanations of economic profits, as developed in the field of strategic management, are (1) a renewed emphasis on the importance of understanding the antitrust implications of competition in the strategic factor markets where firms acquire the resources and capabilities needed to compete in product markets, (2) an appreciation of the role of intangible and tacit resources and capabilities in generating efficiencies in mergers and other industry consolidations, (3) a reinterpretation of the role of patents in encouraging innovation in an industry, and (4) an appreciation of the limits that costly imitation of resources and capabilities puts on government actions to break up dominant firms and to encourage entry by new firms.

REFERENCES

Arthur, W. B. 1989. Competing Technologies, Increasing Returns, and Lock-In by Historical Events. *Economic Journal* 99: 116–31.
Bain, T. 1956. *Barriers to New Competition*. Cambridge, MA: Harvard University Press.
Barnett, W., H. R. Greve, and D. Y. Park. 1994. An Evolutionary Model of Organizational Performance. *Strategic Management Journal* 15: 11–28.
Barney, J. B. 1986a. Strategic Factor Markets: Expectations, Luck, and the Theory of Business Strategy. *Management Science* 32: 1231–41.
    1986b. Organizational Culture: Can It Be a Source of Sustained Competitive Advantage? *Academy of Management Review* 11: 656–65.
    1988. Returns to Bidding Firms in Mergers and Acquisitions: Reconsidering the Relatedness Hypothesis. *Strategic Management Journal* 9: 71–78.
    1991. Firm Resources and Sustained Competitive Advantage. *Journal of Management* 17: 99–120.

1997. *Gaining and Sustaining Competitive Advantage*. Reading, MA: Addison-Wesley.

Bernstein, A. 1990. The Baseball Owners Get Beaned. *Business Week*, October 15, 122.

Brennan, T. 1987. Why Regulated Firms Should Be Kept Out of Unregulated Markets: Understanding the Divestiture in *United States vs. AT&T*. *Antitrust Bulletin* 32: 741–93.

Caves, R., B. Gale, and M. Porter. 1977. Interfirm Profitability Differences: A Comment. *Quarterly Journal of Economics* 91: 667–76.

Cohen, W., and D. Levinthal. 1990. Absorptive Capacity: A New Perspective on Learning and Innovation. *Administrative Science Quarterly* 35: 128–52.

Demsetz, H. 1973. Industry Structure, Market Rivalry, and Public Policy. *Journal of Law and Economics* 16: 1–9.

Dierickx, I., and K. Cool. 1989. Asset Stock Accumulation and Sustainability of Competitive Advantage. *Management Science* 35: 1504–11.

Hambrick, D. 1987. Top Management Teams: Key to Strategic Success. *California Management Review* 30: 88–108.

Henderson, R., and I. Cockburn. 1994. Measuring Competence? Exploring Firm Effects in Pharmaceutical Research. *Strategic Management Journal* 15: 63–84.

Itami, H. 1987. *Mobilizing Invisible Assets*. Cambridge, MA: Harvard University Press.

Jensen, M., and W. Meckling. 1976. Theory of the Firm: Managerial Behavior, Agency Costs, and Ownership Structure. *Journal of Financial Economics* 3: 305–60.

Klein, B., R. Crawford, and A. Alchian. 1978. Vertical Integration, Appropriable Rents, and the Competitive Contracting Process. *Journal of Law and Economics* 21: 297–326.

Klein, B., and K. Leffler. 1981. The Role of Market Forces in Assuring Contractual Performance. *Journal of Political Economy* 89: 615–41.

Levin, R. 1986. A New Look at the Patent System. *American Economic Review* 76: 199–202.

Lippman, S., and R. Rumelt. 1982. Uncertain Imitability: An Analysis of Interfirm Differences in Efficiency under Competition. *Bell Journal of Economics* 13: 418–38.

Mancke, R. 1977. Causes of Interfirm Profitability Differences: A New Interpretation of the Evidence. *Quarterly Journal of Economics* 83: 181–93.

Mansfield, E. 1986. Patents and Innovations: An Empirical Study. *Management Science* 32: 173–81.

Mansfield, E., M. Schwartz, and S. Wagner. 1981. Imitation Costs and Patents: An Empirical Study. *Economic Journal* 91: 907–18.

Meese, A. 1999. Monopoly Bundling in Cyberspace: How Many Products Does Microsoft Sell? *Antitrust Bulletin* 44: 65–116.

Nelson, R., and S. Winter. 1982. *An Evolutionary Theory of Economic Change*. Cambridge, MA: Harvard University Press.

Prahalad, C. K. and G. Hamel. 1990. The Core Competence of the Corporation. *Harvard Business Review* 68 (May–June): 79–91.

Porras, J., and P. Berg. 1978. The Impact of Organizational Development. *Academy of Management Review* 3: 249–66.

Porter, M. 1980. *Competitive Strategy*. New York: Free Press.

1981. The Contributions of Industrial Organization to Strategic Management. *Academy of Management Review* 6: 609–20.

1985. *Competitive Advantage*. New York: Free Press.

Reed, R., and R. DeFillippi. 1990. Causal Ambiguity, Barriers to Imitation, and Sustained Competitive Advantage. *Academy of Management Review* 15: 88–102.

Robbins, J., and M. Wiersema. 1995. A Resource-Based Approach to the Multi-business Firm: Empirical Analysis of Portfolio Interrelationships and Corporate Financial Performance. *Strategic Management Journal* 16: 277–99.

Rukstad, M. J., and J. Horn. 1989. Caterpillar and the Construction Equipment Industry in 1988. Harvard Business School, Case No. 9-389-097.

Rumelt, R. 1984. Toward a Strategic Theory of the Firm. In R. Lamb, ed., *Competitive Strategic Management*, 556–70. Englewood Cliffs, NJ: Prentice-Hall.

1991. How Much Does Industry Matter? *Strategic Management Journal* 12: 167–85.

Rumelt, R., D. Teece, and D. Schendel. 1991. Strategic Management and Economics. *Strategic Management Journal* 12: 5–29.

Scherer, F. M. 1980. *Industrial Market Structure and Economic Performance*. Boston: Houghton Mifflin.

Schmalensee, R. 1985. Do Markets Differ Much? *American Economic Review* 75: 341–51.

Spence, M. 1973. *Market Signalling*. Cambridge, MA: Harvard University Press.

Teece, D., G. Pisano, and A. Shuen. 1997. Dynamic Capabilities and Strategic Management. *Strategic Management Journal* 18: 509–33.

Wernerfelt, B. 1984. A Resource Based View of the Firm. *Strategic Management Journal* 5: 171–80.

Wernerfelt, B., and C. Montgomery. 1988. Tobin's q and the Importance of Focus in Firm Performance. *American Economic Review* 78: 246–50.

Williamson, O. 1985. *The Economic Institutions of Capitalism*. New York: Free Press.

Zaheer, A., and N. Venkatraman. 1995. Relational Governance as an Interorganizational Strategy: An Empirical Test of the Role of Trust in Economic Exchange. *Strategic Management Journal* 16: 373–92.

3

Innovation and Antitrust Enforcement

Daniel L. Rubinfeld and John Hoven

In evaluating markets with relatively homogeneous products and a fixed or slowly evolving technological base, the Antitrust Division of the Department of Justice (DoJ) often focuses on the price effects of potentially anticompetitive behavior. In dynamic industries, however, technological change and innovation receive particular attention. Innovation affects not only the prices that consumers pay for given products but, more important, the quality of products available in the marketplace. Moreover, the force of the innovation process can lead to dramatically higher-quality products being offered at lower prices to consumers in the future. An understanding of the particulars of competition in dynamic industries is, consequently, a vital part of a sound antitrust policy.[1]

Some observers have questioned whether the antitrust laws are adequate to handle the complexities associated with rapidly innovating industries. The antitrust laws, of course, were passed initially to confront issues in "smokestack" industries in which rates of innovation were slow. However, the statutory standard set by Congress is a flexible standard that can be and has been applied to dynamic industries. The specifics of how that standard is to be applied remain open for serious debate. We are of the view that in dynamic innovative industries antitrust enforcement should be forward-looking as much as possible and that accelerated antitrust enforcement must be given serious consideration before the path of innovative activity is set in stone. We believe that this view has been borne out by antitrust activity at the Antitrust Division in recent years.

Rubinfeld served as deputy assistant attorney general at the Antitrust Division of the U.S. Department of Justice from July 1997 through December 1998. Hoven is an economist at the division. The opinions contained herein do not necessarily reflect the views of the Department of Justice.

[1] See the discussion in the second section. See also Federal Trade Commission (1996: 11–24) for a discussion of new and improved products.

The number of matters under investigation at the Antitrust Division in which innovation has been a significant issue has been growing rapidly. The division has responded by delving deeply into innovation questions. This effort is especially appropriate in light of the fact that the losses in economic efficiency that can result from the reduced incentives of firms to innovate can easily dwarf the more traditional static efficiency losses often considered by the division.

THE ANALYSIS OF INNOVATION ISSUES
AT THE ANTITRUST DIVISION

The treatment of innovation issues by the antitrust authorities is not new. A close reading of the working documents of the competition authorities shows that innovation is taken into account in both the *Antitrust Guidelines for the Licensing of Intellectual Property* (*IPG*) and the *Horizontal Merger Guidelines* (*HMG*). In the following two subsections, we describe the treatment of innovation in each.

The Intellectual Property Guidelines

In the 1995 *Intellectual Property Guidelines* there is a single unifying theme: the enforcement agencies apply "the same general antitrust principles to conduct involving intellectual property that they apply to conduct involving any other form of tangible or intangible property" (*IPG* 2.1). While the division appreciates the fact that patents may confer market power, the division does not presume that they do, any more than property rights in mines, trademarks, or taxicab medallions (*IPG* 2.2).[2]

Even where antitrust issues do arise, the division is sensitive to the need to preserve the procompetitive benefits of licensing. These include the quick and efficient commercialization of new products, and enhanced incentives to invest in R&D resulting from broader opportunities to appropriate the rewards of innovation (*IPG* 2.3).[3]

Nevertheless, antitrust issues do arise, typically in relation to licensing restraints. While once again being sensitive to the need to preserve the

---

[2] These core principles had been previously adopted in the 1988 *Antitrust Enforcement Guidelines for International Operations*. See Gilbert and Shapiro (1997: 287).

[3] According to Katz and Ordover (1990: 139), "The inability to appropriate all the gains from ex post sharing of R&D results [from imperfect intellectual property rights] has two negative effects on a firm's incentive to conduct R&D: (1) it reduces the expected return to innovation; and (2) since a firm can gain from the R&D conducted by its rivals, it reduces the firm's potential loss from failing to conduct its own R&D." However, Cohen (1995: 229) cautions, "Despite a growing body of evidence on inter-industry differences in appropriability conditions, there is no clear empirical consensus about whether greater appropriability encourages innovative activity."

procompetitive benefits of these restraints,[4] the division is also aware that firms may use licensing restraints as the basis for cartel behavior[5] or to achieve vertical foreclosure.[6] According to the guidelines,

Harm to competition from a restraint may occur if it anticompetitively forecloses access to, or increases competitors' costs of obtaining, important inputs, or

[4] Ordover and Baumol (1988: 22) offer a list of intellectual property benefits that suggests a restricted role for antitrust enforcement: "As usual, our view is that the licensing process ought to be relatively free of antitrust scrutiny. The bases for this view are as follows: (1) To the extent that private firms already have inadequate incentives to engage in *ex post* dissemination, policies that interfere with dissemination may only exacerbate the problem; (2) To the extent that contracting for the sale and purchase of information through licensing is fraught with significant transactional difficulties, a good deal of latitude should be granted to licensors, who must protect themselves against free riding and uncompensated disclosure; (3) To the extent that price and non-price vertical restraints improve vertical efficiency, when those restraints are applied to the sale of information they are even more likely to be conducive to social efficiency; (4) To the extent that revenues from licensing add to the innovator's profit, they enhance entrepreneurial incentives to invest in the production of information and knowledge; (5) To the extent that licensing improves dissemination and adds to the effective stock of knowledge, it can reduce wasteful duplication of R&D efforts and can redirect R&D funds toward less imitative pursuits."

[5] According to Katz and Ordover (1990: 143), "The biggest [antitrust] concern is that firms will use licensing contracts as a means to subvert competition in markets for downstream products." As an example, Gilbert and Shapiro (1997: 315) cite the Justice Department's complaint against the Pilkington Company alleging that Pilkington's licenses sustained a worldwide cartel in the manufacture and sale of flat glass. Of particular interest is their claim in a footnote that "the cartelmeister theory enunciated in the Pilkington case by the Justice Department could not support PPG's private claim that Pilkington excluded PPG from the market with worthless trade secrets. Under the cartel theory, a firm that is not a member of the cartel would benefit from its formation." However, this overlooks the fact that a cartel beneficiary like PPG may develop its own superior technology, decide to market the technology outside its cartel-assigned territory (even if this causes the cartel to collapse), and be deterred by sham trade secret litigation. According to the Government's Complaint in *United States v. Pilkington* (1994: para. 25), "Pilkington's license agreements provided a framework for a worldwide cartel, created and controlled by Pilkington, for float glass technology and the design and construction of float glass plants." As the Competitive Impact Statement (1994: I.B) explained, "Pilkington has routinely used litigation, and threats of litigation, to enforce its anticompetitive license restrictions. . . . In a 1985 arbitration concluded in 1992 . . . arbitrators determined that, while much of Pilkington's alleged secret know-how was publicly known by 1985, PPG had failed to prove that 45 specific items were publicly known. The arbitrators did not consider the question of whether any of those items were valid trade secrets."

[6] Segal and Whinston (1996: 19) show "that when an incumbent firm can make discriminatory offers of exclusive contracts to buyers, it need not rely on buyers' disorganization to successfully exclude. Rather, by exploiting the externalities present among buyers, an incumbent firm can profitably exclude potential rivals. The ability to make offers to buyers over time further strengthens the possibilities for profitable exclusion, and in many cases can allow the incumbent to exclude for free." Cf. Rasmusen, Ramseyer, and Wiley (1991) and Hoven (1987).

facilitates coordination to raise price or restrict output. The risk of anticompetitively foreclosing access or increasing competitors' costs is related to the proportion of the markets affected by the licensing restraint; other characteristics of the relevant markets, such as concentration, difficulty of entry, and the responsiveness of supply and demand to changes in price in the relevant markets; and the duration of the restraints. (*IPG* 4.1.1)[7]

Licensing issues also arise in the context of settlement negotiations after the division has made the decision to challenge a proposed merger. Occasionally, the parties will propose that a new competitor be created through the licensing of one or both of the merging firms' intellectual property. This could, in principle, be more desirable than a divestiture remedy to a competitive problem because it brings new assets into the market. It is certainly possible that a prospective licensee may have all of the necessary complementary assets to commercialize the product, but that licensee would not have entered the market if it needed to develop the intellectual property on its own. The crucial question is whether this new licensee-entrant is an adequate replacement for an established incumbent.

Licensing solutions to competitive problems created by mergers create a number of difficult, but potentially significant, practical issues that the division takes into account:

- The grant of rights. Does the license grant include the results of unsuccessful designs and experiments? Does the grant include access to ancillary technology licensed from third parties? Does it impose territorial or customer restraints that expose the licensee to a higher risk of trade secret litigation (because the licensee cannot easily demonstrate that its sales to the restricted territories or customers do not use the licensed know-how) or to a higher risk of business failure?
- The transfer of know-how. Is the extent of the know-how transfer specifically delineated?[8] Will the licensee be given all manuals,

---

[7] Gilbert and Shapiro (1997: 333) offer a helpful list of additional indicia of anticompetitive impact: "The dangers of exclusive dealing provisions in licenses are most pronounced when the following conditions are present: (1) the licensor has a first-mover advantage, signing contracts before other potential innovators are themselves in a position to negotiate with licensees, as often occurs when one firm succeeds in innovating before its rivals; (2) there are multiple licensees who find it difficult to coordinate, so that each alone gives up little in agreeing to deal exclusively with the dominant firm, but collectively the cost is large; (3) there are scale economies and the incumbent licensor employs long-term, staggered licenses with exclusivity provisions; and (4) there are strong network effects in the market."

[8] According to Simpson (1995: 249), "The extent of a know-how transfer must be specifically delineated. Know-how does not involve a statutorily created and defined right such as a patent or copyright. A patent is the right to exclude others from making, using,

instructions, and development tools that the merging parties give their own engineers? Whose responsibility is it to make sure that the licensed technology works?[9] Does the agreement include a timetable for transfer of the know-how, and some agreement as to what happens if someone fails to adhere to the timetable?[10]

- The protection of intellectual property. Does the agreement describe the licensed know-how with enough specificity to ensure a common understanding of what information is claimed to be a trade secret and what is not?[11]
- The termination of an agreement. Does the agreement include termination dates for the licensor's obligation to provide technical assistance, the licensee's right to use the licensed technology,[12] and the licensee's obligation to maintain confidentiality of the licensor's proprietary know-how?[13]
- Production and marketing. Does the agreement include a supply agreement, or a requirement to divulge preferred sources of essential materials?[14]

The Horizontal Merger Guidelines

When mergers are being evaluated, reference to the 1997 *Horizontal Merger Guidelines* suffices for the treatment of most common

---

offering to sell, selling or importing the claimed invention or a product made by a claimed process for the life of the patent in that country.... However, for know-how, there is no such careful definition of the extent of the intellectual property in time, in technical area, or in type of recorded medium." Cf. Goldscheider (1996: 39): "A mere general statement relating to 'all trade secrets used by the company in relation to a particular product or persons' will not do." Byrne (1994: 119) offers a model clause that suggests the appropriate degree of specificity for know-how.

[9] Young (1996: 335), Byrne (1994: 210), Street (1994: 186).

[10] Goldscheider (1996: 66).

[11] According to Goldscheider (1996: 336), "legal protection of the legitimate interests of innovating firms in trade secret information by prohibition of use or disclosure by former employees should be denied unless, in most cases, the firm notified the departing employee what information the firm claims to be trade secrets." Cf. Robison (1983: 393).

[12] Byrne (1994: 212) argues persuasively for no time limit on the licensee's right to use the licensed technology: "Either party to a licensing agreement may suffer serious consequences if the right to use confidential know-how expires or terminates with the agreement. If at all possible, the common law courts will not allow a business to be devastated in that way. Subject to an express contrary intention, as a general rule know-how transferred under a technology licensing agreement is given for all time and may be used freely by the recipient after termination of the agreement."

[13] To put a definite end to the risk of sham trade secret litigation, confidentiality agreements should have a fixed termination date, especially for technology that becomes obsolete quickly: "Confidentiality agreements are important and should have a time limit. Don't be inflexible but realistic. Limit them to what is really needed, both ways" (Manfroy, Paterson, and Stockman 1996: 398). Cf. Goldscheider (1996: 328).

[14] Byrne (1994: 119).

innovation issues. The Antitrust Division encounters innovation questions in its analysis of product market definition, the identification of firms that participate in the relevant market, market concentration, entry, and the analysis of anticompetitive effects.

Product Market Definition

When competitive interactions take place mainly through innovations in product quality and features, the division looks for evidence that buyers shift purchases between products in response to relative changes in those competitive variables.[15] (An interesting special case described in the *Intellectual Property Guidelines* is the "technology market" where rights to intellectual property are the relevant product market.)[16]

The Identification of Firms That Participate in the Relevant Market

In general, the guidelines' preferred approach is to define discrete product markets, and to include as market participants any firm that "has existing assets that likely would be shifted or extended into production and sale of the relevant product within one year, and without incurring significant sunk costs of entry and exit, in response to a 'small but significant and nontransitory' increase in price for only the relevant product." However, "if production substitution among a group of products is nearly universal among the firms selling one or more of those products ... the Agency may use an aggregate description of those markets as a matter of convenience" (*HMG* 1.321). In particular, if production substitution is determined by core competence in a particular technology (and all firms with this technology have the ability to market

---

[15] "In considering the likely reaction of buyers to a price increase, the Agency will take into account all relevant evidence, including, but not limited to, the following: (1) evidence that buyers have shifted or have considered shifting purchases between products in response to relative changes in price or other competitive variables; (2) evidence that sellers base business decisions on the prospect of buyer substitution between products in response to relative changes in price or other competitive variables; (3) the influence of downstream competition faced by buyers in their output markets; and (4) the timing and costs of switching products" (*HMG* 1.11).

[16] "Technology markets consist of the intellectual property that is licensed (the 'licensed technology') and its close substitutes – that is, the technologies or goods that are close enough substitutes significantly to constrain the exercise of market power with respect to the intellectual property that is licensed. When rights to intellectual property are marketed separately from the products in which they are used, the Agencies may rely on technology markets to analyze the competitive effects of a licensing agreement.

"To identify a technology's close substitutes and thus to delineate the relevant technology market, the Agencies will, if the data permit, identify the smallest group of technologies and goods over which a hypothetical monopolist of those technologies and goods likely would exercise market power – for example, by imposing a small but significant and nontransitory price increase" (*IPG* 3.2.2).

the products that emerge from it), the division may use an aggregate description of those products (i.e., the products generated by that technology) for convenience and clarity. (This differs from the concept of "technology markets" in the *Intellectual Property Guidelines* because the focus is not on a developing technology, but rather on a relatively stable technology that generates a cluster of new products.)[17]

Market Concentration

The division takes into account the reasonably predictable effects of innovation trends on market concentration and the market shares of particular firms. As the *Horizontal Merger Guidelines* state,

Market concentration and market share data of necessity are based on historical evidence. However, recent or ongoing changes in the market may indicate that the current market share of a particular firm either understates or overstates the firm's future competitive significance. For example, if a new technology that is important to long-term competitive viability is available to other firms in the market, but is not available to a particular firm, the Agency may conclude that the historical market share of that firm overstates its future competitive significance. The Agency will consider reasonably predictable effects of recent or ongoing changes in market conditions in interpreting market concentration and market share data. (*HMG* 1.521)

Entry

The division takes into account reasonably predictable effects of innovation on the likelihood of entry. Occasionally, the division encounters markets where competitive interactions occur through innovation on a very long time scale. In these settings, even if entry takes more than two years, the division considers entry to be timely so long as it would deter or counteract the competitive effects of concern within the two-year period and subsequently.[18]

---

[17] Dussuage, Hart, and Ramanantsoa (1992) refer to this product cluster as a "technology cluster." According to the authors, "Porter defines an industry as 'a group of firms which manufacture substitutable products.' However ... firms which grow as technology clusters do not compete in one specific industry, but in all the industries where their technological potential can provide them with an advantage" (p. 111). A firm that competes in the technology cluster needs "the capacity to develop rapidly a wide range of applications, in the form of many different products to be sold in a large number of markets" (p. 106) and the ability to "assess the competitive advantage its technology could create, and evaluate whether this advantage offsets its lack of familiarity with a particular market (distribution networks, customer behavior, behavior of firms already in the market, etc.)" (p. 111).

[18] "In order to deter or counteract the competitive effects of concern, entrants quickly must achieve a significant impact on price in the relevant market. The Agency generally will

Anticompetitive Effects

The *Horizontal Merger Guidelines* recognize that "Sellers with market power also may lessen competition on dimensions other than price, such as product quality, service, or innovation" (*HMG* 0.1, n. 6). As Gilbert and Sunshine (1995) explain,[19] coordinated effects are not usually a major focus when innovation questions arise (although anticompetitive coordination of innovative activities can be accomplished through market allocation). Unilateral effects in either of two forms are more likely in innovation cases. The first is where the merging firms compete more directly with each other than with other firms.[20] (One would have to demonstrate in a particular case that the incentive to innovate would be reduced by the loss of competition.) The second unilateral effect is the loss of diversity because the number of independent innovators has been reduced by one; in particular, there is a considerable body of anecdotal evidence that diversity is particularly important for major technological advances, and that pathbreaking technological breakthroughs have often been made by niche players or by leading firms working outside their main areas of specialization.

On occasion, a different analytical framework is needed to demonstrate that a merger will lead to higher prices and reduced output. One example is the division's use of innovation markets, defined as the research and

consider timely only those committed entry alternatives that can be achieved within two years from initial planning to significant market impact. Where the relevant product is a durable good, consumers, in response to a significant commitment to entry, may defer purchases by making additional investments to extend the useful life of previously purchased goods and in this way deter or counteract for a time the competitive effects of concern. In these circumstances, if entry only can occur outside of the two year period, the Agency will consider entry to be timely so long as it would deter or counteract the competitive effects of concern within the two-year period and subsequently" (*HMG* 3.2).

[19] "The conditions required to sustain a collusive agreement . . . are particularly difficult to satisfy when the coordinated activity is research and development. Firms are likely to benefit in different ways from a successful R&D program and agreement over the "spoils" of coordinated R&D activity is likely to be difficult. Monitoring will also be difficult since R&D typically involves private information. A firm that succeeds in an R&D program gains a substantial advantage over its competitors and retaliation by its unsuccessful rivals may be difficult or even impossible. In addition, when R&D does not require specialized assets, any collusive agreement to suppress R&D will be vulnerable to entry from innovators who are not members of the agreement." Gilbert and Sunshine (1995: 591).

[20] "In some markets the products are differentiated, so that products sold by different participants in the market are not perfect substitutes for one another. Moreover, different products in the market may vary in the degree of their substitutability for one another. In this setting, competition may be non-uniform (i.e., localized), so that individual sellers compete more directly with those rivals selling closer substitutes" (*HMG* 2.21).

development directed to particular new or improved goods or processes, and the close substitutes for that research and development.[21] The first division challenge of a merger on innovation market grounds occurred in 1993, when the division investigated the proposed acquisition by ZF Friedrichshafen of General Motors' Allison Division.[22] Allison and ZF together produced 85 percent of the world output of heavy-duty automatic transmissions for trucks and buses, but they actually competed in few markets. Nonetheless, the division concluded that even regional markets whose concentration would be unaffected by the merger would be harmed by the merged entity's reduced incentive to develop new designs and products.

Joint Ventures

While there is clearly a tension between intellectual property protection and competition policy (one enhances rewards to the innovator, whereas the other constrains it), the two policy areas have a common goal: to enhance economic performance and consumer welfare. This balancing between innovation incentives and competition has been recognized in the National Cooperative Research and Production Act, which provides a limited safe harbor from antitrust enforcement for qualifying R&D joint ventures. (In fiscal year 1998, thirty-seven such joint ventures were registered with the Department of Justice.) It has also been recognized by the Antitrust Division in a number of its business review letters. For example, the 1997 MPEG-2 Business Review Letter (Klein 1997) provides support (under appropriate assumptions) for a patent pooling of intellectual property for the provision of advanced video compression technology into a single license, which, when granted, would be done on a nondiscriminatory basis.

---

[21] "A licensing arrangement may have competitive effects on innovation that cannot be adequately addressed through the analysis of goods or technology markets. For example, the arrangement may affect the development of goods that do not yet exist. Alternatively, the arrangement may affect the development of new or improved goods or processes in geographic markets where there is no actual or likely potential competition in the relevant goods.

"An innovation market consists of the research and development directed to particular new or improved goods or processes, and the close substitutes for that research and development. The close substitutes are research and development efforts, technologies, and goods that significantly constrain the exercise of market power with respect to the relevant research and development, for example by limiting the ability and incentive of a hypothetical monopolist to retard the pace of research and development. The Agencies will delineate an innovation market only when the capabilities to engage in the relevant research and development can be associated with specialized assets or characteristics of specific firms" (*IPG* 3.2.3). Cf. Gilbert and Sunshine (1995).

[22] Complaint, *United States v. General Motors et al.* (Nov. 16, 1993).

The importance of joint ventures for innovation and competition policy was the subject of Federal Trade Commission (FTC) hearings in 1998. In April 2000, the FTC and the DoJ issued draft *Antitrust Guidelines for Collaborations among Competitors*. Although the new guidelines raise innovation issues, they do not offer a new analytical framework. Rather, the "Collaborations Guidelines" put forward a general competitor collaboration policy that relies heavily on the *Intellectual Property* and *Horizontal Merger Guidelines*.

ACCOUNTING FOR INNOVATION: INTELLECTUAL THEMES

In its analysis of innovation issues, the Antitrust Division makes an effort to keep abreast of developments in the academic literature on the economics of innovation. In this section, we briefly characterize several themes in that literature that have particular importance for antitrust enforcement.

Schumpeterian Competition

At the core of antitrust analysis is the question of how market structure and firm size affect innovative effort. Traditional innovation–market structure analysis views innovation as a manufacturing process in which R&D spending is the input, innovation is the output, and firms are virtually identical except for market share (Tisdell 1995: 30). In this paradigm, a principal innovation focus in a merger investigation is the determination of the merger's impact on incentives to invest in R&D.[23] While the effect of a particular merger on innovative activity can be very significant, the general relationship between market structure and innovation is an unsettled issue in the literature. For example, in his review of the empirical literature Symeonides (1996: para. 44) emphasizes the inconclusiveness of the R&D–market concentration relationship,[24] and Cohen and Levin (1989: 1078) concur: "These results leave little support for the view that industrial concentration is an independent, significant, and important determinant of innovative behavior and performance."

Empirical studies on innovation and firm size are somewhat more definitive, finding that smaller firms (beyond a minimum threshold) are

---

[23] For example: "Having defined the innovation market, an analysis of a merger involving R&D must consider whether the merged firm's share of R&D is sufficient to affect the total level of R&D in that market." Gilbert and Sunshine (1995: 596).

[24] "First, there is little evidence of a positive relationship between R&D intensity and concentration in general, although there may be circumstances where such a relationship exists. Second, there is even less evidence of a positive relationship between innovative output and market structure. Third, industry characteristics such as technological opportunity explain much more of the variance in R&D intensity or innovation than market structure." Symeonides (1996: para. 44).

as research-intensive as larger firms and more productive.[25] However, the contribution of small firms to innovation is known to vary greatly by industry. For example, researchers at the U.K. Science Policy Research Unit noted that the industries in which small enterprises contribute a large share of innovations are those in which they also contribute a large share of output – typically, industries in which capital intensity or innovation costs are lower (Freeman and Soete 1997: 236–37). Audretsch (1995) found that small enterprises enjoy a relative innovative advantage in industries that are highly innovative, and Dorfman (1987) found from her study of computer and semiconductor industries that innovative small firms tend to be start-ups: "Innovations have generally been initiated by either large established companies or relatively new ones. The small mature firm was almost conspicuous by its absence among innovators" (Dorfman 1987: 10).

There is also a substantial body of evidence that leading incumbents prefer a different path of innovation than challengers. According to Dorfman (1987), "Leading companies . . . generally use technology as a means of reinforcing their position without changing the fundamental rules of the game. . . . Because it may disrupt the nature of competition in a given industry, a new technology which modifies the key factors for success tends to be perceived as a strategic opportunity by marginal competitors, and as a threat by the leading competitors, even if they are the ones which developed the new technology."[26] As a consequence, path-breaking technological breakthroughs have often been made, not by leading incumbents but by small start-ups or by major firms working outside their main area of specialization. One policy implication for antitrust is the need to preserve a larger number of firms in industries where the best innovation strategy is unpredictable.[27] (This was an important consideration, for example, in the division's challenge to the

---

[25] Cohen (1995: 189) concludes, "Thus, the robust empirical patterns relating R&D and innovation to firm size are that R&D increases monotonically – and typically proportionately – with firm size among R&D performers within industries, the number of innovations tends to increase less than proportionately than firm size, and R&D productivity tends to decline with firm size." See also Symeonides (1996: para. 29). Cohen and Klepper (1992) offer an alternative interpretation of the apparent productivity advantage of small firms, arguing that large firms have an advantage in appropriating the rewards of innovation and so are willing to pursue R&D projects with a lower probability of success.

[26] Dussauge et al. (1992: 14, 61). Tushman and Anderson (1986) distinguish competence-destroying and competence-enhancing innovations. Christensen (1997) says that established firms find it extremely difficult to pursue a rapidly evolving "disruptive technology" that isn't mature enough yet to serve their current customers.

[27] Swann and Gill (1993: 211). See also Metcalfe (1995) for an evolutionary perspective on the importance of variety (differences in R&D strengths and strategies) and selection (allowing particular R&D strengths and strategies to survive or die).

proposed Lockheed-Northrop merger.) Another implication is Scherer and Ross's (1990: 654) observation that "Technical progress thrives best in an environment that nurtures a diversity of sizes and, perhaps especially, that keeps barriers to entry by technologically innovative newcomers low." (Again, a concern in the proposed Lockheed-Northrop merger was that the merged entity would foster an industry-wide trend to keep innovative activities within vertically integrated chains rather than collaborate with outsiders.) A third implication is the awareness that dominant firms may have an incentive to act so as to deter innovative activities that threaten the dominant position (as, for example, with Pilkington's trade secret licensing restraints, which were challenged by the division).

Innovation Management and Evolution

Important inferences for merger analysis can also be drawn from the innovation management and evolutionary literature. These paradigms depart from the Schumpeterian tradition by emphasizing distinctive firm competencies and strategies, and the cross-fertilization of information among firms that know different things. For example, Dorfman (1987) emphasizes the importance associated with having a rich exchange of ideas among differently situated firms:

There are, thus, complementary roles for large established firms and small, new enterprises in advancing technology, a complementarity that is augmented by a mutual dependence in gaining technical knowledge and know-how. This was manifest by a tendency for established firms to obtain expertise by acquiring newer firms at the same time that other new firms transferred technology and know-how from the research laboratories and production facilities of established firms. These observations lead us back to the conclusions of Jewkes and his collaborators that were cited in the very first chapter of this book: "It may well be that there is no optimum size of firm but merely an optimum pattern for an industry, such a distribution of firms by size, character and outlook as to guarantee the most effective gathering together and commercially perfecting of the flow of new ideas." (Dorfman 1987: 244)

Similarly, Rothwell (1994) observes:

There is considerable evidence to show that innovation today has become significantly more of a *networking* process. During the 1980s the number of horizontal strategic alliances and collaborative R&D consortia have increased dramatically, vertical relationships, especially at the supplier interface, have become more intimate and strategic in nature and innovative SMEs [small- and medium-sized enterprises] are forging a variety of external relationships with both large and small firms. (Rothwell 1994: 43)

The innovation management view is anchored in a literature that builds on the view that because of trade secrets and tacit know-how,[28] knowledge varies among firms, with innovation being driven by a flow of ideas among partners and rivals, not just by R&D spending. These ideas define core competencies that give firms a sustainable competitive advantage over rivals that do not have the same know-how. In fact, as Hamel (1991: 83) argues, "It is possible to conceive of a firm as a port-folio of core competencies on one hand, and encompassing disciplines on the other, rather than as a portfolio of product-market entities."[29] In this view, innovation competition is a race to learn: "Conceiving of the firm as a portfolio of core competencies and disciplines suggests that inter-firm competition, as opposed to inter-product competition, is essen-tially concerned with the acquisition of skills. . . . The traditional 'com-petitive strategy' paradigm, with its focus on product-market positioning, focuses on only the last few hundred yards of what may be a skill-building marathon" (Hamel 1991: 83).

According to this view, innovating firms approach their dealings with teammates and subcontractors as opportunities to learn. For example, Hamel, Doz, and Prahalad (1989) assert that "Successful companies view each alliance as a window on their partners' broad capabilities. They use the alliance to build skills in areas outside the formal agreement and systematically diffuse new knowledge throughout their organizations" (Hamel et al. 1989: 134).

Although learning is an unambiguous social benefit, it is not clear whether these spillovers have a positive or negative effect on incentives to invest in R&D. On the one hand, firms have a greater incentive to invest in R&D when they can appropriate most of the rewards for them-selves.[30] On the other hand, spillovers also generate incentives to invest in R&D, either to develop learning capacity ("absorptive capacity") to capture others' spillovers[31] or because spillovers raise the marginal

---

[28] "Following Michael Polanyi (1967), *tacitness* refers to those elements of knowledge, insight, and so on that individuals have which are ill-defined, uncodified, unpublished, which they themselves cannot fully express and which differ from person to person, but which may to some significant degree be shared by collaborators and colleagues who have a common experience." Dosi (1988: 1126).

[29] See also Prahalad and Hamel (1990) and Teece, Pisano, and Shuen (1994: 14–15): "The very essence of capabilities/competences is that they cannot be readily assembled through markets. . . . [They] cannot be bought and sold short of buying the firm itself, or one or more of its subunits."

[30] "Know-how leakage and other spillovers impair incentives to innovate by redis-tributing benefits to others, particularly competitors and users." Jorde and Teece (1992: 52).

[31] Cohen and Levinthal (1989: 569) show that "contrary to the traditional result, intra-industry spillovers may encourage equilibrium industry R&D investment." Howells

product of other firms' R&D.[32] Cohen's (1995: 229) survey of the literature concludes that "The empirical findings to date do not establish whether the net effect of appropriability on R&D incentives is positive or negative, nor do we yet know the extent to which the net effect varies across industries."

Firms adopt a variety of strategies to maximize the private benefits of these spillovers. They try to be good learners and bad teachers (Hamel et al. 1989; Hamel 1991), they choose alliances that promise more incoming spillovers than outgoing spillovers (Cassiman and Veaglers 1998), they avoid collaborating with competitors (Cassiman and Veaglers 1998: 20; Tidd, Bessant, and Pavitt 1997: 20), and they acquire prospective partners rather than collaborate.[33] Firms may also forgo the benefits of collaboration and rely on internal capabilities, even if collaboration would yield higher quality and lower cost. According to Hobday (1994: 164–65),

While the network system may be suited to fast innovation, it is unsuitable for building corporate competences over the long term. . . . Large firms are unlikely to distribute their core capabilities within a network for economic, technological and strategic reasons. To do so would expose them to predatory behaviour from other large firms and risk their long-term investments in human and physical capital. Where large firms do participate in dynamic networks, the boundaries of its participation are likely to end where its core assets and advantages begin.

Similarly, the Defense Science Board Task Force on Vertical Integration and Supplier Decisions warns that "To develop their internal businesses, prime contractors may favor their new in-house capabilities over external suppliers in new weapon systems bids. . . . Firms might also 'cherry

(1997: 2) notes that "The internal R&D process is changing, it is no longer the sole generator of a firm's innovation stream; it now has an important technological scanning role and as a purchaser and adapter of other organisations' technology."

[32] "The more capable firms there are in the economy, the more potential spillovers will be created and, therefore, the more potential spillovers each capable firm will have access to. Increasing the volume of spillovers in this way will, of course, have an effect on the relationship between R&D input and innovative output analogous to increasing returns to scale. . . . Under the circumstances, there is something to be said for the view that public policy makers might try to maximize spillovers rather than try to minimize them." Geroski (1995: 92).

[33] Merger greatly enhances the incentives and opportunities for a flow of ideas between the previously separate entities, but it may also create negative synergies: "To the extent that a company's knowledge and capabilities depend on its culture and spirit, a merger threatens to destroy the very thing that it was intended to secure. [Also,] an acquisition makes little sense when a company is interested in learning only one of the many capabilities of another organization or when markets or technology may change quickly. Tomorrow's needs may differ from today's, and an acquisition may become an albatross around a company's neck." Badaracco (1991: 104).

pick' the highest value, most sophisticated work for their in-house suppliers to build corporate skills, leaving routine, lower-margin areas for external suppliers."[34]

To summarize, this literature emphasizes that firms know different things, innovation is driven in part by a flow of ideas among partners and rivals, spillovers are not unambiguously negative as some authors suggest, and firms have incentives to exercise an "in-house bias" that constrains this flow of ideas. All of this gives rise to a possible anticompetitive harm from vertical mergers. The risk is that innovation may be impaired because the flow of ideas becomes narrowly confined within vertically integrated firms, without the stimulus of suppliers and producers interacting with a variety of partners and serving as a conduit of ideas from one firm to another. This risk is especially evident in defense industries, for two reasons. First, key defense technologies are sometimes very market-specific, with only a few knowledgeable producers and suppliers. Second, U.S. defense strategy is predicated on being technologically far superior to potential adversaries, so unpredictable innovations triggered by an unexpected convergence of ideas are of paramount importance. These innovation-related risks were given serious consideration in the analysis of vertical issues of the proposed Lockheed-Northrop merger.

The analytical work undertaken by the Antitrust Division builds on the work of the many contributors to the rich academic literature on innovation. Of course, actual merger investigations often present interesting issues relating to market structure and conduct.

Network Effects

With network goods, the value to either consumers or producers increases with the breadth of use of others. As a result, when network effects are present, there may be substantial efficiencies on either the demand or the supply side that lead to the creation of firm dominance in a market. Many network industries are dynamic, in which case the market is a moving target, evolving as technology changes in response to innovation. Antitrust analysis must occasionally focus, therefore, not

---

[34] Defense Science Board (1997: 21–22). The report identifies "Firm's desire to capture or keep leading technology or product position in key areas" (p. 24) as one of the pressures encouraging harmful effects from vertical integration. Additional motives listed for in-house bias include "desire to have a larger base for overhead cost absorption" (p. 24) and divisional incentives that don't perfectly match those of the corporation: "Systems integration divisions seek 'best value' supplier selections while supplier divisions pursue their own financial goals. Corporate leaders may have a policy to make fully competed supplier choices, but their subordinate divisions may act on local economic incentives" (p. 26).

only on static competition within the market as it is currently constituted, but also on dynamic competition for the market of the future, that is, competition to control the next market standard (if there is one).[35]

There are a number of aspects of markets with network effects that make the relationship between innovation and antitrust especially complex and subtle. First, because of network effects small firms can become dominant very rapidly; in loose parlance, the market can rapidly "tip" toward monopoly.[36] In such a case, incentives to innovate are often determined at an early stage when competition for the market is most severe; at a late stage the path of innovation may already to a large extent be determined. Second, in network industries, the literature makes it clear that the forces that drive the winner to be the most efficient may not be as reliable as they would be in non-network markets.[37] The process by which firms and industries move from one standard to another are also a subject of study, especially in light of the possibility that lock-in effects can make it difficult to change a standard, and the social cost of changing the standard may exceed the benefit of changing.[38] Even ascertaining the rate at which particular innovations are made in network industries is itself a complex undertaking. There remains substantial debate, therefore, as to whether the best product will necessarily become the standard. If an "inferior" good gets a decisive advantage by creating an early installed base of users, the switching costs may be sufficient to discourage existing customers from moving to the superior standard. Further, new customers may find that with substantial network effects generated by the dominant firm, price or design advantages may not be sufficient to encourage a switch.

Switching costs can also discourage innovative efforts that might otherwise lead firms to enter markets, especially if the new products to be designed cannot interconnect with those already in the market. In other words, the potential stability of network-dominant firms can reduce the incentives of those firms to introduce innovative products and service offerings.

Third, network effects can create complex vertical issues. A dominant network firm may have an advantage in selling complementary goods

---

[35] Rubinfeld (1998) discusses the relationship between networking and antitrust enforcement in high-technology industries.

[36] Network effects are not necessary for tipping; tipping can occur in any market with substantial scale-related economies, whether on the demand or the supply side.

[37] Katz and Shapiro (1994) suggest that path dependency and timing are likely to be less significant in a strategic setting because a dominant firm can and will act to tip the market in its preferred direction.

[38] Farrell and Katz (1998) analyze how the degree of compatibility affects the nature of competition in network markets.

that allow it to extend its dominance from one market to another.[39] One means of accomplishing this is to condition the sale of the tied product on the purchase of the distinct tying product. Another is to technologically tie the products together so that the option to purchase the two products separately is not readily available. As in the previous cases, the advantages to an incumbent dominant firm are not necessarily anticompetitive. It is quite possible that a dominant provider of a complementary good may be able to take advantage of economies of scale and/or scope to become the most efficient provider. Distinguishing such procompetitive behavior from the anticompetitive aspects of tying and other practices that link vertical markets is a substantial challenge for antitrust law and policy.

RECENT ANTITRUST INNOVATION CASES AT THE ANTITRUST DIVISION

In the past year, innovation has come into even greater prominence at the division. In each of the following four subsections we describe some recent innovation cases. The first three are treated briefly, and the fourth, Lockheed-Martin, is considered in more extensive detail.

The Halliburton-Dresser Merger

Innovation has had a major impact on oil production in recent years, letting oil drillers extract large amounts of previously uneconomical oil without any increase in the cost per barrel. Logging-while-drilling (LWD) tools are the subsurface sensors of this new drilling technology. From their position directly behind the drill bit, they transmit to the surface real-time data about the type of formation (e.g., limestone vs. sand), whether the formation contains oil, and how porous the formation is. LWD services are important in the exploration of oil and gas because they allow the producer to obtain data from the well bore without interrupting the drilling process, particularly in offshore drilling applications, where daily rig rental costs are substantial, and the ability to obtain downhole information in this manner is important for cost-efficient exploration.

LWD innovation has been led by four firms that design and test the cutting-edge technologies, staying always a few years ahead of lesser competitors who imitate and improve once the technologies are well understood. These four industry leaders command a large share of the LWD market and are, of course, the only suppliers of the more advanced

---

[39] For an explanation of why tying can be an effective device for raising rivals' costs and thereby strategically foreclosing competition, see Mathewson and Winter (1997). See also Whinston (1990).

tools. Halliburton Company and Dresser Industries, Inc., are two of the "Big Four." The Antitrust Division challenged their proposed merger on September 29, 1998, because of anticompetitive effects on price and innovation.

The principal focus of the innovation inquiry was to understand what drives innovation in this particular industry. Does the initiative come from customers, from component suppliers, from collaborations? Do the Big Four all play similar roles, or do some lead and others follow quickly with major improvements? Are the merging firms important players? These market-specific, firm-specific inquiries elicited the facts that supported the merger challenge. The division concluded that important innovations in LWD services had come solely from the Big Four; and that fringe players tended to play follow-the-leader, offering last-generation products that had already been superseded by the next generation of innovations. Interestingly, a number of important customers were more concerned about innovation effects than price effects.

The investigation's emphasis on innovation dictated the scope of the divestiture ordered by the consent decree. The divestiture remedy included virtually all of Halliburton's LWD tools, plus the following, needed to ensure a viable innovative business entity: worldwide, royalty-free, irrevocable, nonexclusive intellectual property licenses, and sublicenses covering the use of third-party technology; R&D equipment and records, including the results of unsuccessful designs; manufacturing, testing, and repair equipment and facilities; all assignable contracts and customer lists worldwide; an inventory of measurement-while-drilling (MWD) tools (used in combination with LWD tools); and the right to hire Halliburton employees as the purchaser requires to operate the business.

The Visa–MasterCard Investigation

On October 7, 1998, the Department of Justice filed a Section 1 Sherman Act action against Visa and MasterCard, alleging that the overlapping ownership and governance of these two associations by the same major banks had anticompetitive effects, particularly with respect to innovation at the credit card network level.[40] To understand the nature of the issues raised in the current suit, some background is useful.

Network effects are predominant in the credit card industry. As use and acceptance of a credit card increase, the card becomes more valuable for both businesses and consumers. In analyzing the competitive issues associated with the credit card industry, two related markets are

---

[40] At the time this article went to press, the Visa complaint had been amended and expanded to some extent, but the case was still in litigation.

of particular interest. Consumers and merchants deal primarily with the market for card issuance and card acceptance services. In this market, the individual banks and other institutions that issue cards compete for customers on the basis of interest rates, annual fees, payment terms, customer service, and other enhancements and bonuses. The same issuing institutions provide card acceptance services to merchants on the basis of various fees and services. The suit filed by the Department of Justice relates directly to the second market, the market for the underlying card networks. Those networks provide services to card issuers, including implementation of systems and technologies for card use and clearance, development of card products, promotion of the card brand, and setting fees for use and participation in the card network.

To the extent that many institutions can join a credit card network and issue cards, competition for consumers of general credit card services and for merchants requiring acceptance services will be substantial. However, competition at the network level is more complex and more difficult. Establishing brand name, developing processing and information systems, and building a base of merchants and card users is slow and expensive. Entry is difficult because a new entrant must enter the market at two levels: the issuance and acceptance-services market as well as the network-services level. In fact, only one new network has successfully entered the market in the past thirty years.

Visa and MasterCard began as separate, competing networks that were owned and governed by their card-issuing members. Each eventually accepted the other's members onto its network as participating owners, and the two networks now have substantially overlapping ownership and governance. The Department of Justice is concerned in its case about the innovation-reducing consequences of the Visa–Master-Card arrangement. In its suit, the department alleges that the governance arrangements have the effect of stopping both networks from introducing new products and services because improvements in one network would shift profits from the other. Because Visa and MasterCard have a 75 percent share of the credit card market by volume of transactions, the joint governance arrangement creates little incentive to implement new initiatives in the systems jointly. The particular innovations that were allegedly delayed include the decision by MasterCard to withhold introduction of "smart card" technology, which involves the use of integrated circuits in the cards to store more data, perform a greater array of functions, and better monitor fraud and credit risk. According to the complaint, when Visa did not want to introduce smart cards, MasterCard's board refused to continue its planned development. The department's case also challenges Visa and MasterCard rules that make entry or expansion by smaller networks more difficult.

The Microsoft Investigation

The Justice Department has also challenged what it alleges are a series of anticompetitive practices by Microsoft whose purpose is to maintain its monopoly power in the market for desktop operating systems for personal computers (PC).[41] This power, according to the Antitrust Division, was threatened by Netscape's Internet browser – a software package that provided a means of access to the Internet that had the potential to provide an alternative "platform" that would support any operating system, not solely Microsoft's Windows operating systems.[42] Central to the monopoly power argument is the view that the necessity of producing a range of successful applications along with an operating system (which controls and allocates the hardware resources of the computer and allows the computer to run applications) creates an "applications barrier to entry." Further, the tendency for a single firm to become dominant in the operating systems market flows in part from the fact that operating systems are subject to substantial network effects – the greater the number of programs that are developed to be compatible with popular operating systems, the more popular those systems are to consumers who naturally desire increased options for complementary programs. The result of the network effects and the applications barrier to entry is a market for operating systems that is "tippy," with the consequence that a single operating system type will tend to dominate the market, and entry by potential competitors will be difficult. Currently, the "Windows" operating system, including Windows 95 and Windows 98, dominates the PC desktop market, and Microsoft is alleged by the division to have monopoly power in the Intel-based desktop operating systems market.

The Department of Justice claims, among other charges, that Microsoft has misused its dominance in the market for operating systems in an effort to gain dominance in the complementary market for browsers and maintain its current dominance of the personal computer operating system market. According to the division, Microsoft has required computer manufacturers to agree, as a condition of receiving licenses for installation of Windows, not to remove Microsoft's browser from the computer or to allow the more prominent display of a rival browser. Because consumers demand Windows pre-loaded by manufac-

---

[41] At the time this article went to press District Court Judge Jackson's ruling in favor of the Department of Justice had just been appealed.

[42] Netscape's Navigator web-browsing software is a particular threat to Microsoft because it serves as a mechanism for the distribution of Sun Java, a software program that is cross-platform – programs written in Sun Java can in principle be run on any operating system.

turers onto their PCs, manufacturers have no real choice but to accept these terms. Similarly, the department claims that Microsoft has refused to list Internet service providers (ISPs) in the Windows display screen (or in its ISP referral service) unless the ISPs agree in turn to withhold information about non-Microsoft browsers to their subscribers and to adopt proprietary standards that make their services work better in conjunction with Microsoft's browser than with others. Microsoft is also alleged to have contractually limited the ability of some ISPs to ship non-Microsoft browsers even in response to an explicit customer request for that browser. Microsoft has responded that the integration of its Internet Explorer browser with the Windows operating system expands the functionality of the operating system as well as increasing the features and functionality of programs written for use with the Windows operating system, which ultimately increases consumer welfare. Microsoft also claims that the contractual arrangements with ISPs are cross-promotional agreements that are common within the computer industry.

The department's case reflects an effort to protect competition in Internet markets and to maintain incentives for the development of innovative software by preventing anticompetitive actions against successful products. The challenge for competition policy makers in this context is to preserve competitive opportunities without punishing successful competitors. At issue is where to draw a line: on one side of that line is a successful company's legitimate use of aggressive, competitive tactics, regulation of which might reduce future innovation incentives and consumer welfare; on the other side of that line is the misuse of market power to engage in predatory, exclusionary conduct that forecloses competition and innovation to the ultimate detriment of consumers. Striking the right balance is essential for promoting innovation and protecting consumer welfare in the fast-moving environment of network competition.

The Proposed Lockheed-Northrop Merger

The department's challenge to Lockheed Martin's proposed acquisition of Northrop Grumman – the largest proposed challenge to a merger at the time – illustrates a broad spectrum of the innovation-related issues that we have been discussing. Lockheed and Northrop were two of the leading suppliers of aircraft and electronic systems in the United States. The complaint (filed March 23, 1998) alleged that the acquisition would have tended substantially to lessen competition in numerous product markets, giving the merged entity a monopoly in airborne early-warning radar, electro-optical missile warning, fiber optic–towed decoys, directed infrared countermeasures, and the SQQ-89 integrated antisubmarine warfare combat system, reducing the number of competitors from three to two in high-performance fixed-wing military airplanes, on-board radio-frequency countermeasures, stealth technology, and remote mine-hunting systems, and creating vertical anticompetitive effects in numerous products – for example, through the combination of Lockheed Martin's airframes and Northrop Grumman's fire control radar. Although the complaint alleged substantial price effects, the cornerstone of the challenge was concern that the acquisition would substantially lessen innovation in various products and services for defense applications. In the subsections that follow, we highlight a number of significant economic issues that were raised by the proposed acquisition, including issues in which innovation played a significant role.

Market Definition

The division found that Lockheed and Northrop both participate in the same relevant market for airborne early-warning radar even though they make somewhat different products for that market. Their inclusion in the same market was based in part on the companies' shared core competence. At trial, the division expected to prove that Lockheed and Northrop were the only two competitors in this particular market, with the obvious implication that the two-to-one acquisition would be anticompetitive.

Another relevant market was for the *development* and *application* of stealth technology. The *development* of stealth technology is a technology market in the sense of the *Intellectual Property Guidelines*, and the *application* of stealth technology is a technology market in the sense of a cluster of products generated by a core technology.[43] This technology is critically important for the next generation of warships as well as airplanes, and the consolidation of this market from three independent innovators to two was viewed with great concern.[44] This is an important example of the need to preserve a larger number of firms in industries working at the frontiers of innovation where the best innovation strategy is unpredictable.

---

[43] An alternative approach would have been to regard stealth as an important capability in the market for high-performance fixed-wing military aircraft, but the division concluded that it was sufficiently distinctive to warrant independent standing as a relevant market.

[44] Northrop Grumman was a surprising entrant into the competition for the arsenal ship, and a survivor of the first round of cuts before the program was eliminated. A successful experience in that competition would have positioned it as a prospective bidder for the DD21 class of stealth destroyers.

Market Participants and Ease of Entry

Two issues come up over and over again in identifying the relevant competitors for defense markets. One is the time scale for innovation. In Lockheed-Northrop, the division was concerned about anticompetitive impacts five, ten, or twenty years out. That is clearly a long time to peer into the future, and a long lead time for potential entrants. The division generally takes into account the uncertainties associated with long lead times by being appropriately cautious before concluding that there exist barriers to entry. Nevertheless, the division concluded that the barriers to entry were very high in all of the markets challenged in the Lockheed-Northrop merger. Moreover, although the Department of Defense (DoD) can and does routinely sponsor new entry into particular markets, this is normally done as part of a carefully considered long-term procurement strategy. As an ad hoc response to a Lockheed-Northrop merger, the division in consultation with DoD determined that the possibility of DoD-sponsored entry was not sufficient to deter the expected anticompetitive effects of the proposed merger, that it was not an appropriate response to an otherwise desirable merger, and that the additional cost burden on DoD was properly regarded as an anticompetitive effect.

The second issue is a particular entry barrier, the core competency required to be a "system prime contractor." This is the firm that contracts directly with DoD to produce a weapons system (e.g., a fighter airplane), accepts responsibility for integrating all the needed subsystems, and decides who will supply each of the subsystems (in particular, which subsystems will be produced in-house and what will be offered to outsiders). The requisite competency varies from market to market and is difficult to define. System prime contractors may need to understand what the customer wants but did not specify, they may need in-depth expertise in one or more key technologies, and they probably need a working knowledge of several distinct technologies that have to work together. Note that all of these emphasize institutional know-how. (For example, Northrop can be a system prime for high-performance fixed-wing military aircraft even though it has not won a prime bid in years, and a system prime for the next generation of destroyers even though it has never built a ship.) Physical assets (as emphasized in the traditional industrial organization literature) are sometimes important, too, but know-how (as emphasized in the recent innovation literature) seems always to be a critical entry barrier in rapidly innovating industries.

Horizontal Innovation Effects

If no one knows the correct path of innovation, or if what everyone knows for sure is not so, then innovation is not just a matter of how much

R&D money gets spent. Two aspects of diversity are important: the number of independent innovators, and the opportunity for entry by innovators who have a fresh outlook. Frequently in the history of military aircraft, major pathbreaking advances have been made not by the leading incumbents but by niche firms or by major firms working outside their main areas of specialization.

In the Lockheed-Northrop market for high-performance fixed-wing aircraft, the issue was not whether a consolidation from three airframe manufacturers to two would reduce the intensity of innovative effort. The published literature does not yield a clear conclusion on that, especially because a large share of R&D spending is funded by DoD. Rather, the issue was that the number of independent innovators will be reduced by one, and the literature makes clear that this reduction matters. Moreover, one of the hot prospects for innovation in this market is unmanned aircraft – and that is precisely the kind of competency-destroying innovation that the division believed leading incumbents like Lockheed and Boeing are less likely to encourage.

Vertical Innovation Effects

Vertical innovation effects occur because firms exercise a preference for keeping transactions in-house rather than dealing with outsiders. Taken to an extreme, this becomes an outright refusal to deal (vertical foreclosure), a concern expressed by the Defense Science Board (1997: 22; cf. 3, 16): "Vertically integrated primes may deny competing primes access to key products or technologies they formerly supplied, or may give them access to a lower performance or higher cost product." This was indeed a concern in the Lockheed-Northrop investigation, particularly as regards technologies that defense contractors consider their "crown jewels" – the so-called strategic discriminators that help them win lucrative, strategically important contracts as a system prime rather than a subservient role as subcontractor. For example, Northrop Grumman has an outstanding reputation in composite materials (a critical technology for stealthy airplanes), but it clearly prefers selling stealth B-2 bombers, where they enjoy the profits and decision-making authority of a system prime, rather than act as a subcontractor of composite technology to Lockheed or Boeing. With Northrop as an independent bidder, Boeing has a better chance to obtain access to its composite technology, either because Northrop decides to enter a teaming arrangement with Boeing, or because Northrop happens to lose out in the first round of bidding as a system prime and then tries to get a piece of the action as a composite supplier. Either of these eventualities would be less likely following a merger of Northrop with Lockheed.

These outright refusals to deal, however, are exceptional in the defense industry. Teaming arrangements are commonplace, even among direct competitors.[45] The primary reason is that even direct competitors have complementary capabilities, and teaming can enhance their chances of winning a bid. On the other hand, as discussed earlier, there are also strong incentives favoring reliance on internal capabilities.[46] So defense contractors face a difficult tradeoff. Teaming with an outsider may improve a firm's chances of winning this bid, but keeping the work in-house may position that firm better for the next bid. A Lockheed-Northrop merger would have tilted this decision in favor of keeping the work in-house. In particular, consider the combination of Lockheed's airframes with Northrop's fire control radar. Currently, there are three airframe suppliers (Lockheed, Boeing, and Northrop) and two suppliers of fire control radar (Northrop and Raytheon-Hughes), and teaming arrangements vary from contract to contract. Postmerger, Northrop would become Lockheed's preferred supplier of fire control radar, and a reluctant supplier to Boeing. Raytheon-Hughes would become Boeing's preferred supplier, and a reluctant supplier to Lockheed. As a result, the division expected a tendency toward Lockheed-Northrop competing consistently against a vertical alliance of Boeing with Raytheon-Hughes.

Why is that anticompetitive? One valid but complex argument is that DoD is less likely to get the combination of the best airframe and the best radar after the merger. For example, suppose Lockheed is clearly superior to Boeing in airframes, and Northrop is clearly superior to Raytheon-Hughes in fire control radar. Then a Lockheed-Northrop team creates the best possible combination, but they can win by submitting a bid that is only marginally better than the hypothesized worst possible combination, Boeing-Hughes (Farrell, Monroe, and Saloner 1998). Two considerations argue against this outcome. One is that there is so much uncertainty and so much at stake that Lockheed-Northrop won't take the risk of losing. (But we have already encountered that argument in the context of in-house bias. Defense contractors do trade off the chances of winning a bid against other ways to enhance their profits.) A second

---

[45] Exclusive teaming arrangements have nonetheless become more common, and DoD has had to intervene in significant procurements to ensure that critical competencies were not denied to competing teams.

[46] Defense Science Board (1997: 21–22) observes that "To develop their internal businesses, prime contractors may favor their new in-house capabilities over external suppliers in new weapon systems bids. . . . Firms might also 'cherry pick' the highest value, most sophisticated work for their in-house suppliers to build corporate skills, leaving routine, lower-margin areas for external suppliers."

and more compelling consideration is that, absent the merger with Lockheed, Northrop can bid to be the supplier of fire control radar to both Lockheed and Boeing. In fact, for the Joint Strike Fighter, Northrop competed aggressively to become Boeing's radar supplier at the same time that it was already teamed with Lockheed. Taking all this into account, the mix-and-match scenario presents a valid competitive concern, but a factually and analytically difficult one that may be a challenging subject for further research.

A second effect of in-house bias is the lessening of collaborative learning opportunities. If Lockheed works with Northrop this time and Hughes next time (or both simultaneously), it can learn radar ideas from one and teach the other. Northrop and Hughes, of course, view this with mixed emotions (as do Lockheed and Boeing, when it is their airframe ideas getting funneled through Northrop and Hughes). But from the broader perspective of fostering breakthrough technologies in radar and airframes, a vertical merger that restrains the cross-fertilization of ideas in airframes and radar is a serious concern.

Clearly, the recent innovation literature was enormously helpful to the division's analysis of the proposed Lockheed-Northrop merger, focusing attention on firm-specific core competencies, on know-how as a critical entry barrier, on the flow of ideas between firms as an important contributor to innovation, on the importance of challengers for industry-transforming innovations, on the importance of the predictability of innovation as an industry variable for antitrust analysis, and on the need to preserve a larger number of firms in industries where the path of innovation is especially unpredictable.

CONCLUDING COMMENTS

This chapter has, we hope, made it clear that the Antitrust Division has taken an active role in thinking about innovation issues in recent years. In the process we hope to have made it clear that the current antitrust laws should offer sufficient flexibility so that innovation issues can be properly treated in both merger and non-merger investigations. This is not to say, of course, that all policy issues have been resolved. To the contrary, many interesting and difficult issues remain for antitrust enforcers, economists, and legal scholars to sort out. We hope that this chapter has provided some background and perspective that will aid in that inquiry.

As the chapter has also made clear, there remain a number of difficult and significant policy issues that are likely to continue to be the subject of debate and discussion in the academic and policy arenas for years to come. The Antitrust Division has been, and we expect that it will continue to be, an active participant in those debates.

REFERENCES

Audretsch, David B. 1995. *Innovation and Industry Evolution*. Cambridge, MA: MIT Press.

Badaracco, Joseph L., Jr. 1991. *The Knowledge Link: How Firms Compete through Strategic Alliances*. Boston: Harvard Business School Press.

Byrne, Noel. 1994. *Licensing Technology: Drafting and Negotiating Agreements*. New York: Stockton.

Cassiman, Bruno, and Reinhilde Veugelers. 1998. Spillovers and R&D Cooperation: Some Empirical Evidence. Universitat Pompeu Fabra and Katholicke Universiteit Leuven. Mimeographed.

Chiang, Jeongwen, and William T. Robinson. 1997. Do Market Pioneers Maintain Their Innovative Spark over Time? Paper No. 1098. Institute for Research in the Behavioral, Economic, and Management Sciences, Krannert Graduate School of Management, Purdue University.

Christensen, Clayton M. 1997. *The Innovator's Dilemma: When New Technologies Cause Great Firms to Fail*. Boston: Harvard Business School Press.

Cohen, Wesley. 1995. Empirical Studies of Innovative Activity. In Paul Stoneman, ed., *Handbook of the Economics of Innovation and Technological Change*, ch. 6. Cambridge: Blackwell.

Cohen, Wesley M., and Steven Klepper. 1992. The Tradeoff between Firm Size and Diversity in the Pursuit of Technological Progress. *Small Business Economics* 4: 1–14.

Cohen, Wesley M., and Richard C. Levin. 1989. Empirical Studies of Innovation and Market Structure. In R. Schmalensee and R. D. Willig, eds., *Handbook of Industrial Organization*, 2: ch. 18. New York: North-Holland.

Cohen, Wesley M., and Daniel A. Levinthal. 1989. Innovation and Learning: The Two Faces of R&D. *Economic Journal* 99: 569–96.

Defense Science Board. 1997. *Report of the Defense Science Board Task Force on Vertical Integration and Supplier Decisions*. Washington, DC: Office of the Secretary of Defense, Department of Defense.

Dorfman, Nancy S. 1987. *Innovation and Market Structure: Lessons from the Computer and Semiconductor Industries*. Cambridge, MA: Ballinger.

Dosi, Giovanni. 1988. Sources, Procedures, and Microeconomic Effects of Innovation. *Journal of Economic Literature* 26: 1120–71.

Dussauge, Pierre, Stuart Hart, and Bernard Ramanantsoa. 1992. *Strategic Technology Management*. New York: John Wiley and Sons.

Farrell, Joseph, and Michael L. Katz. 1998. The Effects of Antitrust and Intellectual Property Law on Compatibility and Innovation. *Antitrust Bulletin* 43: 609–50.

Farrell, Joseph, Hunter K. Monroe, and Garth Saloner. 1998. The Vertical Organization of Industry: Systems Competition versus Component Competition. *Journal of Economics and Management Strategy* 7: 143–82.

Federal Trade Commission and the U.S. Department of Justice. 2000. *Antitrust Guidelines for Collaborations among Competitors*. Washington, DC.

Federal Trade Commission Staff. 1996. *Anticipating the 21st Century: Competition Policy and the New High-Tech, Global Marketplace*. Washington, DC.

Freeman, Chris, and Luc Soete. 1997. *The Economics of Industrial Innovation.* Cambridge, MA: MIT Press.

Geroski, Paul A. 1995. Do Spillovers Undermine the Incentive to Innovate? In Steve Dowrick, ed., *Economic Approaches to Innovation*, ch. 4. Brookfield, VT: Edward Elgar.

Gilbert, Richard, and Carl Shapiro. 1997. Antitrust Issues in the Licensing of Intellectual Property: The Nine No-No's Meet the Nineties. *Brooking Papers on Economic Activity: Microeconomics* 1997: 283–349.

Gilbert, Richard J., and Steven C. Sunshine. 1995. Incorporating Dynamic Efficiency Concerns in Merger Analysis: The Use of Innovation Markets. *Antitrust Law Journal* 63: 569–601.

Goldscheider, Robert. 1996. *The New Companion to Licensing Negotiations: Licensing Law Handbook, 1996–97 Edition.* New York: Clark, Boardman, and Callaghan.

Hamel, G. 1991. Competition for Competence and Inter-Partner Learning within International Strategic Alliances. *Strategic Management Journal* 12: 83–103.

Hamel, Gary, Yves L. Doz, and C. K. Prahalad. 1989. Collaborate with Your Competitors – and Win. *Harvard Business Review* 67: 133–39.

Hobday, Mike. 1994. Innovation in Semiconductor Technology: The Limits of the Silicon Valley Network Model. In Mark Dodgson and Roy Rothwell, eds., *The Handbook of Industrial Innovation*, ch. 11. Brookfield, VT: Edward Elgar.

Hoven, John. 1987. Exclusive Dealing Can Sustain a Monopoly. Discussion Paper EAG 87-13, Economic Analysis Group, Antitrust Division, U.S. Department of Justice.

Howells, Jeremy. 1997. Research and Technology Outsourcing. CRIC Discussion Paper No. 6. University of Manchester.

Jorde, Thomas M., and David J. Teece. 1992. Innovation, Cooperation, and Antitrust. In Thomas M. Jorde and David J. Teece, eds., *Antitrust, Innovation, and Competitiveness*, ch. 3. New York: Oxford University Press.

Katz, Michael L., and Janusz A. Ordover. 1990. R&D Cooperation and Competition. *Brookings Papers: Microeconomics* 1990: 137–203.

Katz, Michael L., and Carl Shapiro. 1994. Systems Competition and Network Effects. *Journal of Economic Perspectives* 8: 93–115.

Kennedy, Michael, Susan A. Resetar, and Nicole DeHoratius. 1996. *Holding the Lead: Sustaining a Viable U.S. Military Fixed-Wing Aeronautical R&D Industrial Base.* DRR-1371-AF. Santa Monica, CA: Rand Corporation.

Klein, Joel I. 1997. MPEG-2 Business Review Letter. Letter to Gerrard R. Beeney, Esq., June 26. Washington, DC.: Antitrust Division, U.S. Department of Justice.

Lorell, Mark A. 1995. *Bomber R&D since 1949: The Role of Experience.* MR-670-AF. Santa Monica, CA: Rand Corporation.

Lorell, Mark A., and Hugh P. Levaux. 1998. *The Cutting Edge: A Half Century of U.S. Fighter Aircraft R&D.* MR-939-AF. Santa Monica, CA: Rand Corporation.

Manfroy, Willy, William G. Paterson, and Joachim W. Stockman. 1996. Technology Acquisition Process. In Jay Simon and Woody Friedlander, eds., *The Law* and *Business of Licensing: Licensing in the 1990s*, 1: 385–405. Rev. ed., New York: Clark, Boardman, and Callaghan.

Mathewson, Frank, and Ralph Winter. 1997. Tying as a Response to Demand Uncertainty. *Rand Journal of Economics* 28: 566–83.

Metcalfe, Stan. 1995. The Economic Foundations of Technology Policy: Equilibrium and Evolutionary Perspectives. In Paul Stoneman, ed., *Handbook of the Economics of Innovation and Technological Change*, ch. 4. Cambridge: Blackwell.

Ordover, Janusz A., and William J. Baumol. 1998. Antitrust Policy and High-Technology Industries. *Oxford Review of Economic Policy* 4: 13–34.

Polanyi, Michael. 1967. *The Tacit Dimension*. Garden City, NY: Doubleday Anchor.

Prahalad, C. K., and Gary Hamel. 1990. The Core Competence of the Corporation. *Harvard Business Review* 68: 79–91.

Eric B. Rasmusen, J. Mark Ramseyer, and John S. Wiley Jr. 1991. Naked Exclusion. *American Economic Review* 81: 1137–45.

Robison, Thornton. 1983. The Confidence Game: An Approach to the Law about Trade Secrets. *Arizona Law Review* 25: 347–93.

Rothwell, Roy. 1994. Industrial Innovation: Success, Strategy, Trends. In Mark Dodgson and Roy Rothwell, eds., *The Handbook of Industrial Innovation*, ch. 4. Brookfield, VT: Edward Elgar.

Rubinfeld, Daniel L. 1998. Antitrust Enforcement in Dynamic Network Industries. *Antitrust Bulletin* 43: 859–82.

Scherer, F. M., and David Ross. 1990. *Industrial Market Structure and Economic Performance*. 3rd ed. Boston: Houghton Mifflin.

Segal, Ilya R., and Michael D. Whinston. 1996. Naked Exclusion and Buyer Coordination. Discussion Paper No. 1780. Harvard Institute of Economic Research, Harvard University.

Simpson, P. Martin, Jr. 1995. Key License Clauses for Technology License Agreements. In Gerald Sobel, chair, *Technology Licensing and Litigation 1995*. New York: Practicing Law Institute.

Swann, Peter, and Jas Gill. 1993. The Speed of Technology Change and the Development of Market Structure: Semiconductors, PC Software and Biotechnology. In Peter Swann, ed., *New Technologies and the Firm: Innovation and Competition*, ch. 10. New York: Routledge.

Street, Gary D. 1994. Licensing: Trade Secrets and Know-How. In Gerald Sobel, chairman, *Technology Licensing and Litigation 1994*, ch. 4. New York: Practicing Law Institute.

Symeonides, George. 1996. Innovation, Firm Size and Market Structure: Schumpeterian Hypotheses and Some New Themes. Economics Department Working Papers No. 161. London School of Economics.

Teece, David J., Gary Pisano, and Amy Shuen. 1994. Dynamic Capabilities and Strategic Management. CCC Working Paper No. 94–9. Consortium on Competitiveness and Cooperation, University of California, Berkeley.

Tidd, Joe, John Bessant, and Keith Pavitt. 1997. *Managing Innovation: Integrating Technological, Market and Organizational Change*. New York: John Wiley and Sons.

Tisdell, Clem. 1995. Mainstream Analyses of Innovation: Neoclassical and New Industrial Economics. In Steve Dowrick, ed., *Economic Approaches to Innovation*, ch. 2. Brookfield, VT: Edward Elgar.

Tushman, Michael L., and Philip Anderson. 1986. Technological Discontinuities and Organizational Environments. *Administrative Science Quarterly* 31: 439–65.

United States, Department of Justice, Antitrust Division. 1988. *Antitrust Enforcement Guidelines for International Operations*. Washington, DC.

United States, Department of Justice and the Federal Trade Commission. 1995. *Antitrust Guidelines for the Licensing of Intellectual Property*. Washington, DC.

———. 1997. *Horizontal Merger Guidelines*. Washington, DC.

United States v. General Motors Corp., ZF Friedrichshafen, AG, ZF AG Holding, Inc., ZF Acquisition Corp., and ZF Industries, Inc., Complaint (November 16, 1993).

United States v. Lockheed Martin Corporation and Northrop Grumman Corporation, Complaint (March 23, 1998).

United States v. Pilkington plc and Pilkington Holdings Inc., Complaint and Competitive Impact Statement (May 25, 1994).

Utterback, James M. 1994. *Mastering the Dynamics of Innovation*. Boston: Harvard Business School Press.

Vandevoort, John R. 1971. Trade Secrets: Protecting a Very Special Property. *Business Lawyer* 26: 681–93.

Whinston, Michael. 1990. Tying, Foreclosure, and Exclusion. *American Economic Review* 80: 837–59.

Young, R. B. 1996. An Industry Perspective of Licensing. In Jay Simon and Woody Friedlander, eds., *The Law and Business of Licensing: Licensing in the 1990s*, 1: 323–40. Rev. ed. New York: Clark, Boardman, and Callaghan.

4

New Indicia for Antitrust Analysis in Markets Experiencing Rapid Innovation

Christopher Pleatsikas and David Teece

Economic analysis has come to have strong influence on antitrust analysis. Frequently, however, the economist's vision of a "good" industry is animated by the vision of perfect competition, with its assumption of homogeneous products, identical technologies, and firms competing solely on the basis of price, with prices equal to marginal cost, and earning zero economic profits. The chimera of perfect competition, however, is at odds with the reality of highly competitive technology-driven industries.

Competition policy and antitrust analysis must begin to think differently about certain "monopoly" issues. The nature of competition in markets exposed to the effects of rapid technological innovation is quite different from competition in other markets. Market power is extremely difficult to calibrate, and the traditional models of competition – be they perfect competition, oligopoly, or monopoly – have limited utility. Accordingly, economists and antitrust lawyers must rethink some basic assumptions and recalibrate some metrics or risk promoting litigation outcomes and public policies that harm competition and consumers.

In many industries today new forms of competition dominate the landscape. In particular, innovation (both technical and organizational) animates the process in many sectors. Products are differentiated, often significantly so, due to differences in the technology employed. True high-tech products are rarely commodities.

The introduction of new products and product differentiation accomplished by innovation is key to business success and customer satisfaction. In knowledge-based industries, performance features, quality, reliability, and service take on a special meaning. In the world of high technology, there is high uncertainty and supercharged competition. Prices exceed marginal cost. Waves of new product introductions are frequently accompanied by premium prices initially, followed by a rapid price decline as imitative products emerge. Technology and features are as important to

95

consumers as price, requiring one to talk in terms of price-performance competition rather than price competition alone.

Antitrust economics and the industrial organization literature manifest a limited understanding of the nature of competition in high-technology industries, where competition is driven by innovation. Among the public-policy (and economic) issues that have not been well explored are the evolutionary processes at work, the nature and sources of economic rents derived by participants, the degree of competition (or the lack thereof) in these industries, and the relevance of market structure as a proxy for market power.

The primary focus of this chapter is on market definition and market power analysis. Our purpose is to demonstrate the inadequacies of the traditional structural indicia that have been used by economists and others to define markets and assess market power in high-technology industries and to suggest alternative approaches that are more appropriate for these industries. We do not consider conduct or behavioral issues, except peripherally.

COMPETITION IN HIGH-TECHNOLOGY INDUSTRIES

Companies in high-technology industries experience fierce competition.[1] There are periodic, unpredictable, and discontinuous paradigm shifts[2] that can completely undermine incumbents using existing dominant technologies. Such shifts can and do often result in a total change in the competitive positions in the industry (Andretsch 1995). Incumbents may find themselves left behind by these shifts, as those who develop and successfully commercialize the new technologies often completely overturn the market positions that previously existed. As a result, market shares can shift quite rapidly, and new leaders often emerge. Andy Grove, CEO of Intel, has referred to these as "major inflexion points" in the evolution of an industry. The existence of, but unpredictable arrival of, inflexions underscores the high business risk that exists in these industries. Between inflexion points turmoil occurs as well, though the chances of survival are better.

Recognizing and then seizing the opportunities and threats afforded by major shifts is the essence of entrepreneurial leadership and is criti-

---

[1] For a more complete discussion of these issues, see Teece and Coleman (1998).

[2] Note that, for the purposes of this chapter, the term "paradigm shift" should be construed broadly. That is, it includes both fundamental changes in the character of the technology used in the marketplace (e.g., the shift from mainframe and mini computers to personal computers) and substantial improvements in technologies that do not represent such fundamental changes (e.g., the shift from 16-bit architecture in PCs to 32-bit architecture).

cal to business survival and prosperity. Indeed, entrepreneurial capabilities may be as or more important than technical capabilities. Established firms frequently have the most difficulties in adapting to paradigm shifts, often because they have too great a commitment to the existing technology or because decision making is focused myopically on current problems.

Change can be competency enhancing or competency destroying. Paradigm shifts open new opportunities for newcomers and/or other innovators, particularly when the underlying technology is competency destroying. The inability of incumbent firms in an industry to bridge a discontinuity is frequently observed, as in the semiconductor photolithographic alignment industry. In this industry, over the course of five generations of products, no firm leading in one generation led in the following generation (Henderson and Clark 1990). Utterback (1996), in a more general analysis of discontinuous change, found that in only one-fourth of cases studied did existing competitors either initiate radical innovation or adapt quickly enough to remain among the market leaders.

Investors understand the implications of these paradigm shifts much better than economists do. Investors recognize that competition in such industries is intense – often orders of magnitude more intense than in mature industries. Such intense competition generates high risk, and requires higher than average (across all industries) margins to compensate. High risk for the investor translates to low risk for the antitrust authorities, as incumbent positions are generally extremely fragile and, more often than not, competitive forces are sufficiently powerful to undo monopoly power, should it arise.

SPECIFIC EXAMPLES OF TECHNOLOGY COMPETITION

Technology-driven competition is frequently fierce. Standard ways of viewing competition, and defining markets, are usually inadequate. Here we provide three illustrations.

PPTCs and Other Overcurrent Protection Devices

PPTCs (polymeric positive temperature coefficient devices) are a class of new high-technology overcurrent protection devices (OCPDs) that were developed by Raychem Corporation and first marketed in the 1980s. Raychem has made considerable investments in research and development in this technology, including substantial investments before there were revenues from the product. PPTC devices are used (mainly) in low-current applications, such as in computers and other electronic devices (ranging from toys to medical diagnostic equipment), telecommunications equipment, batteries, and automobiles. PPTCs have been a tremendous spur to competition to all types of low-current OCPDs in the last decade.

Overcurrent protection devices are used in a wide variety of situations to protect electric and electronic circuits from the damage that would result if current flow to the product exceeded design tolerances. The many applications for OCPDs range from the massive circuit protection devices used at electricity network, high-voltage substations to circuit breakers used in homes, to fuses used in most automobiles to protect lighting, power windows, and other circuits.

The technology of PPTCs is ingenious, but employs a straightforward technical principle. Under normal current loads, the devices, which are basically a conductive polymer with two leads, have very low resistance. At much higher current loads, the temperature of the device increases and, at some critical temperature, the polymer undergoes a phase change in electrical characteristics that results in a rapid and substantial increase in resistance, essentially blocking all current. Once the current load is corrected, the device cools down and returns to its former level of resistance. As such, PPTCs work much like a conventional fuse, except that they can reset themselves automatically once the overcurrent situation is corrected.

PPTCs were first commercialized as overcurrent protection devices in the early 1980s. Before they were introduced, overcurrent protection in low-current applications was provided by a variety of technologies, mainly fuses, CPTCs (which are ceramic devices that work in much the same manner as PPTCs), and bimetallics (a type of circuit breaker). Subsequent to the introduction of PPTCs, integrated circuit overcurrent protection devices – sometimes referred to as "Smart Power" – have been introduced.

In the marketplace for overcurrent protection technologies, both radical and incremental technological developments are important. For a lengthy period of time (approximately through the 1980s), the industry was characterized by a slow rate of technological change and displayed some of the characteristics of a mature industry. Technological competition was muted. However, with the introduction of more radical innovations – first PPTCs and then Smart Power – the industry was transformed. As a consequence, innovative activity by developers of all technologies increased dramatically. Currently, the manufacturers of the different technologies are engaged in a continuous process of improving performance characteristics (e.g., susceptibility to nuisance tripping or ability to withstand more extreme operating environments), morphological factors (mainly shrinking the size of these devices, often to a small fraction of their former size), reducing costs (both direct and indirect costs, such as costs to utilize), and other characteristics. In an effort to improve performance, they have even developed hybrid devices (which combine the use of two or more existing technologies). The rapid pace of innovation in the past decade in particular has, in many instances, only served to increase the degree of product differentiation that exists in the industry, as developers of the various technologies strive to introduce products that capitalize on the specific advantages of each of these technologies.

Each of the overcurrent protection device technologies has unique advantages and disadvantages compared with the others. For example, fuses are inexpensive and very small in size but cannot be reset, whereas bimetallic devices have very low resistance (which is important in many devices, such as those powered by batteries, because it increases battery life) but tend to cycle on and off if overcurrent problems persist, which can damage the host product in some conditions. In addition to differences in performance characteristics – which occur across a multitude of dimensions, such as cycle time, trip time, sensitivity to current spikes, and many other factors – products employing the different technologies also exhibit some morphological differences in terms of size, shape, packaging, and other factors that affect design parameters, usage, usability, manufacturing costs, and user costs. Furthermore, the recent increase in innovative activity and the consequential increase in product differentiation that has occurred has strengthened and accentuated the relative advantages and disadvantages of different overcurrent protection products and technologies.

The existence of these advantages and disadvantages has important implications for the specific choices of overcurrent protection devices made by individual buyers. For example, makers of computers purchase mainly fuses, PPTCs, and Smart Power devices but seldom purchase bimetallic devices or CPTCs for applications in their products. Makers of rechargeable battery packs, by contrast, mainly purchase fuses, PPTCs, bimetallic devices, and Smart Power devices but not CPTCs; telecommunications equipment utilizes mainly PPTCs, CPTCs, and fuses but not bimetallic or Smart Power devices.

In fact, in only one important application, inside lithium battery cells, has one device – PPTCs – historically been used to the exclusion of others. In the case of these products, internal, integrated overcurrent protection was necessary to protect lithium cells from catastrophic failure because lithium battery cells could explode and/or cause fires if unprotected from overcurrent problems. Thus, the development of PPTC devices that could be fitted internally (i.e., inside the battery cell) was an enabling technology for this product. At the time lithium battery cells were introduced, there was no alternative to a PPTC overcurrent protection device for internal protection.[3] Recently, however, even this application has seen the introduction of alternatives for overcurrent protection, including inherently fail-safe lithium battery chemistries and alternative positive temperature coefficient materials.

Therefore, with the possible past exception of lithium battery cell applications, each user of overcurrent protection devices has had a choice of technologies. These choices can be represented by a vector of product characteristics, including size, shape, technical performance, and price. For example, Motorola has chosen a PPTC to protect the battery pack in one cell phone and a bimetallic device in another. Alternatively, Compaq has chosen to protect the Universal Serial Bus (USB) port with Smart Power in one model of computer and a PPTC to protect the same device in another model. Thus, despite the fact that alternatives are available – and used – for every other low-current overcurrent protection application, the existence of unique sets of attributes for each technology implies that, for each specific use, a uniquely "best" choice will exist and, presumably, be chosen. This choice may not provide the best technical performance but rather the best technical features at a certain price point.

Vascular Graft Technologies

Vascular graft technologies are used to repair or replace diseased or damaged blood vessels. These technologies are but a subset of a wider range of treatments that are available for this purpose. The vascular solutions that are potentially applicable to patients include:

- Preventive therapies and measures, such as diet modifications and/or exercise regimes.
- Pharmaceutical treatments, such as cholesterol reducing drugs.
- Vascular grafts, including synthetic (e.g., dacron), biological, and saphenous vein solutions.
- Noninvasive or interventional procedures, such as laser angioplasty, balloon angioplasty, and endarerectomies.

Grafts are generally made from materials that do not raise an immune response in the human body so that antirejection drugs are not required. Vascular graft can be categorized by size, materials, and type. Large-size grafts (>10 mm) are used to replace or repair abdominal and thoracic aortas and other very large arteries. Synthetic materials dominate in these applications, in part because there is no way to borrow material from existing large arteries for transplantation (i.e., within the same

---

[3] Internal protection was primarily required in primary (i.e., nonrechargeable) lithium cells.

host). Medium-sized grafts (6–10 mm), for such applications as arteri-ovenous shunts and femoropopliteal grafts above the knee, utilize auto-genous, synthetic, and biologic materials. Small grafts (<6 mm), for coronary arteries and femoropopliteal grafts below the knee, mainly use autogenous and biologic materials, although, less commonly, synthetic materials are used as well.

Among the materials used for grafts are autogeneous saphenous veins, human umbilical veins, bovine carotid arteries, dacron, and PTFE (a resin-based material similar to Teflon). Although each is used only for specific types of grafts, there is considerable overlap in applications, with the choice depending in part on each surgeon's preference and training. For example, all types are used for femoropopliteal replacements, but only PTFE, human umbilical veins, and bovine carotid arteries are used for arteriovenous shunt replacements. There are no important applica-tions, except possibly abdominal-thoracic and aortic applications (in which dacron predominates), where substitute materials are not com-monly used.

Each of these graft materials has unique advantages and disadvan-tages in different types of surgeries. For example, many surgeons believe that the saphenous vein, which in the late 1980s accounted for more than half of all grafts, is, when available, superior for most grafts below the aortic level. However, just as baby formula competes with mother's milk, even though the latter is universally acknowledged (except in unusual circumstances) as the most nourishing infant food, other graft materials compete against saphenous veins on the basis of the performance char-acteristics of these materials and the impact on the health of the patient of attempting to harvest the saphenous (or other) veins for use.

In fact, sales of graft materials are unusual in that the ultimate con-sumer – the person receiving the graft – has little (or, in most circum-stances, no) input into the choice among competing products. Surgeons, sometimes with input from administrators under some health plans, have primary responsibility for selecting among the alternative graft materi-als. Choices among the alternatives for any particular application in a specific patient are made based on peer choice, clinical trial results, expe-rience (particularly during training), and patient health. Brand identifi-cation and customer loyalty are also significant factors in choice. Most surgeons utilize multiple materials in their practices, with one survey demonstrating that more than 80 percent of all surgeons use more than two graft materials in their practices.

Interestingly, cost is an insignificant factor in choice among the alter-natives. This results mainly from two factors. First, patients and their physicians are far more interested in performance than costs, because the consequences of product failure caused by use of an inadequate (or less adequate) material are so great. Second, the cost of the procedure itself usually dwarfs the cost of the material. Thus, low sensitivity to price would be expected.

In addition to considerable demand-side substitutability among materials, there are three salient facts concerning market structure that indicate the competitive nature of the marketplace. First, there is considerable competition among suppliers of the basic PTFE material. Five large manufacturers supply this material to buyers worldwide. Second, although Food and Drug Administration (FDA) approval represents a formidable entry barrier for innovators, many firms have undertaken research in vascular grafts and represent significant potential competition, not least because the possibility of a breakthrough technology (e.g., from biotechnology research) in such an innovative industry is so great. Third, excluding saphenous veins harvested from the patient's own body (an obvious substitute for synthetics), numerous manufacturers compete for share both in the United States and worldwide. Furthermore, the largest supplier of nonsaphenous vein materials supplies only a relatively small percentage of all graft materials (approximately 25 percent of all nonsaphenous vein grafts in the mid-1990s).

Medical Diagnostic Imaging Devices

Diagnostic imaging devices are used by physicians and other health care providers to view inside the human body without intervention.[4] There are several types of these devices, employing a range of technologies. These include traditional X-ray instrumentation, nuclear imaging, ultrasonic devices (ultrasound), computed tomography (CT or CAT scanners), magnetic resonance imaging (MRI), and digital radiography.

Each of these technologies has a unique set of characteristics that help determine when and under what circumstances it is employed as a diagnostic tool, although there is considerable overlap in both capabilities and usage. Table 4.1 presents some of the performance characteristics of the different technologies. Given the substantial performance variation among these technologies and the fact that large price differences persist both within and across these technologies, it is not surprising that performance attributes are of central importance in competition among these products and technologies.

The principal performance attributes recognized in the industry include:

---

[4] This section and subsequent sections that discuss medical imaging devices are drawn largely from Hartman et al. (1993).

Table 4.1. Summary of Performance Characteristics

Technology	Relative Invasiveness	Relative Clarity	Relative Tissue-Specificity
X-ray	High	Low	Low
Nuclear	Low–medium	Low	Highest
Ultrasound	Low	Low–high	Medium
CT	Medium	High	High
MRI	Low	High	High
Digital X-ray	Medium	Medium	High

- Types of tissue applications for each device (although these are broad in the case of each technology, there are some types of applications for which some of the devices are better suited).
- Degree of invasiveness associated with the device.
- Clarity of the image.
- Capability to target specific tissue.

In general, there is a rough tradeoff between price and performance in this industry, but the tradeoff is not and has not been stable. As in most high-technology industries, this instability is magnified by the coincident evolution of price and performance attributes. For example, early nuclear imaging devices could distinguish only between tissues that were centimeters apart, while more recent equipment can provide spatial resolution of a few millimeters or less.

Importantly, as the performance characteristics of the technology improved, often dramatically, prices did not necessarily follow a consistent path. For example, nuclear imaging scanners introduced in the 1950s cost about $10,000, while in the 1990s positron emissions tomography systems can cost in the millions and MRI devices can cost hundreds of thousands. Even within technologies, there has not been a monotonic movement of prices, as prices reflect capabilities. In fact, dramatic improvements in capabilities often are associated with substantial increases in price.

In terms of historical development, the industry began in the 1890s with the development of conventional X-ray devices. Nuclear imaging and ultrasound technology were first developed in the early 1940s, although commercialization of these technologies did not occur until the 1950s. Computer tomography was first developed in the early 1960s and commercialized in the mid-1970s, at about the same time that MRI and digital radiography technologies were first developed. There was considerable lag between commercial introduction and commercial success

104 Christopher Pleatsikas and David Teece

for each of these technologies, although with more recent technologies this lag has decreased to a few years from a decade or more for some earlier technologies.

In terms of sales, X-ray devices dominated the industry until the latter 1970s. By the late 1980s, sales of X-ray devices constituted less than 30 percent of all medical imaging device sales, measured in dollar terms, although they still accounted for the largest share of sales of all medical diagnostic imaging devices (see Table 4.2).

The historical development of each of the technologies is even more interesting and manifests the dynamic nature of the industry. For example, nuclear imaging devices were first introduced in the form of commercial prototypes in about 1950, using hand-held units for imaging thyroid glands. These did not achieve high levels of sales, nor did the mechanical scanners introduced in the middle of that decade. In fact, commercial success for this technology was not assured until the early 1960s, when developments in complementary technologies, such as electronics, resulted in improved functionality and accumulated clinical experience fostered greater acceptance among medical providers.

Through this development period, about a dozen manufacturers of nuclear imaging devices entered and then exited the industry. All were financially unsuccessful because their products did not attain sufficient commercial acceptance despite, in some cases, enjoying a large share of the sales of this technology. Subsequently, the entry of a successful manufacturer of X-ray technology (Picker), with its established distribution system and reputation in the industry, combined with continued advances in the technology, helped to lay the foundation for commercial viability of the technology. Even Picker's leadership did not last long, however, as entrants introduced new, more useful variants such as full-body scanners and cameras to provide stationary images. Among these new technology leaders was Nuclear Chicago, which was subsequently acquired by GD Searle in 1966. Soon, Searle found its leadership in this technology challenged by new manufacturers that combined even more improved camera technology with the imaging device.

The competitive picture within other technologies was very similar. For example, X-ray computed tomography devices (so-called CT or CAT – for computed axial tomography – scanners) were first developed as a practical medical diagnostic instrument by Godfrey Hounsfield, who was employed by the British firm EMI and developed a head scanner. CT scanners obtained radiographic images of single slices of body tissue. They were first widely used in neurological imaging, the primary application for nuclear imaging devices at that time as well. CT scanners, although they were four to five times as expensive as nuclear imaging devices then, produced much clearer images.

Table 4.2. Annual Sales of Diagnostic Imaging Technologies in the United States ($million), Deflated by the Producer Price Index

Year	X-ray	Nuclear Imaging	Diagnostic Ultrasound	CT Scan	Magnetic Resonance	Digital Radiography	All Modalities
1954	45	<1	—	—	—	—	45
1955	43	<1	—	—	—	—	43
1956	42	<1	—	—	—	—	42
1957	41	<1	<1	—	—	—	41
1958	42	<1	<1	—	—	—	42
1959	42	<1	<1	—	—	—	42
1960	42	1	<1	—	—	—	43
1961	48	1	<1	—	—	—	49
1962	53	2	<1	—	—	—	55
1963	69	4	<1	—	—	—	73
1964	77	6	<1	—	—	—	83
1965	84	9	1	—	—	—	94
1966	85	10	1	—	—	—	96
1967	171	14	1	—	—	—	186
1968	180	17	1	—	—	—	198
1969	172	19	2	—	—	—	193
1970	173	24	3	—	—	—	200
1971	190	31	4	—	—	—	225
1972	206	39	7	—	—	—	252
1973	273	40	10	5	—	—	328
1974	281	42	15	13	—	—	351
1975	257	43	23	46	—	—	369
1976	230	46	41	87	—	—	404
1977	232	59	49	185	—	—	525
1978	239	69	60	115	—	—	483
1979	242	70	64	85	—	—	461
1980	238	69	77	97	<1	—	481
1981	242	68	80	133	<1	17	540
1982	262	63	77	175	5	55	637
1983	252	50	78	248	28	56	712
1984	257	47	90	185	39	81	699
1985	250	48	110	161	109	81	759
1986	247	51	127	153	143	82	803
1987	242	50	145	168	160	81	846

Source: Mitchell (1988).

EMI sold its first CT scanner unit in 1972 in London, with its first American sale a year later. Competition quickly became vigorous, with the entry of several firms in 1974–75. During this period entrants improved upon the device, with some introducing the first whole-body scanners. By 1977 twelve companies were making CT scanners for sale in the United States. The competition proved too much for EMI, which, under severe financial pressure, sold its scanner business to Thorn PLC in 1979. Subsequently this business was sold again – the international operations to General Electric and the U.S. operations to Omnimedical, Inc.[5] By the mid-1980s most early entrants into the CT scanner business had exited, while new entrants dominated the sales of this device.

Competition Analysis in a High-Technology Context

Each of these three industries – overcurrent protection, vascular graft technologies, and medical imaging – demonstrates the fierce but nontraditional, competitive forces at work in many high-technology industries. The fundamental question from a public policy perspective is to discern whether some of the traditional tools employed in defining markets and measuring market power can usefully be applied in such contexts. In fact, because each of these three industries has been the subject of antitrust inquiry, either by the agencies or the courts, the applicability of these traditional tools has been tested.

LIMITATIONS OF TRADITIONAL INDICIA USED TO EVALUATE MARKET DEFINITION AND MARKET POWER

The fundamental underpinning of all (noncollusive) competition policy issues is the analysis of market or monopoly power. In traditional antitrust economics and jurisprudence, the starting point for competitive assessment is the concept of a (relevant) market. The presumption is that if a firm has a "high market share" coupled with high entry barriers, it may have a high degree of market power ("monopoly" power). Thus, its conduct can be injurious to competition and ought to be scrutinized most carefully.

Given this presumption, antitrust analysis necessarily finds itself endeavoring to determine whether a firm has monopoly power. Absent monopoly power, noncollusive business conduct never raises antitrust issues. In the presence of monopoly power, business conduct that would otherwise be unobjectionable may become problematic. This has traditionally been determined by defining the market in which a firm competes and then assessing the degree of control that a particular firm has over that market. Indeed, defining markets and the share a firm has within it is the linchpin of traditional antitrust analysis.

In U.S. antitrust jurisprudence, two main categories of traditional indicia are commonly used to define markets and to derive measures of market power: the methods contained in the *Horizontal Merger*

---

[5] GE had wanted to purchase the entire scanner business of Thorn but was deterred from doing so by a Justice Department investigation. Omnimedical's operations survived only into the early 1980s.

Guidelines, and indicia that roughly correspond to those identified in *Brown Shoe*.[6] These have been utilized by the courts as if they are universally applicable, without regard to industry context.[7] Unfortunately, context is extremely important,[8] and these indicia, particularly the *Brown Shoe* indicia, are not well suited for analysis of high-technology industries. In the following subsections, we describe the techniques of analysis that have been developed from these sources and the problems inherent in them for analysis of antitrust problems in high-technology industries.

The Horizontal Merger Guidelines

The *Horizontal Merger Guidelines*, revised in 1997, include several categories of analytical techniques or indicia that have been applied to mergers and, more generally, to the problem of market definition whether in the merger context or otherwise:

- The so-called hypothetical monopolist test is to identify market boundaries. The hypothetical monopolist is, for analytical purposes, assumed to implement an SSNIP (small but significant, nontransitory increase in price). If the SSNIP is sustainable despite any demand-side substitution, a relevant market is said to be identified.
- The Hirshman-Herfindahl Index (HHI) is used as a threshold to identify mergers that are likely to have (or may possibly have) anti-competitive effects. When the thresholds established in the *Horizontal Merger Guidelines* are exceeded, the HHI test indicates whether further analysis is required. High HHIs are assumed to proxy for market power.
- Entry analysis is utilized to identify both uncommitted entrants for purposes of identifying market shares and potential entrants that may be able to constrain behavior of current market participants.

The analytical techniques utilized in the *Horizontal Merger Guidelines* have limitations for application in high-technology industries, whether for mergers or other competition issues. For example, the hypothetical

---

[6] *Brown Shoe, Inc. v. United States*, 370 U.S. 294 (1962).

[7] Although both categories derive from market merger analysis, they have been widely applied by courts and analysts in circumstances where more general allegations of anti-competitive behavior have been made. It should be noted, however, that not all courts have accepted the use of these indicia for non-merger cases.

[8] By context, we mean not only the specific circumstances of the case – for example, whether merger or allegations of anticompetitive behavior not related to a merger – but also the specific circumstances of the industry, most importantly the industry structure and nature of competitive activity in the industry (or industries) of interest.

monopolist test relies implicitly on some measure of cross-elasticities of substitution because demand-side substitution possibilities – geographic and/or product – are critical to assessing market boundaries under this approach. The central question involves identifying products that compete. All reasonable substitutes must be identified. Such identification may be relatively straightforward in many (though probably not all) mature industries. After all, different grades of steel may be good substitutes for one another in the manufacture of certain products, but it may be obvious that iron, aluminum, or titanium is a poor substitute for steel in many uses. Alternatively, different varieties of wheat may be substitutable in many uses (e.g., for making bread), but barley or corn may not be a good substitute for wheat in many circumstances.

With high-technology products, substitution analysis becomes much more difficult. Most obviously, data for estimating cross-elasticities, which are often lacking even for products in mature industries, are seldom available at all for high-technology industries.[9] Even in the absence of definitive cross-elasticity data, it is sometimes relatively easy to identify substitutes for mature products. There is a great deal of experience as to applications and the criteria that are applied by users to decide among alternatives may be well understood and easy to express in economic terms. For high-technology products, however, it is often difficult for nonexperts – including economists, lawyers, judges, and juries – to determine whether and to what extent substitution between (or among) products made by different technologies is feasible.

The ability of customers to utilize specific high-technology products in their businesses is often based on whether that product satisfies arcane technical and economic criteria.[10] Because data relevant to quantifying economic substitutability are incomplete or not available at all, it may be difficult to determine or even to estimate, with an acceptable degree of accuracy, the proportion of users who can avail themselves of existing substitution possibilities.

For example, in the overcurrent protection market, PPTCs, bimetallics, and Smart Power with a fuse backup are all feasible substitutes for rechargeable battery applications. The rationale for choosing a specific overcurrent protection device for use in a particular product,

---

[9] Even where such data are available, of course, they seldom provide definitive views as to the elasticity of substitution between two products.

[10] After all, automakers' needs for mature products, such as rolled steel from a specific producer, may be relatively simple to understand (even by economists). However, their ability to utilize the electronic components produced by a specific manufacture may not at all be obvious to nontechnical analysts. Because, to a great extent, economic substitutability will depend on such assessments, this information is obviously relevant to an antitrust analyst.

however, is not often easy to quantify. As noted earlier, there are trade-offs between PPTCs and bimetallics on a number of dimensions, including resistance, which affects battery life, and failure mode, which may affect warranty costs.[11] Although this tradeoff is easy to comprehend in general, it is difficult to quantify so as to be able to model consumer choice for overcurrent protection devices (and thereby to estimate the substitution elasticities). Given that a third alternative technology, Smart Power, is also available, the assessment of substitution possibilities is even more problematical. This is particularly true because the Smart Power–fuse combination is clearly more expensive than either of the other alternatives in terms of total costs. However, in terms of marginal costs (i.e., when battery management functions are already incorporated into the device that uses the battery) and/or functionality, the Smart Power device with backup may possess some key advantages, at least in some circumstances.

This points to two quite different ways of viewing substitution in some circumstances. According to one view, the particular characteristics that are required for the end product influence (or even determine) the choice of input technology that is incorporated. This requires that the manufacturer of the end product choose, say, the product's performance characteristics prior to designing the final product. According to the second view of substitution, makers of end products choose the input technology (or combination of input technologies) based on the functionality tradeoffs they present, and the manufacturers' views of the value of these tradeoffs. The resulting end products have features or characteristics that reflect these tradeoffs (i.e., the features the product offers are not predetermined but are, to an extent, an outcome of the engineering and design process).

Although the differences between these views may appear to be rather subtle at first glance, the implications for market definition are far-reaching. Under the first view – what may be viewed as a "top-down" approach because it is the desired functionality in the end product that dictates choice of input technology – the scope for substitutability may be limited (or at least may appear so). The manufacturer selects the product attributes (e.g., the characteristics the end product must have to succeed in the marketplace). Substitution is then limited (or, perhaps, nonexistent).

Under the second view – what may be termed a "bottom-up" approach – the choice is more interactive, with costs and values for the

---

[11] For example, because PPTCs will cut current until the fault is corrected, there is no chance of reconnecting a circuit when a fault still exists, a circumstance that may cause damage to the battery under some conditions.

various desired features assessed as a package rather than the desired value for each feature separately derived. The bottom-up approach allows for more freedom of choice among the technological alternatives available and therefore implies much more substitutability. However, the analysis required to establish the degree of substitutability requires a much more detailed (and microeconomic) approach than is generally utilized in defining markets.[12]

The SSNIP test presents a separate set of challenges for analysis of high-technology industries. Absent investigation of a merger or acquisition, when prevailing prices can usually be used as the basis for applying the SSNIP test, the most immediate problem that faces the analyst is the difficulty of identifying the competitive level of prices to be used as a bench mark to assess the impact of a SSNIP. With commodity (or even lightly differentiated) products, this is often relatively easy, because there are many producers, and one can rely upon empirical observation of prices in well-developed markets. Many high-technology products, by contrast, are highly differentiated, rendering price comparisons across different products highly problematical. In addition, markets may appear to be highly fragmented, as customized products are often developed to satisfy the specific needs of particular customers. Further, given the degree of customization and the lack of open, well-developed markets or the dearth of public information on pricing, even assembling comparable price series for competing products may be difficult or impossible.

Another problem associated with attempts to apply the SSNIP test to high-technology industries involves identifying the magnitude of "small, but significant" that should be used in this context. The earlier versions of the *Horizontal Merger Guidelines* specified 5 percent as the appropriate level for analysis. Beginning in 1992, the guidelines were somewhat less prescriptive, stating that "In attempting to determine objectively the effect of a 'small but significant and nontransitory'

---

[12] The two approaches may be illustrated by the following example. Battery makers are concerned about battery life (i.e., the ability to provide power from one charge for a certain amount of time). Under the top-down approach, a battery manufacturer may specify that a particular battery be able to provide maximum battery life prior to any final design of the product. Under such circumstances, the choice of overcurrent protection would almost certainly be a bimetallic device because it has the lowest resistance of any feasible choice. Under the bottom-up approach, by contrast, the battery life would be the end result of tradeoffs made by the manufacturer during the product development, engineering, and design stages. That is, the features of the final product would reflect the tradeoffs in price and performance made during the product development, engineering, and design stages rather than having been specified at the outset of this process. Such a device might incorporate various types of overcurrent protection.

increase in price, the Agency, in most contexts, will use a price increase of five percent lasting for the foreseeable future."[13]

As a practical matter, agencies in the United States use anything from 5 to 20 percent and claim that the answers rarely differ whatever number between 5 and 20 percent is used.[14] In high-technology industries, where nonprice competition is often far more important than price competition, the appropriate price change for antitrust analysis will be larger than 5 percent. Even at 20 percent, the SSNIP test may find a plethora of $20 million or smaller "markets" around new products.

Of course, this points to an even more serious flaw in the use of SSNIP analyses for high-technology industries. Because performance competition is usually the central focus of competitive efforts in these industries, the entire concept of SSNIP is awkward, for at least three reasons. First, unlike more mature industries, where performance features often change in more incremental and predictable ways and, in shorthand terms, competitive efforts are focused on price changes because there is little variation in performance characteristics, performance competition is at the heart of high-technology competition. At times of paradigm shifts, and even in between, substantial performance increases are often achieved by manufacturers. For example, currently Pentium (actually Pentium III) chips operate at speeds (>1,000 MHz) several times faster than earlier-generation Pentium (or predecessor) chips and provide a variety of functions unavailable in earlier versions. Thus, with the competitive focus on performance, considerations of price are often secondary or even tertiary, except where direct (i.e., substantially similar) products are readily available.

Second, the entire concept of SSNIP is rather static. When technology, even during periods of incremental change, rather than revolutionary change, is advancing rapidly – with new product life cycles often only months in length – price-performance relationships change rapidly. The rate of change (i.e., improvement) in this relationship is of interest to buyers. There is a substantial problem, however, attempting to operationalize a SSNIP-type rule that would properly capture the competitive dynamic in a high-technology context. Perhaps the ratio of price to performance measures over time is more appropriate.

Third, because competition in most high-technology industries is focused on performance rather than price, the underlying concept of SSNIP itself has little relevance. It might be more appropriate to focus on those dimensions of competition – that is, specific measures of

---

[13] *Horizontal Merger Guidelines* (1992: 20).
[14] Based on a conversation with the Director of Research, Department of Justice, Washington, DC, December 17, 1998.

performance – that are the focus of competitive efforts. Elsewhere we have suggested an alternative that identifies key performance measures and attempts to discern substitutability when performance is affected (Hartman et al. 1993).

Additional problems occur around the measurement and interpretation of market shares and market concentration. Unless, of course, the market is defined correctly, the HHI is completely meaningless, even if one believes in structural analysis. Because product differentiation in high-technology industries is frequently high, HHI analysis will overstate industry concentration levels if markets are defined with reference to product differentiation. This could well lead analysts and the courts to the erroneous conclusions about the nature and extent of competition in these industries and to policy errors concerning market definition and market power.

Finally, entry analysis must be reconsidered and substantially recast for application in high-technology industries. The standards applied in the *Horizontal Merger Guidelines* – entry within one year for uncommitted entrants (i.e., no sunk costs) for inclusion in consideration of market shares and within two years for committed entrants to constrain behavior – make little sense in dynamic contexts. A more appropriate bench mark to assess entry is the duration of product life cycle. It is not just immediate entry that tempers behavior in high-technology industries; it is also the threat of the next generation of products and services that concerns incumbents. Current leaders must succeed in each round of innovation or lose leadership. In such a dynamic environment, high market shares are often fragile and may confer little, if any, future advantage.

Thus, it would be appropriate to view entry analysis more flexibly in high-technology industries. Although there is always some uncertainty as to the timing of paradigm shifts, it is not "speculative" to take the possibility of such shifts into account. Indeed, the richness of the underlying technological opportunity may help one calibrate the likelihood of fundamental change. Furthermore, the unpredictability of the timing of such shifts, in fact, may help to constrain behavior, as current market leaders can never be sure that a shift won't occur soon. The possibility – or, indeed, inevitability – of major change will help check attempts to exploit market leadership at the expense of customers. This is because the existing customer base may be the only bridge through to the future for the incumbent. Fragile though this link may be, the incumbent will need to build goodwill as its only shield against annihilation.

Brown Shoe *Factors*

While the agencies demonstrate increasing sophistication in dealing with market definition in the context of innovation, the courts are still burdened with case law that does not as yet connect with the realities of the new knowledge economy. In particular, *Brown Shoe* is still utilized from time to time, despite the fact that economic analysis and agency thinking have long eclipsed it. *Brown Shoe*[15] enumerated a number of indicia for identifying markets and "submarkets"[16] (and, indirectly, for assessing market power within those markets). Without discussing the merits (or demerits) of the submarket concept, these indicia are particularly ill-suited to analyzing high-technology markets. There are eight such factors set forth in *Brown Shoe* – one for markets and the others for submarkets. Although seven of the eight factors were described by the Supreme Court as applying to analysis of submarkets, they have been more generally utilized in attempts to define markets by some economists. The eight factors are:

- Interchangeability of use or cross-elasticity of demand.
- Industry or public recognition of the submarket as a separate economic entity.
- The product's peculiar characteristics and uses.
- Unique production facilities.
- Distinct customers.
- Distinct prices.
- Sensitivity (of sales) to price changes.
- Specialized vendors.

Of these eight factors, only cross-elasticity and elasticity ("sensitivity to price changes") of demand have a strong theoretical foundation as a basis on which to identify market boundaries and measure market power. Unfortunately, as we have already indicated, for most high-technology markets insufficient data exist for estimating cross-elasticities and elasticities. Thus, as a practical matter, these measures are not generally useful. As an alternative to rigorous estimation of cross-elasticities and elasticities, the *Brown Shoe* factors allow consideration of "interchangeability of use" and "sensitivity [of sales] to price changes." These suggest less rigorous tests, which consider substitutability more broadly in terms of economic and technical feasibility and, perhaps, in terms of marketplace evidence of actual instances of substitutability. If viewed in this manner, these factors, in fact, can be of assistance in defining high-technology (and other) markets and assessing

---

[15] *Brown Shoe, Inc. v. United States*, 370 U.S. 294 (1962).

[16] The assertion of relevant antitrust submarkets within relevant antitrust markets has justifiably been criticized as inherently contradictory and, thus, not at all useful because it requires the simultaneous existence of two types of economic substitutes. See, e.g., Simons and Williams (1993).

market power. However, determinations of what constitutes sufficient evidence of economic or technical substitutability and/or of marketplace substitution would have to be matters of the weight of the evidence, because no obvious and definitive economic test of sufficiency exists.

Whereas the other six *Brown Shoe* factors may have, at best, limited applicability to defining markets and assessing market power in mature, relatively undifferentiated markets, they present even greater difficulties in the context of high-technology industries. In some cases these factors are entirely inappropriate.

For example, "industry or public recognition of the submarket [or market] as a separate economic entity" is almost impossible to operationalize as a standard or test in an antitrust investigation. What constitutes "recognition"? Even if, in a business sense, a market is treated as separate in some manner, does this have any relevance to antitrust analysis? Given the economic content of the terms "relevant market" and "antitrust market power" (or monopoly power), treatment or analysis of markets by noneconomists, though useful information in an economic inquiry of competitive conditions and consequences, is rarely definitive.

A "product's peculiar characteristics and uses" are even less useful, because products (and services) in many high-technology industries are highly differentiated. Thus, "peculiar" characteristics and uses for individual, but competitive, products may be a fundamental characteristic of the market in question. Subdividing the relevant market based on the very product differentiation that exists risks defining markets much too narrowly and overstating market power, so that power is found where none, in fact, exists.

"Unique production facilities" are presumably an attempt to inject supply-side substitution effects into competition analysis. However, they are only relevant to defining markets and assessing market power where products are undifferentiated or only lightly differentiated. In highly differentiated high-technology industries, it is not uncommon for individual, but competing, products to require unique production facilities. For example, although inkjet and laser printers may compete closely (and indeed be nearly perfect substitutes in many circumstances) in many uses, it would be impossible to produce engines for the former on a production line (or facility) designed to produce the latter. Thus, supply-side substitution is sufficient, but not necessary, to integrate two otherwise separate "markets." This fact substantially limits the applicability of this *Brown Shoe* factor in antitrust market analysis in high-technology industries.

Another *Brown Shoe* factor, "distinct customers," is particularly vague and difficult to put in practice. It could refer to either purchaser (users) or applications (uses). Of course, the key factor in defining relevant markets and assessing power in those relevant markets is substitutability, which is an empirical question. To the extent that an identifiable set of customers has no substitutes practically available – that is, there are no technical and/or economic substitutes that are feasible – the analysis presents few, if any, problems. When such substitutes exist, the issues devolve to an investigation to the degree of economic constraint on the product(s) or service(s) of interest that substitutes provide. Predominance in terms of market share among particular users or uses, while interesting and perhaps even relevant to the inquiry, begs the definition question in many respects because it puts the cart before the horse. In other words, it risks defining the relevant market based on ad hoc collections of identifiable or convenient groupings of users or uses (from the perspective of practically based as opposed to any theoretically based taxonomies), even though, in an economic sense, these collections may not constitute a "market" at all.

Economic theory, of course, provides some support for the notion that parallel movements in prices for two goods may indicate that they compete against one another in one relevant market. However, this condition may be neither necessary nor sufficient for two products to compete.[17] The broader factor specified in *Brown Shoe* – "distinct prices" – has no basis in theory for determining market boundaries. Just because two products (or services) have distinct (i.e., different) prices, this is no indication that they exist in separate relevant antitrust markets, even if such differences are sustained over time. For example, for households, natural gas and electricity may compete for certain uses, but their energy prices are not the same, even on a heat equivalent (Btu) basis. There are many reasons why products may compete, but sustainable differences in prices may obtain. These include, but are not limited to, differences in prices of complementary goods,[18] quality differences, branding, and others.

The distinct prices factor has also been extended, erroneously in our view, to include "distinctive" (i.e., high) price margins as an indicator of market boundaries (and market power). Under this view, producers that enjoy high margins are only able to do so because their prices are insulated from competition by substitutes. In some sense, this argument turns

---

[17] It is generally accepted that price correlation analyses are relevant to defining the boundaries of relevant antitrust markets only where relatively low levels of product differentiation exist.

[18] For example, energy-using equipment, such as hot-water heaters fueled by gas, are generally more expensive than those fueled by electricity, but these differences are offset, to at least some extent, by the lower cost of gas as compared with the cost of electricity that pertains in most locales.

the cellophane trap[19] as well as the problem of market definition on their heads. That is, high margins are viewed as an indicator, in and of themselves, of market power, which must, by inference of proponents of this view, in turn, be evidence of poor substitutability. Completely lost in this analysis, particularly when applied in a high-technology context, are several important concepts. For example, many innovators obtain legal protection from (at least some forms of) competition through copyrights and/or patents. Also, the unique nature of the technology and/or the ability to protect proprietary information may affect the appropriability of the innovation by the wider market. In addition, product differentiation may affect margins.

More important, a focus on margins as an indicator of either market boundaries or market power is entirely inappropriate, particularly in high-technology industries. Most fundamentally, empirical research has not supported the position that market power is particularly correlated with accounting margins (e.g., Scherer 1985: 272–73). In addition, high net margins may merely be reflective of the high returns required on successful products, given the inherent uncertainty and riskiness of such investments.[20] High gross margins, which are even less appropriate in our view as an indicator of market definition or market power, merely reflect the division of costs between direct manufacturing costs and other costs. Research and development costs, which may have to be maintained at relatively high levels to sustain market leadership (or even protect market share), are completely ignored when gross margins are used.

Sensitivity of sales to price changes, another *Brown Shoe* factor, is essentially the own-price elasticity of a product or service. Just as little information is likely to exist on cross-elasticities of substitution for high-technology products, reliable estimates of own-price elasticities are unlikely to be available either. Further, high-technology markets are likely to be characterized by monotonically declining prices (often rapidly declining) and monotonically increasing performance and sales. Deriving any accurate and reliable (i.e., for the purposes of defining market boundaries and identifying substitutes) ceteris paribus quantification of price elasticity would be difficult in such circumstances. Relying on a qualitative assessment of data and market perceptions, by contrast, is imprecise, but, when performed well, such an analysis can be of value.

---

[19] *United States v. E.I. duPont de Nemours and Co.*, 351 U.S. 377 (1956).

[20] Note that most such investments do not produce positive returns; e.g., see Mansfield (1977). These observations he made about success rates remain valid as noted in several sources, both academic and popular (e.g., see *Marketing News* issues from February 1 and June 21, 1993).

The final *Brown Shoe* factor is specialized vendors. Again, whatever the applicability of this factor to mature markets – and it is certainly arguable that it has any relevance even in those circumstances – this factor is particularly inappropriate for deriving market boundaries in high-technology markets. Such vendors are often utilized by producers in high-technology industries for several reasons. These include situations where specialized knowledge is required to apply the technology (or to utilize the product that incorporates it), where complementary assets are required that are more efficiently provided by vendors and/or where there may be free-rider problems (e.g., for obtaining information) if a mix of specialized and nonspecialized vendors are used.

Thus, the *Brown Shoe* factors – all eight, plus extensions – are particularly inappropriate bases for analysis of either market boundaries or market power in high-technology industries. They do not reflect an appreciation of either the manner of competition in such industries or the specific nature of the innovative process.

PROBLEMS IN APPLYING TRADITIONAL INDICIA IN HIGH-TECHNOLOGY CONTEXTS

The traditional indicia for defining relevant antitrust markets (and/or assessing market power in those markets) generally result in markets that are too narrow – that is, these markets exclude substitute products or services that should be included. As a consequence, market power would be overestimated. In the subsections that follow, we discuss three examples where traditional indicia have led to erroneous conclusions regarding market definition.

The Legal System in Action, Example 1: The Overcurrent Protection Market (Bourns v. Raychem)

Recent litigation in federal court[21] concerned allegations that Raychem, the developer of PPTC overcurrent protection devices, had violated antitrust laws in alleged attempts to restrict the entry into the marketplace of a competitor, Bourns, Inc., that had introduced similar PPTC devices. Without discussing the merits of the case, which was brought as a countersuit to Raychem's original claims relating to misappropriation of trade secrets, the issues relating to market definition and assessment of market power aptly illustrate the problems of employing traditional indicia to a high-technology context.

As noted earlier, the development of PPTC overcurrent protection devices involved a lengthy research and development effort by Raychem. Approximately a decade of R&D passed before introduction

---

[21] *Bourns, Inc. v. Raychem Corporation*, No. CV 98-1765 CM. (C.D. Calif.).

of the first commercial product, in the early 1980s. Substantial R&D spending has continued up to the present in an effort to improve the performance of these products, reduce their costs, and extend their application to new uses.

In response to these efforts, makers of other types of overcurrent protection devices have increased R&D spending to develop new product forms, new applications, improve performance, and reduce costs. For example, fuse makers have developed much smaller and less costly fuses in an effort – successful to date – to retain their cost and size advantage over PPTC devices made for the same applications. Also, makers of bimetallic devices for rechargeable battery applications have recently developed a "strap" form factor to compete directly against a similar strap product first introduced for PPTC devices. These and other numerous, similar examples, as well as the introduction of Smart Power integrated circuits, have helped transform what was a marketplace with mature technologies – or at least technologies that were improving at a relatively slow rate – into a dynamic one with rapid technological development.

No rigorous data on prices and sales of all overcurrent protection devices, however, were available for expert analysis in the case. This situation is, of course, quite common in litigation, where only a small proportion of the firms that may be considered for inclusion in the relevant market are parties to the case. Thus, economic experts must rely on data that is anecdotal, incomplete (covering only a few firms or products), qualitative and/or only partly relevant because it was collected for a different purpose than for estimating antitrust relevant markets. The only exception to this circumstance may occur where a specific survey is commissioned to collect the required data, but such a task is expensive and seldom undertaken on a scale necessary to provide definitive answers to market definition and market power assessments. Therefore, the economic analyst must utilize the information and resources that are available, framed within a methodology that is sensitive to the characteristics of the competition that has, is, and/or will be taking place.

This case was no different from the norm in this respect; the information available had obvious limitations, but did provide insight to help answer the relevant questions. But, despite the dynamic and innovative backdrop for the overcurrent protection marketplace, the economic expert for Bourns defined and analyzed the market using a variant of the *Brown Shoe* factors. First, using mainly marketing information from Raychem, he concluded that product markets should be defined by major application categories. He alleged that this indicated at least seven relevant antitrust product markets. He maintained that these seven distinct markets existed despite the fact that many PPTC devices (as well as overcurrent protection devices that employed other technologies) could be and were in fact utilized in more than one (and sometimes several) applications categories. As a consequence, one type of fuse or one type of PPTC device might be used in several different applications that the Bourns' expert labeled as separate "markets." Furthermore, he maintained that these separate and distinct product markets existed even though the types of applications involved were exactly the same across at least some of the different markets. Thus, the predominate application for overcurrent protection in the computer applications (or "market," as the Bourns' economic expert maintained), as well as many or most of the general electronics and low- and high-voltage telecommunications applications (which the Bourns' expert separated into three more separate "markets"), was printed circuit boards.

Bourns' expert separated these markets based on marketing documents, supported to a very limited extent by "customer perceptions" based on less than five customer interviews and some industry literature on applications.[22] He then endeavored to use *Brown Shoe*–like factors to determine the breadth of products in each of these "markets" and, simultaneously, market power in those "markets." The following five factors were specifically used in his analysis.

Customer Perceptions

This factor, of course, is a variant of the "public recognition" factor from *Brown Shoe*. In this case, the Bourns' expert utilized mainly marketing materials developed by Raychem, which separated customers into the application categories that the Bourns' expert used as the basis for his market definitions. As part of his review of "customer perceptions," the expert also reviewed the alleged benefits of PPTC devices compared with devices employing other technologies. This review is related to the "peculiar characteristics" factor noted in *Brown Shoe*. According to the expert, because PPTCs provided certain benefits compared with devices based on other technologies, this was evidence of separate markets for PPTC devices.

Important Characteristics

This element of the "method" employed by Bourns' expert is also related to the "peculiar characteristics" factor in *Brown Shoe*. The economic

---

[22] Nearly all of this literature was from the trade press and virtually all of it had, in fact, been written by Raychem personnel. Thus, it was designed, in large part, to serve a marketing function – accentuating the advantages of PPTCs, highlight their differentiation, and minimize their disadvantages compared with alternative products and technologies.

expert asserted that the particular performance advantages of PPTCs compared with other types of overcurrent protection devices indicated that these other types of devices would be poor substitutes for PPTCs. Thus, he maintained that this factor supported the view that PPTCs existed in a separate market.

Gross Profit Margins

Bourns' economic expert noted that Raychem's gross profit margins for PPTCs were high in an absolute sense, as well as high when compared with industry averages for electronic products and when compared with the firmwide gross margins for manufacturers of other types of overcurrent protection devices. With one exception however, the vast majority of the revenues for these other firms was derived from products other than overcurrent protection devices. For this and other reasons, this index is particularly ill-suited to the definition of markets or the assessment of market power. Beyond the specific facts of this case – Raychem's internal rate of return over more than two decades on its PPTC overcurrent protection investment was well within industry norms – the use of gross margins for these antitrust purposes implies that short-run marginal costs are an appropriate measure of competitive market prices. This is clearly erroneous, because "imperfectly"[23] but workably competitive markets can sustain prices above even long-run marginal costs.

Pricing

Bourns' economic expert investigated several aspects of pricing behavior. First, he utilized information on price levels (the "distinct pricing" factor in *Brown Shoe*). He concluded that PPTCs were priced at a premium to other types of PPTCs. In fact, this conclusion was erroneous; some other types of overcurrent protection devices are typically priced higher than PPTCs. The economic expert also concluded that, because PPTC prices had declined faster than prices for most other overcurrent protection devices over a five-year period, PPTC prices were independent of the pricing of other overcurrent protection devices (also related to the "distinct prices" factor). He stated that information that indicated that PPTCs gained share in terms of overall sales of overcurrent protection devices was not relevant to analysis of price independence. Third, he stated that documents from Raychem that evaluated different pricing strategies being considered indicated that Raychem's PPTC pricing was unconstrained by other technologies. Finally, he concluded that varying

---

[23] Clearly, innovative markets that might be considered "imperfect" using mainstream analysis may be much closer to "perfect" in the sense that they manifest the introduction of competitive new products with superior price-performance characteristics.

margins for sales to different types of customers was indicative of price discrimination by Raychem.[24] In his view, Raychem must have market power.[25] Thus, PPTCs must exist in a separate relevant market.

Price Elasticity

Bourns' economic expert also reviewed "findings" on the own-price elasticity of demand for PPTCs that were developed by Raychem's marketing employees. In fact, none of the information developed by Raychem qualified as an "elasticity" calculation, as economists understand the term. Rather, these calculations simply tracked changes in prices and quantities over time.

As noted earlier, Bourns' economic expert performed a simultaneous analysis of market definition and market power (a methodology that he readily acknowledged). His conclusion was that there were seven relevant antitrust "markets," each defined according to the broad application categories used for marketing analysis by Raychem. He further concluded that each of these relevant "markets" was a PPTC-only market because, for each purchaser of PPTCs, that device provided the best combination of technical features and price; otherwise, as he noted, purchasers would have chosen another device. Not surprisingly, he found that Raychem, as virtually the only maker of PPTCs until very recently, had monopoly power in each of these "markets." He asserted, without any supporting analysis, that technically feasible alternatives existed, but they were not close enough substitutes to constrain Raychem's PPTC pricing. Thus, all alternative products employing other overcurrent protection technologies existed in separate relevant "markets." Further, he asserted that anyone who purchased another type of overcurrent protection device but then switched to a PPTC was not a participant in the relevant market until that person or firm switched to a PPTC. For opposite switches, which he asserted were rare, buyers participated in the PPTC "markets" prior to the switch but left these "markets" after the switch.

In reaching this conclusion, Bourns' economic expert ignored ample empirical evidence of competitive behavior in the overcurrent

---

[24] In doing so, he rejected, without any apparent analysis, the hypothesis that varying margins, by customer, could be the result of other factors. These factors could include different product mixes, different levels of after-sale services provided, and many other factors, even though he admitted that such differences did exist and would affect margins observed for sales to individual customers.

[25] He rejected the view that price discrimination could occur in a competitive market. Recent economic analysis, of course, contradicts his view. See, e.g., Borenstein (1985).

protection industry and failed to grasp the character of competition in high-technology industries. For example, he ignored much (admittedly anecdotal) evidence of switches from PPTCs to other technologies by customers, including a recent switch by the single largest consumer of PPTC devices.[26] Further, he ignored evidence of technological competition such as form factor imitation (practiced by both Raychem and makers of competing devices), dynamic fluctuations in market share (particularly over the medium term, two to five years), and threats from entirely new technologies that had been developed and introduced into the marketplace. Furthermore, he even ignored several prominent examples where PPTCs and competing overcurrent protection devices were used interchangeably in the same product.

This case points to a fundamental flaw in the use of traditional market definition and market power assessment indicia – such as the *Brown Shoe* factors – when they are applied to high-technology industries and any market with highly differentiated products. Most important, the traditional indicia fail to capture the full scope of competition in high-technology markets. Market shares often shift markedly over time frames that, unfortunately, fall outside of the entry analysis specified in the *Horizontal Merger Guidelines*. For example, external port applications for personal computers (e.g., printer ports, mouse ports, and the new Universal Serial Bus or USB ports) have been an evolving and dynamic battleground for overcurrent protection device makers. In the early 1990s, fuses predominated. As computer makers began to appreciate the value of resettability for reducing warranty claims, there was a shift to resettable technologies by many computer makers, especially to PPTCs, which held the predominate share by 1995. Even before this shift in sales, however, the threat from silicon-based solutions began to affect the market. With the development of new USB standards in 1997, there was a widespread shift to Smart Power. Today, Smart Power and PPTCs have approximately equal shares. Entry analysis under the guidelines approach, which focuses on one- to two-year time horizons, artificially narrows the analysis of competition in this and similar markets and masks the dynamic nature of competition and the constraints on the exercise of market power.

In fact, use of traditional indicia, such as the *Brown Shoe* factors, will inevitably lead to the wrong conclusions about market definition in high-technology-relevant markets. Inherently, such indicia favor a piecemeal, narrow approach that obscures the nature of competition and leads to

---

[26] However, the anecdotal evidence consisted of a large number (i.e., literally dozens) of examples of actual or threatened switches by customers that represented a substantial fraction of Raychem's PPTC business.

findings of narrow, separate, and isolated markets. The effect is much like that of putting blinders on a horse. The true nature of the landscape is lost because vision is restricted.

In high-technology markets, products are often physically distinct. Entry with duplicate products is often difficult (because of trade secrets or intellectual property protections) or may even be competitively unwise (because product differentiation can be a source of competitive advantage under some circumstances). Competition is generally based on performance (thereby leading to "distinct prices" for each product) and vendors often utilize specialized vendors (who must have special knowledge to sell them and develop specialized, complementary assets to sell and service them). Narrow focus on such differences inevitably leads to the assertion of narrow markets.

In the Raychem case, given the overwhelming evidence on the fierce nature of intertechnology competition and the high level of innovative activity on the part of makers of the various technologies, both the judge and the jury came to the only reasonable conclusion. Except for primary lithium battery cells – where PPTCs, due to special characteristics, were an enabling technology and where no feasible alternatives had existed until recently – PPTCs were seen to compete in a broad market with other overcurrent protection devices. In fact, the judge labeled the Bourns' economic expert's market definitions a "tautology" based on his view that buyers entered and exited the market depending on which overcurrent protection technology they purchased. Unfortunately, the courts do not always recognize these fallacies. This is not surprising because some distinguished members of the economics profession have also failed to recognize the points advanced in this chapter.

The Legal System in Action, Example 2: The Vascular Solutions Market (Impra v. Gore)

In the early 1990s antitrust claims were filed against Gore, the leading maker of PTFE vascular grafts, that, inter alia, alleged that Gore had monopolized and attempted to monopolize the market (and submarkets) for PTFE vascular grafts. The claims were filed by Impra, one of Gore's competitors, and were wide-ranging.[27] Thus, they concerned allegations of restraint of trade violations relating to PTFE resins – an essential input for the manufacture of PTFE vascular grafts – as well as other monopolization claims and disparagement claims relating to Impra's vascular graft products. As implied by the allegations, Impra defined the relevant antitrust market quite narrowly, confining it to PTFE vascular

---

[27] As is common, these claims (as well as the antitrust claims raised by Bourns in *Bourns v. Raychem*) were advanced as counterclaims to an intellectual property suit.

grafts. It also defined submarkets within this market based on the size (i.e., diameter) of these grafts.

However, there is strong evidence that vascular solutions, a much larger marketplace, were the relevant antitrust market definition in this instance. Vascular grafts and treatments are part of an innovative industry that provides numerous overlapping (in terms of technical applicability) solutions to people with diseased blood vessels. While not every treatment is appropriate in each individual case, advances in nongraft treatments have been providing and will continue to provide competing alternatives to replacing segments of diseased blood vessels. This is particularly applicable in terms of a long-run perspective, because the need for grafts should decline as alternative treatments extend the "useful life" of tissue that might otherwise have to be replaced. In fact, several medical studies have noted the substitution effect of alternative (e.g., drug-based or other invasive procedures) treatments: "a multitude of developments in laser and mechanical atherectomy devices are . . . opening up even more alternative technologies to compete with bypass vascular grafting. . . . The other major threat to the proliferation of vascular bypass surgery could conceivably emanate from a variety of pharmaceutical agents used to decrease both the incidence and severity of coronary and peripheral arterial disease."[28]

Because these treatments are so differentiated from vascular graft technologies and methods of service delivery, traditional relevant market definition methods are unlikely to define markets correctly. There is no question of the competitive threat that these different treatments pose for vascular grafts. As noted, price sensitivity is low for different graft materials; price sensitivity across the multitude of available treatment methods would be even lower. However, there is a very powerful competitive dynamic that works through performance criteria, even more powerful than in most industries, because the consequential benefits and detriments of performance are perceived as so substantial. This performance-based competition provides the basis for broadening the market definition beyond grafts to include at least some other types of treatment.

Further, given the prevalence of arterial diseases, there are considerable research and development efforts on a wide range of fronts by a large number of companies to develop treatments for this problem.

As with overcurrent protection devices, there is no source of information readily available that provides data on the cost and number of treatments purchased. There is considerable information on treatment

---

[28] Source: The Wilkerson Group, Inc., CV/MIS Profile #10-Vascular Grafts, July 1987, pp. 37–39.

methods used and even some data that may be used to derive the gross number of treated individuals, perhaps by broad category of treatment through various medical databases. But there is considerable product differentiation and, indeed, price discrimination by providers of treatment.[29] Furthermore, the technique or technology used to cure and/or alleviate diseased arteries, of course, represents only a portion of the overall medical services provided to individuals that suffer from this condition. These factors render quantitative analysis virtually impossible. Thus, because elasticities and cross-elasticities of demand cannot be estimated, as with overcurrent protection devices, anecdotal and incomplete information must be used. Most important, the key to proper market definition is an appreciation of the nature and type of competition that takes place in this industry.

Again, however, the plaintiff attempted to utilize a static, narrow framework, centered on a mechanistic application of traditional market analysis. The plaintiff's expert focused on the physical differences among the different vascular graft materials and the fact that the decision makers who chose the graft materials in any circumstance (i.e., mainly surgeons) were very insensitive to and often unaware of price. They simply chose the graft material that they believed would perform best. The fact that other, nongraft treatments might compete against grafts was not recognized by the plaintiff. Thus, the plaintiff concluded that makers of PTFE grafts could profitably impose a SSNIP, thereby indicating that PTFE grafts existed in a separate market.

However, the vascular solutions or treatment business cannot be appropriately analyzed using conventional tools. Orthodoxy is clearly at odds with reality when nearly all participants freely acknowledged that price was unimportant, yet fierce competition was readily apparent and widely recognized.

In fact, the basis for competition in this industry, as in most high-technology industries undergoing rapid innovation, is performance. Suppliers consistently strive to improve the performance characteristics of their products – making them safer, stronger, smaller or larger, less apt to cause clots, and better able to facilitate full recovery. These dimensions of competition are no less tangible and important than price. In fact, to decision makers and recipients alike, they are far more salient indicators of desirability. Ignoring them, in a single-minded and narrow focus on pricing, can be compared with assessing competition in the automobile industry based on the colors of the cars offered when there are so many other, more obvious, dimensions on which competition takes place.

---

[29] Such price discrimination is, of course, broadly practiced in the delivery of medical care (i.e., it exists independently of the delivery of treatments for vascular diseases).

The Legal System in Action, Example 3: The Medical Imaging Market (GE's Attempted Acquisition of the Thorn EMI CT Scanner Business)

As with overcurrent protection and vascular solutions, medical imaging devices are highly differentiated on various dimensions. Although there has been no recent litigation testing ideas concerning market boundaries, the attempted acquisition of Thorn EMI's CT scanner business by General Electric in 1980 brought the market definition question to the fore. The resolution of that case manifested the problems that persist in trying to identify markets in high-technology industries. GE was ultimately frustrated in its efforts to acquire Thorn EMI's U.S. scanner business because the Department of Justice was concerned that such an acquisition would increase GE's U.S. share of the CT scanner business to levels that would raise competitive concerns in that narrow "market."

Subsequent developments have demonstrated that such concerns were misplaced. As Table 4.2 shows, sales of CT scanners were already generally declining in 1980. Although sales increased again and reached a global peak in 1983, they never again attained those levels. The key to these sales trends was competition from other medical imaging technologies.

Indeed, the intertechnology competition in the medical imaging business is the key to understanding the competitive pressures and competitive strategies more broadly in this market. For example, as Searle's Nuclear Chicago unit struggled to maintain its leadership in sales of nuclear imaging devices in the early 1970s, it faced competition from two fronts: introduction by entrant manufacturers of nuclear imaging devices with improved cameras, and newly introduced X-ray computer tomography devices (CT scanners). CT scanners were first introduced in 1973 and were first widely used in neurological imaging, the primary application for nuclear imaging devices in the early 1970s as well. CT scanners, although they were four to five times as expensive as nuclear imaging devices at that time, produced much clearer images. Fierce competition ensued between makers of both types of devices. Importantly, although CT scanners were outselling nuclear imaging devices within three years (i.e., by 1975), CT scanners only partially supplanted them as diagnostic tools.

CT scanners were followed by MRI equipment. Introduced commercially in 1980, MRI devices produced even clearer images and with less invasiveness (i.e., no ionizing radiation). Thus, though more expensive than CT scanners, MRI devices posed a formidable sales threat and, in turn, partially supplanted CT technology in the marketplace. Despite this technological success, however, the first three firms to introduce MRI technology had either exited the industry or were facing financial trouble by the late 1980s. Later entrants, which had introduced technically superior products and had provided better customer support, gained the major share of sales and enjoyed commercial success.

A review of the development of each of the new medical imaging technologies introduced in the past few decades actually manifests strikingly similar patterns. Each of the technologies has exhibited extremely high HHIs during the early period of commercial development. Initially, there was only one (or at most just a few) participant(s). In a very short period of time, however, there had been substantial entry and very dynamic competition, driving down HHIs over periods of five to ten years (see Tables 4.3 and 4.4). In virtually all cases, the early pioneers in the industry did not even survive as leaders in the business through the first decade after market introduction.

Within each technology, the HHIs, when viewed statically, might lead one to conclude that market power existed, but dynamic considerations would completely undermine such a conclusion. Even ignoring the impact of other technologies on competition, market leadership in any specific technology during these early years conferred no real market power. Early "monopolists" were generally and with alacrity displaced by competitors producing improved products employing the same basic technology or, even more significant, producing differentiated but highly efficacious products employing a totally different technology.

In addition, the tenuous character of technology leadership was often quite apparent contemporaneously with these market developments. This strongly suggests that static structuralist frameworks and techniques for identifying market boundaries, assessing market power, and characterizing the competitive process are inappropriate and misleading in the context of industries undergoing rapid technological change. It would be far more accurate and useful in the medical diagnostic imaging industry, for example, to look at the combined impact of all relevant technologies when evaluating competition and market power. Among these technologies, performance competition was particularly fierce.

It is also significant that the competition that developed did not develop in a manner that may be familiar to those who study the long-term history of many industries that are now considered "mature." The technological competition in the medical imaging industry did not, as in railroad transportation or steel manufacturing, result in the complete replacement of older technologies by newer technologies (e.g., the replacement of the steam engine by the diesel electric engine). Competition in the medical imaging industry followed a path that is quite common in high-technology industries (such as overcurrent protection)

Christopher Pleatsikas and David Teece

Table 4.3. Number of Participants in Diagnostic Imaging Modalities in the United States

Year	X-ray	Nuclear Imaging	Diagnostic Ultrasound	CT Scan	Magnetic Resonance	Digital Radiography	All Modalities
1954	13	2	—	—	—	—	15
1955	13	3	—	—	—	—	16
1956	14	3	—	—	—	—	17
1957	13	3	1	—	—	—	17
1958	14	5	1	—	—	—	20
1959	13	3	3	—	—	—	18
1960	14	3	2	—	—	—	18
1961	13	3	2	—	—	—	17
1962	14	4	4	—	—	—	21
1963	14	4	10	—	—	—	27
1964	17	4	10	—	—	—	30
1965	21	3	10	—	—	—	32
1966	22	4	11	—	—	—	35
1967	25	4	14	—	—	—	40
1968	24	7	18	—	—	—	46
1969	24	7	16	—	—	—	44
1970	23	11	25	—	—	—	51
1971	30	15	27	—	—	—	63
1972	28	18	31	—	—	—	67
1973	31	22	37	1	—	—	78
1974	30	25	43	2	—	—	86
1975	28	29	48	8	—	—	91
1976	30	31	54	8	—	—	96
1977	32	29	57	12	—	—	99
1978	32	27	56	15	—	—	94
1979	31	25	63	13	—	—	96
1980	29	26	73	12	1	—	106
1981	30	26	68	13	3	3	103
1982	31	23	68	12	6	17	108
1983	32	24	72	12	9	23	111
1984	30	24	68	16	12	21	111
1985	38	25	71	15	13	20	124
1986	39	25	76	14	18	17	134
1987	40	25	71	12	16	18	129

Source: Mitchell (1988).

– older technologies have been spurred to more vigorous technological development by new technologies that have entered the marketplace. In this manner, the older technologies have been "renewed" and continue to enjoy market success. Such responses clearly indicate that different technologies compete, even though a mechanical application of the SSNIP test or the *Brown Shoe* factors are likely to indicate otherwise. In

Table 4.4. Implied Hirschmann-Herfindahl Indices (HHI), 1961–1987

Year	X-ray	Nuclear Imaging	Diagnostic Ultrasound	CT Scan	Magnetic Resonance	Digital Radiography	All Modalities
1961	1,469	5,048	5,000	—	—	—	1,464
1962	1,467	4,718	4,950	—	—	—	1,461
1963	1,548	4,859	2,904	—	—	—	1,533
1964	1,529	4,719	3,004	—	—	—	1,494
1965	1,326	4,472	2,293	—	—	—	1,281
1966	1,239	4,582	2,143	—	—	—	1,173
1967	1,158	4,638	2,152	—	—	—	1,102
1968	1,158	4,715	2,292	—	—	—	1,060
1969	1,268	4,019	2,363	—	—	—	1,122
1970	1,273	3,089	1,944	—	—	—	1,089
1971	1,284	3,054	1,353	—	—	—	1,060
1972	1,631	3,894	1,836	—	—	—	1,297
1973	1,578	2,353	2,293	10,000	—	—	1,253
1974	1,507	2,130	1,190	9,608	—	—	1,133
1975	1,527	1,807	1,141	5,335	—	—	1,005
1976	1,556	1,733	1,073	3,570	—	—	928
1977	1,508	1,648	1,117	2,468	—	—	961
1978	1,675	1,438	1,072	2,268	—	—	1,033
1979	1,813	1,354	830	2,428	—	—	1,122
1980	1,842	1,319	822	3,620	10,000	—	1,361
1981	1,965	1,424	860	3,802	5,000	3,464	1,418
1982	1,965	1,578	945	2,992	3,082	1,404	1,519
1983	1,957	1,450	942	2,385	2,794	1,511	1,408
1984	1,948	1,317	915	1,848	2,024	1,220	1,240
1985	1,949	1,426	772	1,826	2,489	1,491	1,341
1986	1,949	1,285	743	2,212	1,843	2,043	1,328
1987	2,414	1,794	1,475	2,576	2,374	2,222	1,637

addition, increasing specialization has occurred as competing technologies strive to serve niches with products optimized to perform certain tasks. For both reasons, the importance of price in competition has declined as performance competition assumes greater importance.

Thus, being more realistic about competition and market share in the medical diagnostic imaging industry, one would develop a combined HHI that embraced all six technologies. The resulting measure of concentration (Table 4.4), in contrast to the HHIs within each technology, is actually quite low throughout the period. This lower measure of market power more accurately characterizes the competitive dynamic in this industry.

In attempting to evaluate the level and nature of competition in the industry, however, a very pertinent question concerns the type of analytical framework that would best capture the reality that has occurred (and continues to occur). For example, the *Horizontal Merger Guidelines* framework, with its emphasis on small, but significant, price changes as the basis for market definition, seems particularly inappropriate in this context.[30] The medical diagnostic imaging industry has, for decades, experienced numerous successful challenges to existing technology by more expensive technologies that possess improved performance. Furthermore, and as important, these new technologies, although successful in their own right, have not eliminated incumbent technologies but have spurred developers of incumbent technologies to improve their own products. Each may find a distinctive niche, but it is silly to characterize such niches as relevant markets.

For example, prices of CT instruments, when they were new to the market, were several orders of magnitude greater than those of nuclear imaging or conventional X-ray devices. However, substitution to CT scanners occurred anyway, driven by the increased performance they offered. In fact, the competitive challenge delivered by the new technology as compared with that of the old technology had little to do with price (and certainly not price in isolation from other performance characteristics). If the price of competitive technologies had been lowered by 5 percent (or the price of CT scanners had been increased by 5 percent) in 1973, there would almost certainly have been little measurable impact on the sale of CT scanners. However, as Hartman et al. (1993: 334) noted:

This insensitivity of competition to price does not imply that the two modalities . . . [did not compete]. Indeed, competition was vigorous, but was simply not price dependent. Rather it was performance dependent. . . . To ask what incremental competition to CT instrumentation a hypothetical monopolist would confront from an assumed 5% price increase thus frames the market definition question incorrectly and produces the wrong answer.

In addition to ignoring the importance of performance competition in a high-technology context, the analytical framework developed within the *Horizontal Merger Guidelines* also implicitly undervalues the importance of potential competition, from vendors of both improvements in existing technologies and entirely new technologies. In particular, the short time horizon – one year for uncommitted entrants and two years for committed entrants – is biased against the logic of competition in high-technology industries. For example, in the medical diagnostic

---

[30] Even raising the "small but significant" threshold to 20% (which we understand the agencies do from time to time) may not cure the problem in part because competing technologies may not yet be "observable" in the marketplace.

imaging industry, the lead time from research and development to commercial success was much longer than one or two years, but vendors of existing technologies have had to respond to potential threats as a matter of course. Even after introduction of new technologies, the full extent of the threat to incumbent technologies was not manifest within a short time period but, nevertheless, required vigorous competitive responses (i.e., both short-run and long-run strategic action) from manufacturers of existing technologies. This is consistent with the observation that, in high-technology industries it is potential and emerging competition that is often most threatening. Yet this aspect of the competitive process is usually difficult or impossible to incorporate into static assessment methods.

NEW INDICIA FOR ANTITRUST ANALYSIS OF HIGH-TECHNOLOGY MARKETS

As noted in Teece and Coleman (1998: 826–28), defining markets from a static perspective when innovation is rapid will inevitably lead to the identification of markets that are too narrow. This will, in turn, tend to overstate market power in many circumstances. Thus, the emphasis in the *Horizontal Merger Guidelines* on short-term entry – one to two years – and price rather than performance competition will reinforce the bias toward findings of monopoly power in high-technology markets. Put differently, a mechanical application of the guidelines and *Brown Shoe* will find high-technology industries riddled with monopolists, despite the obvious truth that high-technology markets almost always present competitive circumstances that are far more vigorous than in more mature markets. Because monopolies will be "found" when they do not exist, business practices will be scrutinized unnecessarily. In high-technology markets, there is a substantial chance that traditional antitrust analysis and tools will result in findings of monopoly power where none exist and in findings that anticompetitive behavior exists when such behavior is likely to be procompetitive.

What is needed is a set of tools and analytical techniques that would eliminate or, more likely, reduce the chance for such errors, to ensure that the incentives for innovation are not harmed. Others, such as Yao and deSanti (1993) and Ordover and Baumol (1988), have recognized some of the particular problems in assessing market definition and market power in high-technology industries but have proposed no real alternative analysis.

Hartman et al. (1993: 336–43) have suggested a potential candidate technique for defining high-technology markets that may be appropriate. This was advanced again in Teece and Coleman (1998: 855–56). A hedonic framework is suggested to analyze the interaction of price and performance, and a tentative 25 percent threshold for performance parameters and four-year entry horizon for analysis within the general framework set forth in the *Horizontal Merger Guidelines*. Such a threshold would, in fact, generally be quite conservative, because multidimensional performance attributes are common in these markets. In such circumstances, a 25 percent change in one performance parameter would be equivalent to a small change in overall performance, particularly if interaction terms were important (i.e., customers were interested not only in single, stand-alone attributes but the interaction of those attributes on performance).

We recognize that the earlier proposal is not the only way to proceed. Here we suggest several alternative approaches. None of these, by itself, may be sufficient for defining markets and/or assessing market power, but in combination they should be more effective than the static-based analysis embodied in the *Horizontal Merger Guidelines*. In developing these measures we have tried to be pragmatic to assist the courts, as well as competition policy authorities.

Defining High-Technology Markets

First, as a very pragmatic and qualitative measure, a wide-angle lens is needed to assess competition. This is because, in high-technology industries, there are often market niches where one differentiated product may gain an advantage – in some cases a substantial advantage – over the alternative solutions available to users. If one focuses on these niches, one is led to the conclusion that a myriad of very narrow markets occupied by pygmy monopolists exists. But common sense tells us that a myriad of such narrow niches cannot be relevant antitrust markets. For example, analysts necessarily ignore the more important fact that price discrimination in these narrow niches may not be possible. Arbitrage from other buyers may occur. It is also possible that buyers possess far better information than sellers on alternatives, reducing opportunities for price discrimination even where they, theoretically, may exist.

Of particular importance in constructing a broad view of competitive activity is technology competition. If technology competition has "depth," with a number of firms' products and/or technologies advancing along a number of dimensions and applications, competition is likely to be very robust indeed. In fact, rapid innovation from a number of sources – even in dissimilar technologies (as long as they have similar applications) – should be recognized as a hallmark of broad competitive activity and should shift the burden to those who argue for narrow markets. In such circumstances, price differences are sustainable because performance differences may be sustained. Further, and more important, participants in such a market are forced to improve their products continuously to maintain share.

In fact, an inquiry into the dimensions of competition would almost certainly be useful. Competition driven by new products and features is especially important. It may be useful to identify customer views about the extent of competition. In addition, such research may help to quantify the relative importance of various performance parameters, which may assist in developing a performance-based index akin to the one suggested in Hartman et al. (1993). Finally, by quantifying customer needs and customer response to product innovation by various suppliers, the information gained may help to determine whether the innovative and other "competitive" activity that has occurred (or is being alleged) constrains behavior sufficiently to support a particular market definition. In the example of overcurrent protection devices, because behavior by suppliers is directed mainly toward performance parameters that are very important to customers (i.e., that the customers value highly), then the finding of broad markets can likely be sustained.

Another indicator of a broad competitive market in high-technology markets would be substantial shifts in share over time – certainly at least four to five years. Where this has occurred and, more important, is (or has been) expected to occur, this should be viewed as definitive evidence of competitive forces and a broad market. In such circumstances, monotonic gains by one product or technology are not necessarily an indication that such a product or technology is insulated from competitive forces. If this gain is sustained only by out-innovating others in the market, competition may be broad and powerful.

For example, in 1992 Raychem viewed the threat from Smart Power as potentially powerful and likely to emerge in the next three to four years (sooner in some cases). The fact that it had not yet emerged as powerfully as expected by 1997 should not be taken as an indication that potential competition from that source had not constrained Raychem's behavior, particularly given the advances in semiconductor technology that had occurred over the interim. It may only have been Raychem's ability to press on and succeed in its innovative activity for PPTCs that kept the threat of Smart Power at bay. Such market conditions do not in any way indicate narrow markets or unconstrained monopolies.

Thus, indicia for defining high-technology markets must focus on competitive conditions and competitive activity. There must be an investigation of behavior and actions and over a longer time horizon than the standard one to two years. Standard indicia, and particularly the hypothetical monopolist test, using the SSNIP (at or near a 5–10 percent level) will surely define markets too narrowly. If it is difficult to determine an appropriate SSNIP (whether the "P" is interpreted as "price" or "performance") so that markets can be confidently defined, then one can endeavor to assess whether monopoly power exists by assessing:

- Innovative activity (e.g., research and development expenditures and trends, product innovations and introductions, and performance enhancements).
- Competitive activity (e.g., shifts in share, the impact of potential entry, shifts in customer purchases).
- Pricing responses and flexibility.

Where innovative activity is high, one should presume that monopoly power does not exist. If a firm can "price without regard to competition" (a definition of monopoly advanced by the Supreme Court), then why would it spend a large proportion of its revenues on R&D? High R&D spending relative to sales is generally an indication that participants view product performance as the ultimate arbiter of competitive strength. Furthermore, potential competition can also generally be assessed in such terms, as potential entrants attempt to match or even leapfrog existing technology to secure a foothold in the market. Unfortunately, particularly for potential entrants or even current participants with diversified activities, assessing the magnitude and specific impact of R&D activities is usually problematic. However, this does not excuse the analyst from investigating such issues and attempting an evaluation of their impact on market definition – whether quantitative or, more likely, qualitative.

Evaluating Market Power

Of course, once the market is properly defined, there may be no need to proceed further to assessing market power. Where markets are broad, shares may be so small that there is little or no likelihood that anti-competitive behavior is possible. Where some question remains, however, there may be scope for developing or specifying new indicia for such purposes.

If high profit margins are being advanced as indicia of monopoly power, the burden should fall upon the complainant to establish the extent and source of any rents being earned. As noted in Teece and Coleman (1998: 818–22), the source of profits can generally be subdivided into three types – monopoly (Porterian), scarcity (Ricardian), and entrepreneurial (Schumpeterian). They are not always easy to distinguish. In high-technology contexts, Ricardian and Schumpeterian rents will be common. The long-term economic consequences of discouraging the creation of scarcity and entrepreneurial rents could well be severe. Extreme care should therefore be used in making decisions about the existence of monopoly power.

Clearly, the use of high margins as an indicator either of market definition or market power is inappropriate in high-technology contexts. Most obviously, many (some would say most) innovative efforts fail to result in a commercially successful product, even by firms that are well known as successful innovators. Thus, successful products, in successful firms, require high returns to "pay back" the cost of unsuccessful R&D efforts. Absent the chance to earn high returns on research and development and innovative activities, firms would normally avoid such activities, given the high risk they entail. Certainly, a competition policy that simply (and rigidly) classified high returns as monopoly returns, with concordant antitrust liability, would only increase risk, thereby increasing further the returns that investors require.

Even more irrelevant to assessing monopoly power (or to defining markets) are indicators like gross margins. Gross margins do not include the research and development expenditures, nor do they even include incremental selling costs. In competitive high-technology markets, substantial, ongoing R&D costs may be mandatory to increase or even to maintain share, as competitors race to develop improved products or even to initiate the next paradigm shift. High incremental selling costs may also be incurred for innovative products as consumers may require educational services, value-added services, or other specialized assistance to employ the product.

If high margins on innovative products are poor indicators of market power, what would be of use? It is possible that an analysis of a firm's R&D portfolio may be of assistance in evaluating whether monopoly returns are being earned. Thus, even if high rates are being earned on one or even a few such projects, a competitive rate of return on the portfolio is indicative – although not definitive – that monopoly returns are not present.

Finally, some analysis of the likely duration of the monopoly or monopoly power must be undertaken. Where power is relatively transient (or thought likely to be), it is generally (perhaps always) innocuous. In such cases intervention action may even be counterproductive, since it might disrupt the smooth functioning of the existing market.

Only if both market analysis and the analyses of rents and R&D portfolio returns indicate monopoly power should the inquiry pass to the next stage of the inquiry – specification and evaluation of alleged anticompetitive behavior.

Further, assessing the impact of R&D on market structure and behavior is as important to assessing market power as it is on market definition. The information that capable rivals are developing competitive (or, often, superior – in performance terms) products can be a powerful influence on the behavior of current market participants even if the R&D

may not result in viable products within the one- to two-year framework identified in the *Horizontal Merger Guidelines*. Thus, a qualitative and, if possible, quantitative analysis of the likely impact of R&D activity on market power is critical for understanding the competitive dynamic in high-technology or rapidly innovating industries and contexts.

CONCLUSIONS

No hard and fast indicia lend themselves to precise definitions of markets in high-technology contexts. However, the traditional indicia will typically define markets too narrowly and should not be used, at least not mechanically.

In their place, a qualitative analysis is likely to be less flawed. One should endeavor to address and analyze competitive circumstances rather broadly. Particularly if innovation competition across producers and/or technologies can be established on a wide front (i.e., beyond just isolated anecdotes), the burden should shift to the narrow market advocates to establish their case.

Survey research may be required and may be desirable to establish the most important dimensions of competitive efforts and the attitudes of customers. Such a survey could in fact establish a performance-based SSNIP that could be used to define markets.

For assessing market power in such industries, the market definition exercise may provide obvious answers. If market power is provisionally identified, an analysis of rents would be useful to identify whether market power is in fact potentially troublesome or simply the outcome of innovation and/or natural scarcity.

We are disturbed by the low degree of attention to these issues in the literature. The agencies and the courts appear extremely reluctant to tackle the issues we have identified. Academic scholars have been quite slow to assist, perhaps because the issues seem so daunting and the ramifications too hostile to received wisdom. Whatever the reason, the imperative exists. Mainstream scholars will have much to answer for if they do not engage these issues vigorously. In our view, serious treatment of these issues is long overdue.

REFERENCES

Audretsch, David B. 1995. *Innovation and Industry Evolution*. Cambridge, MA: MIT Press.

Borenstein, Severin. 1985. Price Discrimination in Free Entry Markets. *Rand Journal of Economics* 16: 380–97.

Hartman, Raymond, David Teece, Will Mitchell, and Thomas Jorde. 1993. Assessing Market Power in Regimes of Rapid Technological Change. *Industrial and Corporate Change* 2: 317–50.

Henderson, Rebecca M., and Kim B. Clark. 1990. Architectural Innovation: The Reconfiguration of Existing Product Technologies and the Failure of Established Firms. *Administrative Science Quarterly* 35: 9–30.

Mansfield, Edwin. 1977. *The Production and Application of New Industrial Technology*. New York: Norton.

Mitchell, W. 1998. Dynamic Commercialization: Innovation in the Medical Diagnostic Imaging Industry. Ph.D. dissertation, Haas School of Business, University of California, Berkeley.

Ordover, Janusz, and William Baumol. 1988. Antitrust Policy and High-Technology Industries. *Oxford Review of Economic Policy* 4: 13–34.

Scherer, F. M. 1985. *Industrial Market Structure and Economic Performance*. Chicago: Rand McNally.

Simons, Joseph, and Michael Williams. 1993. The Renaissance of Market Definition. *Antitrust Bulletin* 38: 799–857.

Teece, David, and Mary Coleman. 1998. The Meaning of Monopoly: Antitrust Analysis in High Technology Industries. *Antitrust Bulletin* 43: 801–57.

United States, Department of Justice and Federal Trade Commission. 1992, 1997. *Horizontal Merger Guidelines*. Washington, DC.

Utterback, James. 1994. *Mastering the Dynamics of Innovation*. Boston: Harvard Business School Press.

Yao, Dennis, and Susan deSanti. 1993. Innovation Issues under the 1992 Merger Guidelines. *Antitrust Law Journal* 38: 113–41.

5

Innovation and Monopoly Leveraging

Franklin M. Fisher

The concept of monopoly leveraging – the idea that a firm with monopoly in one market can use its power to gain monopoly power in another – is an old and persistent one. And why not? The picture of the ever-expanding empire of a "malefactor of great wealth" has at least the appeal of a well-told horror story. In the past few decades, however, economists and others have cast doubt on the realism of the tale, and the current state of thinking is that profitable monopoly leveraging is possible, but not so often as might be supposed without analysis.

In some industries, the presence of technical innovation lends a new dimension to the story. Innovations can provide the ability to leverage or can threaten a monopolist who does not leverage. Moreover, where leveraging involves innovation, the analyst and the antitrust authorities are presented with the problem of deciding whether the benefits to consumers of the innovation itself outweigh the anticompetitive effects of leveraging. Indeed, they may be presented with the problem that the leveraging monopolist seeks to disguise its actions as socially beneficial innovation precisely to evade antitrust sanctions.

In this chapter, I discuss (relatively informally) three antitrust cases in which I have been involved and which, in one way or another, illustrate these issues. These are: the computer reservations systems (CRS) cases, the *IBM* antitrust case of the 1970s, and the recent *Microsoft* case.[1]

---

[1] *Continental Airlines, Inc. and Texas Int'l Airlines, Inc. v. American Airlines, Inc., and United Airlines, Inc.*, No. CV 0696 ER (Mex) (C.D. Cal), and *USAir, Inc. et al. v. American Airlines, Inc. and United Airlines, Inc.*, No. CV 84-8918 ER (Mex) (C.D. Cal) and associated cases; *United States v. Int'l Business Machines Corp.*, Docket number 69 Civ. DNE (S.D.N.Y.); *United States v. Microsoft Corporation*, Civil Action No. 98-1232 TPJ (D.D.C.). I was the principal economics witness for Continental Airlines in one of the CRS cases, for IBM, and for the Department of Justice in the *Microsoft* case. Not all issues are covered in the present chapter. The opinions here expressed are my own and should not be taken necessarily to represent the views of the attorneys with whom I have worked

The first of these shows how innovation can aid monopoly leveraging; the second, how innovation can lead to socially beneficial actions that competitors dislike; and the third, how leveraging, packaged as innovation, can be used to forestall the possibility that innovation will destroy an existing monopoly.

I begin, however, with a discussion of the theoretical issues involved in monopoly leveraging.

THEORY

Although it is not the only example (and not the only one involved in the three cases discussed in this chapter), it will aid the exposition if I focus on tying as the means of monopoly leveraging.

For later purposes, it will be convenient to distinguish *tying* and *bundling*. Tying occurs when a seller of product A requires all purchasers of A also to purchase product B from it. Sometimes this means that purchasers are required also to purchase B from the same seller if they purchase A (e.g., block booking in movie exhibition); sometimes it means that purchasers of A, *if they wish to buy B*, must do so from the seller of A.

Bundling is different at least in form. In bundling, the seller of A automatically includes B as part of the sold package, but does so at no separately stated charge. This is just a different form of the first kind of tying, the one in which customers who buy A must also buy B. The difference is that the price of B is not separately stated but is bundled into the price of A. Here I use this form of tying or bundling as an example.[2]

To begin the analysis, suppose that the seller of A has a monopoly in that product. Suppose that it requires every purchaser of A who wishes to purchase B to do so from it. If such purchasers are a large enough segment of the buyers of B, will not this enable the A monopolist to become a monopolist of B?

---

or, especially, their clients. This is particularly true as regards the Antitrust Division of the United States Department of Justice.

    In previous publications, I have thanked those who contributed to my testimony in the computer reservations and *IBM* cases. For assistance in the *Microsoft* case, I am particularly indebted to David Boies, Wayne Dunham, Karma Giulianelli, Joen E. Greenwood, Diane Owen, Mark Popovsky, Daniel Rubinfeld, and Mary Beth Savio. As already indicated, they are relieved of responsibility for the views and also any errors in the present chapter.

[2] The question may arise whether there is anything to be said about the first form of tying – the requirement that B must be bought if A is – that is not covered here. The answer is affirmative. When products are not sold at a fixed price but rather at auction or through negotiated sales, there are circumstances in which block booking can increase seller profits by permitting the seller to take advantage of different valuations on the part of different buyers. This will not concern us further. An excellent discussion of the theory of these practices can be found in Whinston (1990).

The answer is affirmative if production of B requires some minimum scale, but the question is misleading. The real question is whether this is a profitable strategy for the producer of A and whether it might not achieve equal or greater profits in some other way.

To see what is involved here, suppose first that every purchaser of a unit of A also requires exactly one unit of B. Then the A monopolist is effectively selling a package of one unit of each and charging the combined price. (Note the similarity to bundling here.) Let the monopoly price for the bundle of A and B considered as a unit be denoted by M. Let the monopolist's price for A and B be denoted by P_A and P_B, respectively. Then the profit-maximizing action for the monopolist will be to set $P_A + P_B = M$. Now suppose that the monopolist were simply to set the price for A, P_A, and permit B to be purchased elsewhere. Suppose that the outside price of B is X. Then the monopolist can certainly set $P_A = M - X$, collecting the remainder of the monopoly price for the bundle after B is purchased.

But this is the equivalent of the monopolist farming out the production of B at a cost of X per unit. If X is less than the monopolist's per-unit cost of B, then the monopolist will make more profits by doing so than by producing B in-house. If, on the other hand, X is greater than the monopolist's own cost of B, then the monopolist need only set P_B a little below X, set $P_A + P_B = M$, as before, and not bother with the requirement that all purchasers of A also purchase B from it; they will do so anyway.

What is involved here can also be described (somewhat incompletely) by saying that the monopolist can exercise its power only once. It can set P_B a trifle below X and impose no tie, or it can charge a higher price for B and impose the tie. But customers who are just willing to pay M for the bundle will pay one dollar less for A for every dollar that the price of B is raised. In effect, if $P_B > X$, the customer's willingness to pay for A will be reduced by the requirement that B be purchased from the monopolist.

It is perhaps unsurprising that this analysis has been championed by members of the Chicago School, including Posner (1976) and Bork (1978), and used to argue that the idea that tying can (or, more properly, will) be used to leverage monopoly power from A into B is an illusion. But that is not the end of the story.

Before proceeding, however, I want to discuss a different issue. Particularly when two products, A and B, are used in fixed proportions, a monopolist of A who wishes to tie or bundle B together with it could instead accomplish the same end by charging a low or zero (or even negative) price for B together with a high price for A. Then why should the monopolist bother with tying or bundling? The answer, of course, is that if this leads to monopoly profits in B (or, as we shall see, to protection of the A monopoly), the price for B would be predatory and easily seen to be so. Hence tying or, especially, bundling may be a way of disguising a predatory price.

Returning to the question of whether leveraging through tying is profitable, it turns out that it can be so once we drop the assumption that A and B are always used in fixed proportions. Here there are two cases to consider, one that applies when either other firms or final consumers are the purchasers of A and B and one that applies only to the case in which A and B are used to produce some other output.

The first of these situations can be illustrated by considering not the *IBM* case of the 1970s but the much older 1930s case that IBM lost.[3] Those were the days of punch-card accounting machines, and the allegation was that IBM had tied punch cards to machines, requiring every user of an IBM machine to purchase its punch cards from IBM as well.[4] Similarly, Xerox used to require users of its machines to purchase paper and supplies from it. Why does not the above analysis apply and show that such a practice would be unprofitable? Indeed, because there can hardly be much profit in monopolizing punch cards or copying paper, why bother?

The answer has long been known to reside in a phenomenon known as "metering" (Bowman 1957). IBM and Xerox had to charge the same price to all customers. Had that not been the case, they could have increased their profits by charging higher prices to customers with a low elasticity of demand than to those with a high one. But customers who used the machines intensively were likely to be relatively price insensitive, so IBM and Xerox could profitably price discriminate by tying supplies to the machines and charging supracompetitive prices for the supplies. In this way, the intensive-use, low-price-sensitive customers would end up paying more than the low-use, high-price-sensitive ones.[5]

Two features of this should be noted. First, the fact that tying is profitable in such situations has little or nothing to do with monopoly leveraging. Tying is profitable because of its effects on profits in the monopolized market. Any effects on the market in the tied product (punch cards or copying supplies in the examples given) are incidental or at least secondary.

---

[3] *International Business Machines Corp. v. United States*, 298 U.S. 131 (1936).
[4] This was, in fact, a practice not limited to IBM. Remington-Rand also engaged in the same practice but settled the case against it.
[5] The use of tying to effect price discrimination extends beyond metering. See, e.g., Burstein (1960).

Second, even the IBM and Xerox examples involved a technological issue. In those cases, the companies involved could (and did) defend their actions by claiming that they needed to ensure that the tied products were of sufficient quality that the performance of the tying products (the machines) would not be downgraded. Claims of this sort are common and may sometimes be correct.

The second case of profitable tying occurs when A and B are used to make another product, C, possibly in addition to other uses. Suppose that the A monopolist were to attempt to capture monopoly profits by charging a high price without tying. If A and B are not used in fixed proportions in the manufacture of C, then makers of C will substitute B for A to the extent possible. If the A monopolist ties B to A, it can avoid this.

Indeed, even if A and B are used in fixed proportions in the manufacture of C, a similar phenomenon occurs if A has other uses. In that case, a high price for A will not lead to substitution of B for A in the manufacture of C but will lead to substitution away from A in other uses. This case is also one of variable proportions: A and B are not *always* used in fixed proportions. The case is also similar to that of metering: tying permits the A monopolist to charge a high price to the producers of C and a lower one to more price-sensitive customers for A.

In all the cases so far examined, monopoly leveraging has been incidental to maximizing profits in the original monopolized product. The next case need not have that property, nor does it depend on whether the products involved are used in fixed proportions.

Suppose that B is not produced competitively but is itself subject to market power. Then B will be sold at prices above marginal cost. The A monopolist will not view this as desirable, especially if B is used in fixed proportions with A. For, if A and B are complements, sales of A will be higher with a low price of B than with a high one. From the point of view of the A monopolist, the circumstance is equivalent to one in which it purchases B and then sells a combined A-B package. Clearly, the lower the price at which it can purchase B, the better off it is. In this case, the A monopolist can avoid paying monopoly rents to the makers of B if the A monopolist can take over the production of B itself. Further, if B has uses other than as a complement for A, then the A monopolist may be able to earn monopoly rents on B sales to others by taking over the market for B.

Of course, "taking over the market for B" can be profitable even if that market is originally competitive. If B has other uses than merely as a complement for A, then the A monopolist by leveraging its power into the market for B can create monopoly rents in that product where none previously existed. (Naturally, whether or not the original market for B is competitive, the A monopolist's ability to do this will depend in large part on how important sales for use with A are as part of the total demand for B.)

We have now come upon a second reason for monopoly leveraging in addition to the cases in which doing so increases profits in the original product. The monopolist of A may be able to organize the market for B so as to create monopoly rents where none previously existed.

There is still a third possibility, allied to the first but sufficiently important to deserve a separate statement. In order for the monopoly in A to continue, entry into the market for A must be difficult. Suppose that the independent production of B makes it easier for firms to enter the market for A. Then the A monopolist will have an interest in controlling the market for B that goes beyond its short-run profit-maximizing calculation. This can happen if the technology for making B is similar to but less complicated than that for making A, so that learning to make B is a good first step toward making A. But, as we shall see, it can also happen in other ways.

To sum up, there are three circumstances in which leveraging monopoly power (through tying or otherwise) from the monopolized market for A into the market for another product, B, can be a profitable strategy:

- Such leveraging can increase monopoly profits in the monopolized product. This can happen if not every customer always uses A and B in fixed proportions or if B is itself not competitively sold.
- Such leveraging can serve to "organize" the market for B, transferring monopoly rents or creating them where they did not previously exist.
- Such leveraging can protect the original monopoly in the market for A.

I now turn to particular cases that, as it happens, exemplify the last two cases more than they do the first and involve technological innovation.

COMPUTER RESERVATION SYSTEMS

Computer reservation systems (CRSs) were developed in the late 1970s from the internal reservation systems of airlines and grew rapidly in capability and importance.[6] They extended to travel agents the ability to interface with the computer systems of airlines. This facilitated not merely the providing of information but also the ability to make reser-

---

[6] For a more detailed history of computer reservation systems and a discussion of the policy issues that they raise, see Fisher and Neels (1999).

vations directly, issue boarding passes, deal with hotel and rental car bookings, and so forth. The travel agency business became seriously automated.

Unfortunately, that gain in efficiency did not come without costs to competition. American Airlines and United Airlines – which, not incidentally, had the best-developed internal CRS – refused to cooperate in a joint industry development and developed their own systems (called SABRE and APOLLO, respectively). Moreover, they quickly discovered and took advantage of a particular phenomenon.

When a client calls and requests a flight from Hither to Yon (two medium-sized American cities) at 9:00 A.M., say, there will typically be many options available. If traffic between Hither and Yon is not very heavy, there may be no direct flights leaving close to 9:00 A.M., but there may be a number of connecting flights involving different times and different connections. The CRS must use an algorithm to decide the order in which these options are presented to the travel agent. Indeed, because only about eight options fit on a screen, the algorithm must decide which flights will be presented on the first screen and which relegated to later ones. This involves weighing the inconvenience of connecting against the inconvenience of departing at a different time of day as well as other tradeoffs.

But the order in which flights are presented to the travel agent matters. Not surprisingly, the travel agent tends to begin at the top of the list and work down until the client accepts an option. The flight that appears in the first line is chosen much of the time; a flight on the first screen nearly always.

American and United took advantage of this phenomenon to favor their own flights. In American's case (United was subtler), the algorithm worked in terms of "penalty minutes." A flight leaving an hour later or earlier than the desired time received a penalty of sixty minutes on that account; the inconvenience of connecting was assigned a number of minutes, and so forth. Flights were then listed in ascending order of penalty minutes. It just so happened that all non-American flights were assigned an additional sixty penalty minutes assuring that American's own flights would generally appear first.

Indeed, the practice went beyond this. Other airlines were invited to become "cohosts" on American's CRS. This meant that for a large fee, the number of penalty minutes assigned to them would be smaller than for noncohosts (although never as small as for American Airlines itself). United behaved similarly. Further, airlines that particularly competed with American or United claimed to have experienced difficulties in the ease with which their flights or fares could be found.

While, in principle, travel agents could have worked around the "display bias" (as it was called), this did not happen widely enough in practice to offset the effects. This is not surprising. To work around the bias would have required the agent first to know the ways in which the bias was present and then to be willing to spend time offsetting it. While agents may have been willing to do this for particular customers, they quite naturally did not do so generally. If customers were satisfied with the choice they were getting, there was little incentive to spend time in improving those choices, even were that an easy task.

The situation did not go unnoticed forever. In 1984, the outgoing Civil Aeronautics Board (CAB) issued rules to prohibit the use of carrier identity in algorithms. American and United responded by greatly increasing their booking fee, the fee charged another carrier for a booking made through the CRS.[7] Antitrust litigation followed, with American and United winning one case (brought by USAir and a number of other carriers) and settling the other (brought by Continental and its associated family of airlines) greatly to the satisfaction of the plaintiffs. For my present purposes, more details are unnecessary.

In analyzing these events, the first question to ask was whether American and United had monopoly power. The answer is plainly yes. Although there was considerable competition in the marketing of CRSs to travel agents, monopoly power resided in the sale of booking services to airlines. Both United and American had contracts with a very large number of travel agents. As a result, an airline not participating in both of the two systems was at a severe disadvantage, a fact dramatically illustrated by Continental's disastrous experience when it temporarily withdrew from one of the *minor* CRSs.[8] Moreover, the presence of both United and American (as well as others) in this activity did not prevent each of them from having monopoly power. An airline had to be listed in both. It could not offset a high price for a SABRE listing by somehow being listed more in APOLLO.

Before the CAB promulgated its 1984 rules, American and United chose not to exercise their monopoly power by charging high prices in the monopolized market, a point to which I shall return. Rather they exercised it in the provision of biased displays. To see why this was profitable, consider the economics of airline operation.

---

[7] In fairness, I should add that American and United were not the only proprietors of such systems. But they were by far the largest.

[8] Continental did not even cease to be listed, but tickets on it could not be purchased through the CRS.

Given that a flight is to operate, the marginal cost of filling an empty seat is extremely low relative to the cost of flying the aircraft. Hence relatively small differences in load factors (the fraction of seats that are occupied) can make a large difference to an airline's bottom line. By using display bias, American and United successfully diverted passengers from other airlines to their own flights. This both raised the cost of their rivals and increased American and United's profits. Indeed, monopoly power is the sustained ability to charge significantly supranormal prices without losing so much business as to make such action impossible. Display bias gave American and United the ability to keep prices up without losing so many customers as they would otherwise. Hence it is no exaggeration to say that this part of the history of CRSs involved the leveraging of monopoly in computer reservation systems into air transportation. This is an example of the use of monopoly leveraging to "organize" a second market.

After the CRS rules, however, display bias became more difficult (although not altogether impossible).[9] American and United then began to exercise their monopoly power in the markets in which they had it, raising the fee for bookings. This had two effects. First, it produced more profits from bookings fees. Second, because other airlines had to purchase at a high price what American and United could obtain at cost, it raised rivals' costs, again permitting American and United to charge higher prices for air transportation than would otherwise have been possible, although the leveraging effect here was plainly much less than in the case of display bias.

There remains the question of why American and United did not raise their fees *before* the rules. Why did they not both profit from display bias and charge higher prices? I do not know the answer, but here are some possibilities.

First, display bias was hidden; high booking fees would not have been. With the airline industry still in the first years of deregulation, American and United may simply have thought it best not to attract the attention of the regulatory agency, or, indeed, of the antitrust authorities.

Second, high booking fees would have prompted other airlines to book customers directly. Although that could not have eliminated the profits from such fees, it might have reduced them to some extent. More important, keeping customers booking through their display-biased CRSs was doubtless much more profitable for American and United than is measured by the direct fees paid by other airlines. (Recall, in this connection, the fees paid by "cohosts" for a reduction in bias.)

---

[9] See, e.g., Fisher (1987); but cf. Fisher and Neels (1999: 475 n. 39).

Whatever the reason, however, the fact is clear that American and United did not charge the short-run monopoly profit-maximizing price until after their other purposes had been restricted by the rules. (A similar statement is true of Microsoft, which chose not to exercise its monopoly power simply in the short-run price of its operating system.)

The story of computer reservations systems is one of an innovation with undoubted large benefits used for anticompetitive purposes. Some of the anticompetitive acts involved a form of monopoly leveraging. The nature of the industry was such that no satisfactory nonregulatory remedy for the acts involved was ever found, but that is another story.

THE *IBM* CASE

The *IBM* case was perhaps the greatest antitrust fiasco of all time. Brought in January 1969 as the last act of the Johnson administration's Antitrust Division, it went to trial in 1975 and remained there until 1981. In early 1982, the case was dismissed by stipulation, both sides agreeing that it had been "without merit." It spawned a large number of private suits, a few of which were settled and all of which were won by IBM. I have had much to say about the reasons for the fiasco and, especially, about the bad economics of the Justice Department, and shall not linger over those subjects here except as they are relevant to the analysis of innovation and monopoly leveraging.[10] It is popularly supposed that the *IBM* and *Microsoft* cases have much in common, but that superficial view has no validity.

Among IBM's actions that were alleged to be anticompetitive were some of the bundling or tying variety. These fell into two main categories: the bundling of software or services with hardware, and the bundling of formerly separate hardware components together. While it is the latter that bears most directly on the *Microsoft* case, I discuss them both.

Bundling Software and Services with Hardware

Until 1968, IBM offered systems support and software to purchasers or lessees of its computer systems at no separately stated charge.[11] The government alleged that this was anticompetitive because it raised entry barriers into the computer systems market that IBM was said to have monopolized.[12] As discussed earlier, monopoly leveraging can make

[10] For a full discussion, see Fisher, McGowan, and Greenwood (1983).
[11] IBM tied services to hardware in a different area, requiring lessees of its computers to take maintenance from it. I do not discuss this here, save to observe that IBM *owned* the computers in question and hence had a direct interest in how they were maintained. For a full discussion, see Fisher et al. (1983: 215–18).
[12] The government never actually formulated a sensible definition of the market it thought IBM had monopolized, but taking that into account in this chapter would be tedious at best.

sense as a device to protect against entry into the originally monopolized market, so such a claim requires one at least to know some facts before dismissing it.

Unfortunately for the claim, the facts are dispositive. The government's position was that bundling forced other hardware producers also to offer such a bundle and that this made entry more difficult. This was quite untrue. In the first place, IBM's bundling did not prevent the enormous growth of an independent software industry with very many participants, so that it would have been (and was) easy for hardware manufacturers to acquire the necessary software to produce a bundle. This made the supposed entry barrier merely a question of raising capital, and there were no capital barriers to entry.

Second, IBM's bundling in the relatively early days of the computer industry was a response to consumer demand.[13] The bundle effectively provided insurance, a guarantee that computers would function and solve users' problems. That was highly desirable in a period in which computers were great, unfamiliar, frightening beasts. When a community of users arose that did not need the bundle, bundling diminished, starting in 1968.

The important point here is the following: had consumers *not* wanted the bundle, IBM's bundling would have made entry *easier*, not harder. Other hardware manufacturers could have offered hardware without the bundle to customers who wished to dispense with the latter. This would have made their products more attractive relative to IBM. Instead, most manufacturers offered their own bundle. It is noteworthy that, when IBM unbundled, Honeywell ran advertisements proclaiming that they still offered "the same old bundle of joy."

This was not a case of monopoly leveraging. IBM neither succeeded nor could reasonably have expected to succeed in monopolizing software and services. Moreover, as should now be plain to any sensible person, IBM had no monopoly to leverage or protect. There were (and are) competitors aplenty.

Bundling Formerly Separate Hardware Components Together

There were also occasions on which IBM effectively bundled together formerly separate hardware components, including them within the central processing unit. Two of these involved disk-control functions and one involved memory.

Until the early 1970s, much of the control circuitry for disk drives was located in a separate box (the "controller"). Such boxes became obsolete when IBM introduced two devices, the integrated storage controller

---

[13] It is also relevant that property rights in software were unclear, at best.

(ISC) and the integrated file adapter (IFA) in connection with the announcement of the System/370 line of computer systems. The ISC and the IFA (which ran on different machines) replaced the old controller with circuitry inside the central processor itself.

The government contended that these introductions were anticompetitive acts designed to extend or preserve IBM's power over the supposed "market" for disk drives attachable to IBM systems and, of course, to eliminate competition in control circuitry.

The allegation as to memory was much the same. Here, in the mid-1970s, IBM introduced new memory devices, far smaller than the old. It then offered its new central processing units (CPUs) with a certain amount of memory included. (This had always been done to an extent, since CPUs will not run without memory, but the new minimum memory capacity was substantially larger than the old one had been.) Larger amounts of memory could be purchased separately, but the days of stand-alone large memory boxes were over. The government claimed that this was an attempt to stifle competition in the supposed "market" for memory used with IBM systems.

Both of these cases present essentially the same set of issues. First, each involved an innovation. The speed of light is very high, but signals moving at that speed travel only about three inches in a nanosecond, making the minimization of the distance that signals have to travel an important factor in computer design. Largely as a result of this (as well as because of the floor space involved), the placing of control circuitry and memory inside the CPU was a major goal. Further, the IFA and ISC were less expensive than the old controller boxes. Finally, the new disk drives and memory devices worked faster than the old.

That does not settle the issue, however. If it did, then anticompetitive bundling, no matter how large its effects, could be justified as being accompanied by consumer benefits from innovation, no matter how small. Further, the consumer benefits here necessarily required the placing of additional circuitry inside the CPU. Removing that circuitry would certainly have affected the functioning of the machines involved (although that does not mean that the devices could not have been sold separately). If the provision of technological improvement were the end of the story, companies would be encouraged to design their products so as to make a bundle difficult to take apart. (This is what Microsoft did in Windows 98 as regards the integration of its web browser.) Hence such cases must still be examined for anticompetitive effects and, if necessary, any such effects must be weighed against the advantages produced by the bundled innovation.

This is not much of a problem in considering the case of IBM. First, the disk-control devices did not change any connections between exist-

ing CPUs and existing disk drives. Second, anyone who wished to attach
to the new CPUs in the old way could still do so. Third, competing manufacturers of disk drives could, and soon did, attach their products to the
new control devices. The innovation essentially made the old controller
boxes obsolete and expensive.

This is not a complete answer, however, because IBM did not offer
the new control devices for separate sale, and the same was true of the
minimum amount of memory supplied. Hence one can imagine IBM's
actions to have had negative effects on competition for those items even
though the allegation as to the "market" for disk drives attachable to
IBM systems seems patently baseless.

Before proceeding, we can dispose of the memory case (although the
subsequent analysis also applies to it). For the bundling of minimum
memory to have been anticompetitive, a sufficient section of the memory
business would have had to be foreclosed to drive out other manufacturers. This did not happen, even though those manufacturers now had
to compete only to supply additional memory. In part, that is because
there was a good deal of such additional memory; in part, it reflects the
fact that memory manufacturers could easily supply memory for non-
IBM processors.

And, in case anyone has forgotten, there were many non-IBM processors. Some of these were part of full computer systems; some, such as
those made by the Amdahl Corporation, were plug-compatible replacements for IBM CPUs. As suggested by the peculiar definition of one of
the relevant markets as the "market" for disk drives attachable to IBM
CPUs, there was a wider world out there and wider competition than
the government apparently saw.[14]

Therein lies the most powerful answer to the claim that IBM's
bundling was anticompetitive or even monopoly leveraging. IBM was
(and is) engaged in competition with many other firms. That competition
involved both individual "boxes" such as disk drives or CPUs and complete systems. Had consumers not found the bundled offering of the new
products sufficiently attractive, then, as in the case of bundled software
and services, there would have been an opportunity for, rather than a
foreclosure of, IBM's competitors.

Monopoly leveraging through bundling requires monopoly power. It
can serve to preserve that power, but, so long as entry is not difficult for
other reasons, bundling that is undesired by a significant group of customers only creates an opportunity for rivals.

---

[14] The disk-drive issue was not (to put it mildly) the only blinkered and peculiar market
definition put forward in the case. Similar "markets" were defined for tape drives and
other peripherals, and the government managed to define Amdahl and the other makers
of perfect substitutes for IBM products out of the market altogether.

THE *MICROSOFT* CASE

The *Microsoft* case presents a very different phenomenon. To see why requires a brief examination of Microsoft's monopoly power and the reasons for it.

Application software is typically written to connect or call on application programming interfaces (APIs). These APIs permit the application to use the services of an underlying software platform, typically (but not always) an operating system. In general, application programs written for a given operating system will not run on other operating systems, and "porting" them to another operating system is a matter of considerable effort and expense.

Now, the production and sale of software involves considerable economies of scale. Most of the expense is fixed cost, the cost of writing and debugging the software itself. The marginal cost of licensing additional customers is nearly zero. As a result, writers of applications programs have an incentive to write for those operating systems that have a very large number of users.

On the other hand, operating systems themselves are subject to "network effects." In the present context this means that the desirability of an operating system to a given user increases with the number of others who are using it. This occurs largely (but not only) because users naturally wish to have an operating system that has a large number of applications written for it.

As a result, there is a positive feedback phenomenon in operating systems. The more users of a given operating system there are, the more applications will be written for it. The more applications are written for a given operating system, the more users there will be.

Microsoft is the beneficiary of this phenomenon (the "applications barrier to entry"). At least since the triumph of Windows 95, it has had roughly 90 percent of the operating systems installed on Intel ×86 chip personal computers (PCs).[15] Indeed, as this suggests, Microsoft has monopoly power in such operating systems. This is well illustrated by considering the fact that most operating systems are sold through licensing PC manufacturers (called OEMs, original equipment manufacturers). There is ample testimony from OEMs that they feel that they have no choice but to ship their computers with Windows, which is, to all

---

[15] It does not matter to the analysis here whether or not Apple computers are included in the same market. They are a small percentage of the total. More important, it is simply not the case that a small increase in the price of Windows would induce a large number of customers to shift from PCs to Apple computers or other devices. The price of Windows is a small percentage of the total price of a PC.

intents and purposes, the only game in town. Given the positive feedback described earlier, no alternate operating system vendor has been able or will be able to gain more than a niche.

This does not mean, however, that there can never be a threat to Microsoft's monopoly. Such a threat can arise in ways other than the direct entry of a new operating system vendor. In recent years, there have been two major potential threats and at least the possibility of other ones.

The most important such threat was provided by the innovation of the browser, first made commercially successful by Netscape. Netscape's Navigator browser was an instant success, being acquired by users to enable them efficiently to browse and use the World Wide Web. As such, it was a major piece of applications software.

But browsers have another aspect as well. It turns out that it makes sense for them to provide some of their own APIs so that software developers can use them to make efficient use of Internet resources. But then an extremely popular browser could itself be the beneficiary of the effects already described. In particular, if enough software developers were to write applications using the browser rather than the underlying operating system as a platform, and if computing, as seems at least quite possible, were to become more and more a matter of using Internet resources, then users and OEMs would become more and more indifferent as to which operating system underlay the browser.

This threat to Microsoft's monopoly power was enhanced by a second one – the creation by Sun Microsystems of the Java programming language and associated software. In principle, programs that are written in Java will run on any operating system that supports Java.[16] If successful, this would mean that application programmers would be indifferent as to the operating system and would write more and more in Java. Netscape actively promoted Java, supporting and distributing it with its browser. Naturally, were Java to be successful, the positive feedback barrier to entry enjoyed by Microsoft would simply disappear.

Microsoft took steps to rid itself of these threats, and I shall explain how. Before doing so, however, it is useful to point out that Microsoft had a pattern of vigorously attempting to suppress any innovation that offered application writers even a partial alternative platform on which to build their software. During the late 1990s, it successfully bullied both Intel and Apple into discontinuing such attempts. It did so by threats. In the case of Apple, in particular, this took the form of threatening to withhold Macintosh development for Microsoft Office – the extremely popular suite of applications that includes Work and Excel – and threat-

---

[16] More accurately, on any operating system that has a "Java Virtual Machine."

ening to put very large development teams to work in the audio-video area in which it felt challenged, "even if," as the Microsoft representative put it, such action made "no business sense."

Actions that "make no business sense" except for their destructive effect on competition are predatory and anticompetitive. Microsoft succeeded in coercing Apple and, indeed, used that coercion to get Apple to support Microsoft's browser, Internet Explorer (IE), as its default choice.

In the meantime, Microsoft took action directly against Java and further actions against Netscape.

In the case of Java, Microsoft appeared to embrace the innovation but in fact worked to render it harmless. It introduced its own version of Java for Windows. That version, called "J/Direct," offered application programmers writing in Java the ability to call on certain Windows facilities directly rather than through the original Java system. This could be useful to those developers, but the programs thus created would not run on operating systems other than Windows. This was also true of programs written using Microsoft's developer aids for Java, unless the developer was very careful and informed.

Microsoft was internally clear as to what these actions would do. One document speaks of containing Java by promoting "polluted Java." With Windows still by far the most popular operating system, application programmers would naturally write first for Windows. If many or most of them swallowed Microsoft's bait, then the threat that Java represented to the barriers to entry sustaining the monopoly would dissipate.

It is the actions directed at Netscape and its browser that aroused the most attention, however, and which directly relate to the monopoly-leveraging-and-innovation theme of this chapter.

First in later releases of Windows 95 and then much more tightly in Windows 98, Microsoft bundled its own browser, Internet Explorer, with its operating system. In the first instance, this means that customers obtained IE at no separately stated charge; indeed, most customers could not and cannot obtain Windows 98 without also getting IE.

In this regard, it is important to note that the main customers are the OEMs, the makers of personal computers who ship their computers together with the operating system. This is the most important channel of distribution for operating systems and for browsers. Microsoft required its OEM customers not to remove IE.

Microsoft attempted to justify these practices with two technological claims. The first is that the so-called integration of IE with Windows 98 provides a benefit for consumers, permitting them to have a single browsing experience whether browsing the World Wide Web or looking for files on their own hard disk. The second is that IE cannot be removed from Windows 98 without damaging the workings of the operating system.

Neither of these claims had much real content. First, it is not clear that the "common browsing experience" either amounts to much or is actually desired by consumers. Further, it would be perfectly possible to provide that experience with other browsers.

As for the integration claim, it arose only because Microsoft chose to design its products so that IE and Windows 98 shared a good deal of code. That did not have to be the design choice. Moreover, while the shared code could not be removed without affecting the functioning of the operating system, the Internet browsing functions could be in the sense that access to IE itself could be removed and another browser substituted instead without any degradation. It appears clear that Microsoft designed its products with an eye on the antitrust issues.

It is also worth noting that Microsoft pressured Apple into agreeing to make the version of IE written for the Mac operating system its default browser. No claim of technical improvement for Windows can explain that.

Microsoft also claimed that bundling the browser was a normal procompetitive act because the demand for browsers helps to sell Windows. In that case, however, it is strange that Microsoft should have pushed Apple into adopting IE. Moreover, even if true, such a phenomenon merely suggests the profitability to Microsoft of having a browser available. There is no reason that the available browser had to be IE. Indeed, on this line of argument, Microsoft should have welcomed sales of any browser.

That Microsoft definitely did not do. Having ensured that IE would appear on the computer of nearly every new computer purchaser, it set out to tie up the other most important distribution channel for browsers. This is the provision of browsers by Internet service providers (ISPs) including on-line services (OLSs), of which the most important is America on Line (AOL). In exchange for prominent positions on the Microsoft desktop and sometimes cash payments, Microsoft required such entities to make IE the browser they placed with their subscribers unless there was a specific request for another and, in a fairly typical case, to be sure that IE constituted 85 percent of all their browser placements.[17]

---

[17] There is no reason to believe that the acquisition of Netscape by AOL that occurred during the trial will make any difference here. Before the merger, Netscape would have paid AOL to adopt its browser an amount only slightly less than what that adoption was worth to Netscape. That amount is unlikely to change as a result of the merger. If Microsoft's desktop placement was worth more than that to AOL previously, it will still be worth more than that after the merger. Indeed, even if the use of Netscape's browser

Microsoft also signed restrictive contracts with Internet content providers (ICPs) such as the Walt Disney Company. In exchange for prominent appearance on the desktop, such companies had to agree that, in any similar placement by Netscape,[18] the ICP could not use its company logo or other items such as the Disney characters. More important, the ICP was prohibited from paying Netscape any consideration for such placement.[19]

That last provision is a dead giveaway as to why the restrictions were imposed. Microsoft cannot have had any interest in preventing such payments save as a way to reduce Netscape's revenues. This is not a normal, profit-maximizing, procompetitive act. It is the act of a predator determined to "cut off Netscape's air supply," a quote from a high Microsoft executive on the subject of Microsoft's browser bundling.

Of course, as Microsoft repeatedly pointed out, there were other channels of distribution open to Netscape. These are principally the downloading of Navigator by users and the sending out of voluminous mailings of compact discs (CDs) that enable the installation of Navigator. Neither of these channels enabled Netscape to avoid the effects of Microsoft's actions, however. Downloads are extremely time-consuming and difficult for the uninitiated. The hit rate for CD mailings is low, and the costs per installation quite high.[20]

Moreover, the fact that the consumer's computer already has a perfectly capable browser loaded onto it very greatly reduces the incentive to install a second one. As in the case of computer reservation systems, there is no reason for most consumers to bother. The same thing is true for OEMs thinking of adding Navigator to their shipped PCs – an act that would also increase their support costs. Further, even adding Navigator to a PC with Windows 98 would not remove IE. Microsoft designed its software so that a number of different applications result in IE being used even if the user specifies Navigator as the browser of choice.

---

by AOL is worth more to the merged company than it would have been to Netscape alone, Microsoft, with monopoly rents to protect can surely offer AOL enough to overcome that fact. AOL's executives have repeatedly stated their intention to continue the use of IE, and AOL did not exercise its option to exit from the arrangement in early 1999, choosing instead to go forward as before for the next few years.

[18] The contracts typically did not mention Netscape by name but dealt with "other browsers" defined as the two most popular browsers apart from IE. There is some doubt as to who the very minor number three browser is; there is no doubt as to who was being targeted.

[19] Some of these restrictions on ICPs and others were waived by Microsoft on the eve of the trial.

[20] Microsoft pointed to the successful experience of AOL with mailings, but the cases are not comparable. AOL was not mailing to a customer group, most of whom already had an OLS. Further, a successful hit by AOL brought in a continuing stream of revenues from the customer involved.

There is another important point to notice in all this. Microsoft went beyond bundling, beyond offering IE at no separately stated charge. It actually paid to have its browser adopted despite the fact that the browser was a "no-revenue product." In the case of ISPs and ICPs, that payment took the form of offering valuable space on the desktop, space that could otherwise be sold. Indeed, in the case of AOL, Microsoft, in addition to cash payments, offered such space despite the fact that this removed the advantage that its own on-line service, MSN, possessed. In the case of OEMs, the placing of an unwanted burden reduced the license fee that Microsoft could have charged.

Why then did Microsoft do all this? First, we can dispose of the proposition that its actions were purely competitive and profit maximizing regardless of their effect on competition. That is plainly not so.

Second, operating systems and browsers are not bought or used in fixed proportions. So Microsoft was not merely accomplishing something that it could have done by charging a high price for Windows.

There are two remaining possibilities. The first of these is that Microsoft was attempting to monopolize the market for browsers so as to earn monopoly profits therein. This may be true. Even with no charge for browsers, there are ancillary revenues that come with browser sales. It is interesting to note, however, that there is no hint in the contemporaneous Microsoft documents that their actions had anything to do with these. Indeed, the fact that Microsoft executives claimed that Netscape's business model would not look good without revenues from browser sales suggests that, at least in a competitive environment, they did not regard the ancillary revenues as important.[21]

The correct answer is not hard to find and has already been suggested. Microsoft took these actions in a deliberate attempt to protect its monopoly power in platforms. The growth of someone else's browser, particularly in conjunction with Java, would have threatened that power by making it attractive to application writers to connect with browser or Java APIs. With Microsoft not controlling those APIs, the importance of Windows and the barrier to entry that preserves the monopoly would be lessened or disappear.

Note the contrast with IBM. IBM's bundling, if undesired by customers, provided an opportunity for IBM's competitors who could offer computers without the bundled products or services. In the case of Microsoft, the parallel statement does not hold. When Microsoft bundled its browser, it did not risk the entry of competing operating systems

---

[21] Late in the trial, Microsoft introduced the claim that its actions were in fact merely aimed at securing such ancillary revenues. As observed in the text, there is not a shred of contemporary evidence that such revenues were even considered.

that are attractive because they do not offer a bundled browser. No such entry could be significant because of the applications barrier to entry – the very barrier to entry that Microsoft's actions were designed to protect.

On the contrary, by bundling its browser and by means of its other acts, Microsoft was removing a threat that entry would later arise. Because of the applications barrier to entry, no operating system vendor could effectively constrain Microsoft's power. But if enough users were to acquire independent browsers to use with Windows, especially browsers that offered Java, such constraints might very well have arisen. Microsoft recognized that threat and took actions to prevent it from becoming a reality. That is anticompetitive monopoly leveraging aided by and disguised as innovation.

LEVERAGING, THE INCENTIVE TO INNOVATE, AND PUBLIC POLICY

The fact that monopoly leveraging can be assisted by innovation may require some further discussion, however. A referee of this chapter has suggested that I should comment on the tradeoff between the inefficiencies caused by leveraging and the possible gains that may result from a greater incentive to innovate if doing so brings the ability to leverage monopoly power. There are several things to say in this regard.

- There is, of course, a general presumption that competition brings about an efficient allocation of resources. The theorems on which that presumption rests, however, involve static equilibria. It is well known that the result does not necessarily apply when innovation is an important factor. Hence it is possible that encouraging innovation at the expense of competition may actually improve social welfare. We do this in the patent and copyright laws.
- On the other hand, it is not true that higher rates of innovation are necessarily socially preferable to low ones. Policies that generate the socially optimal rate and type of innovation are not known. (Indeed, it is far from clear that seventeen years is optimal for the life of a patent.)
- Still less is it true that *any* given innovation, no matter what its nature, is worth giving up the beneficial effects of competition and permitting anticompetitive inefficiencies, no matter how large. There is a long-standing doctrine of patent misuse, and appropriately so.
- Moreover, it is very important not to lose sight of the fact that permitting a monopolist to leverage its monopoly through innovation may increase the *monopolist's* incentive to innovate but may very

well hamper or prevent innovation by others.[22] Perhaps the most harmful effect of Microsoft's actions was the strong message they sent that innovations that interfered with Microsoft's monopoly in operating systems would not be tolerated.

Given all this, it is hard to see any merit in an antitrust exemption permitting monopoly leveraging if done through innovation. There can certainly be innovations that necessarily involve the extension of monopoly power – innovations that bring consumer benefit, that cannot be realized in any way less restrictive of competition, and that would be profit-maximizing to pursue even without the increase in monopoly rents that they may bring. Those innovations should be allowed on the general principle that acts that one would in any case see under competition should not be prohibited.

Innovations that do not meet such a standard, however, should not be encouraged. In this connection, note that neither the development of computer reservation systems nor the integration of the browser by Microsoft simply and inevitably led to monopoly leveraging. In both cases, they were accompanied by deliberately anticompetitive acts. There would have been nothing wrong with Microsoft offering its browser and operating system together had it also offered them separately, charging a positive and remunerative price for the browser (both separately and as part of the bundle). To the extent that integration of the browser really did bring consumer benefits, consumers would have preferred that version and there would have been no need to offer the browser at what was, in effect, a predatorily low price.

I see no merit in a rule of law that would permit the predatorily low price because it was associated with an innovation. Further, although an innovation by a legal monopolist that *merely* makes its product more desirable (and does so in the least restrictive way) should not be prevented, I see no merit in the idea that one wants to encourage anticompetitive innovations that would not have occurred save for the increase in monopoly rents associated with them.

REFERENCES

Bork, R. H. 1978. *The Antitrust Paradox.* New York: Basic Books.
Bowman, W. S. 1957. Tying Arrangements and the Leverage Problem. *Yale Law Journal* 67: 19–36.
Burstein, M. L. 1960. The Economics of Tie-In Sales. *Review of Economics and Statistics* 42: 68–73.

---

[22] I am indebted to Wayne Dunham for emphasizing this point.

Fisher, F. M. 1987. Pan American to United: The *Pacific Division Transfer Case.* *RAND Journal of Economics* 18: 492–508. Reprinted in F. M. Fisher, *Industrial Organization, Economics, and the Law*, ch. 3. Cambridge, MA: MIT Press; London: Harvester-Wheatsheaf, 1991.

Fisher, F. M., J. J. McGowan, and J. E. Greenwood. 1983. *Folded, Spindled, and Mutilated: Economic Analysis and U.S. v. IBM.* Cambridge, MA: MIT Press.

Fisher, F. M., and K. Neels. 1999. Estimating the Effects of Display Bias in Computer Reservation Systems. In F. M. Fisher, *Microeconomics: Essays in Theory and Applications*, ch. 28. Cambridge: Cambridge University Press.

Posner, R. A. 1976. *Antitrust Law: An Economic Perspective.* Chicago: University of Chicago Press.

Whinston, M. D. 1990. Tying, Foreclosure, and Exclusion. *American Economic Review* 80: 837–59.

6

Network Effects and the *Microsoft* Case

Stan Liebowitz and Stephen E. Margolis

Much of our work has examined the logic and empirical support for concepts of lock-in and path dependence. These topics have now entered the realm of public policy in what may be the most important antitrust action, or at least the most famous, since the Standard Oil case almost one hundred years ago.

Network effects occur when the value consumers receive from a product increases as the number of users of that product increases. Archetypal examples are fax machines and telephones, which have virtually no value to a consumer if only one consumer has one, but have increasing value as additional users adopt the product.

As long as other factors, such as increasing costs, do not overpower network effects, larger firms or networks will have advantages over smaller firms or networks. Following through the logic of the model, this leads, naturally enough, to a single winning firm or network.[1] Network effects share an important characteristic with economies of scale. In particular, both confer an advantage on larger firms in an industry, although the former does it by increasing demand and the latter by decreasing costs.

A portion of this literature claims that network effects tend to keep a leading firm's position intact, even if there is a superior product available, a result otherwise known as lock-in.[2] We need to make clear that

This chapter is based on research conducted for our book, *Winners, Losers, and Microsoft: Competition and Antitrust in High Technology* (Oakland, CA: Independent Institute, 1999). Graphs and excerpts are reprinted with permission of The Independent Institute. Those interested in greater detail should consult the book.

[1] Differences in taste, however, can allow incompatible standards to coexist.

[2] We have focused on a form of path dependence we call third-degree path dependence, meaning that the inability to coordinate their activity causes consumers to continue to use a product even when there would be an alternative product that would provide benefits net of switching costs.

our definition of lock-in does not just imply that costs of switching make it uneconomic to switch. If it is uneconomic to switch, switching should not occur. Failure to switch is not an inefficient lock-in. Instead, we define lock-in to mean that a superior product is not adopted even though all costs (except coordination costs) are less than the benefits. In case it appears that we are setting up a straw man, the reader should note that it is exactly this form of lock-in that generated so much excitement about the typewriter keyboard fable in the profession (David 1985). Our previous investigations of supposed real-world cases of lock-in, however, forced us to conclude that there were as yet no known real-world instances (Liebowitz and Margolis 1990, 1995).

The first use of these concepts against Microsoft, in the mid 1990s, was the claim that network effects in software would lead to lock-in, or the wrong choice of software products.[3] The more recent use of network effects has modified this claim very slightly. For example, Franklin Fisher, in his testimony against Microsoft, claims that network effects enhance Microsoft's monopoly power. Judge Jackson, in his finding of fact,[4] claimed that the "chicken-and-egg" nature of software markets led to an "application barrier to entry," meaning that incumbent operating system producers were protected from competitors by the fact that network effects and coordination costs would be working against the challenger. The implication would seem to be that the challenger might or might not be superior, but that the barrier to entry prevents the rival product from ever getting a chance to compete with the incumbent.

This concept of entrenched incumbents is, apparently, a beguiling idea because it has seduced a large portion of the economists who have encountered it. This is so in spite of the fact that the economic theory is itself ambiguous, as demonstrated by the concept of excess momentum (Farrell and Saloner 1985). Perhaps an even more telling criticism is the fact that it is unclear that there is any empirical support for this claim. Nonetheless, this concept has achieved considerable acceptance, perhaps in part riding on the coattails of the popularity of the concept of network effects, which itself has been the focus of only a very limited and suspect empirical literature, particularly as regards software markets.[5]

---

[3] See Reback et al. (1995).

[4] *United States v. Microsoft Corp.*, GSF. Supp. 2d 1 (D.D.C. 1999) (findings of fact).

[5] We are aware of two empirical attempts to test the strength of network effects in spreadsheet markets, Gandal (1994) and Brynjolfsson and Kamerer (1996). Both run hedonic regressions with putative proxies for network effects as independent variables. Gandal uses Lotus file compatibility and the ability to link to external databases to measure the strength of network effects. Brynjolfsson and Kamerer use Lotus menu structure and installed base as a measure of network effects. In general, however, these varables will

Because it has been claimed that software manifests network effects, and because increasing returns in production (decreasing average cost as output increases) are also likely in the software industry, the conditions would seem to be in place for software to be an incubator for lock-in or inertia. In the following section we examine some implications of these theories. The analysis of software markets that follows examines evidence regarding the general predictions of these theories and some specific allegations of Microsoft's "monopolistic" behavior in these markets.

IMPLICATIONS OF NETWORK EFFECTS

Network effects are thought to be common in many high-technology industries. A virtual mountain of papers has been written about these effects in spite of the lack of evidence of their overall strength, such as their theoretical appeal. In the *Microsoft* case it has just been assumed that network effects are pervasive, which does not seem out of line with many academic articles. Legal standards, however, probably should require more stringent standards than current academic fads because so much is at stake, but in antitrust at least, standards have historically not been high. Just because there is so much uncorroborated agreement about network effects, however, does not mean that the common beliefs about network effects are all true. It is important that we try to verify these beliefs. In the following, we suggest some implications of network effects. If these implications are not found in software (or other network) markets, then many beliefs about the importance of network effects in software or other markets should be reexamined.

Price: The Neglected Implication

We start with this not because it is easily testable, but because it has been entirely ignored in the literature and because it is about as direct an impact as one can find.

Network effects increase the demand for a product. Ceteris paribus, as network effects get stronger, prices should rise. This should be true for individual firms as they increase their market shares and also for the market as a whole as the size of the network increases, at least as network

---

not measure network effects. Lotus file compatibility cannot distinguish between consumers who, when upgrading, wish to remain compatible with their old files, not a network effect, from the network effect of wishing to be compatible with others. The same problem afflicts the installed base variable. These variables might perform as hoped if the samples were limited to first-time buyers, which they were not. The ability to link to external databases is a useful function, but not a network effect. The Lotus menu structure variable measures the importance of remaining compatible with one's old learned habits, also not a network effect.

effects are usually modeled. This is in complete contrast with the impact of economies of scale, which by lowering the costs of the firm, should lower the price of the product for any given level of monopoly power exerted in the market.

Surprisingly, this clear implication of network effects has not received much attention in the literature. The higher prices that should be caused by the increase in demand brought about, in turn, by larger networks, the relationship at the very core of this theory, has been neglected.

Because so many factors are involved in setting market prices, it may be difficult to generate a definitive test relating prices to network size, but the general claim of higher prices as networks get larger should be observable in some fashion. The reader should keep this in mind as actual prices in various markets are examined.

Winner-Take-All (or Most)

The implication of network effects that has received most attention is the winner-take-all (or winner-take-most) result coming from increasing returns. A potential problem in testing this implication is that it applies equally well to old-fashioned economies of scale. For many high-tech products, particularly software, economies of scale seem very likely, thus making it difficult to distinguish separately the impact of network effects.

Another difficulty is that software has a characteristic that we refer to as "instant scalability," meaning that the output can be increased very rapidly without the usual additional costs associated with sudden increases in output. This instant scalability is due to the fact that reproduction equipment is not specialized. Instant scalability will also be found for compact disc music recordings and long-playing records prior to that.

Note that this is not the same as zero or low reproduction costs. Printed books using specialized plates can be reproduced at very low marginal cost, but the scale of output is limited to that one printing location using those plates because it is time-consuming to create other plates.

Software has this attribute because disc-reproducing machines are not specialized for any particular software title and thus it is considerably easier to increase output of a software title than to increase output of automobiles or even books. In a world where output can be changed so quickly, market shares can adjust to meet every whim of consumers. The market need not have unfilled orders or higher prices – no Cabbage Patch dolls or Furbies here.[6] Instant scalability provides yet another

---

[6] Furbies are toys that were in short supply in the 1998 Christmas season, Cabbage Patch dolls were in short supply during the late 1980s. The shortages in both cases caused a minor sensation.

potential explanation for winner-take-all outcomes in software. The difference, however, is that market shares can change dramatically here because a product that better strikes a fancy will quickly come to dominate the market. The software markets that we look at appear to change in a manner consistent with this property.

We believe that this concept of instant scalability may have been at work for some time and is worthy of further examination to determine how important its impacts may be. We hope some readers will join us in putting this concept to some empirical testing.

Winner-take-all results, therefore, are consistent with network effects, but also with economies of scale and instant scalability.

Lock-In or Inertia

The concept of lock-in would seem to apply to software if it applies anywhere. Network effects should be stronger in most software markets than would have been expected in the other suspected havens of lock-in – typewriters or video recorders, for example.

If large firms have advantages over small firms, then we have the possibility of what we have defined elsewhere (1995) as third-degree lock-in or inertia. Obviously, this is not to say that an incumbent remains forever entrenched, but only that when a better product comes along it might not get adopted even if there were economic advantages to its adoption. This is to be distinguished from weaker cases of lock-in, where real costs of switching make it uneconomical to switch to another product.

Confirmation of the lock-in hypothesis requires finding better products that are not adopted.[7] Testing for inertia would require that we know the optimal switching speed and compare that to the actual speed with which a switch is made. Testing for inertia obviously requires more detailed knowledge than testing for lock-in, and considerably more detail than we are likely to find. Instead, we ask the reader to compare the speed of changes in software markets to speed of changes elsewhere, admittedly an imperfect measure.

As already mentioned, Judge Jackson, in his finding of fact, converted the lock-in concept to a barrier to entry. As we all know, barrier to entry is a slippery concept, meaning anything from a high cost of entry to a cost incurred by the challenger but not the incumbent. The latter definition has always seemed correct to us, and in that case it is unclear how network effects, economies of scale, or any of the other factors at work

---

[7] Better here means that the costs of switching are less than the benefits, on a social scale. Obviously, any rational consumer would switch any time his personal benefits were greater than his costs..

favor the incumbent relative to the challenger. The incumbent had to coordinate consumers to adopt his product, whether it was first in the market or replaced a previous incumbent. In either case, getting consumers to come on board is a cost imposed on all market entrants, late or early, and does not necessarily favor early firms.

In contrast to much of the path dependence literature, which focuses on excess inertia, we note the possibility that the speed at which market leaders replace one another might be greater in software markets than in many "ordinary" markets due to the *instant scalability* feature of software. In fact, the software markets that we examine here exhibit extremely rapid changes in market leadership. Although we are not aware of any precise bench marks with which to make comparisons to other industries, it appears on casual inspection that changes in market share occur at a far more rapid rate in software markets than in other markets.

Tipping

Tipping is a term that has been used rather vaguely in the literature and in Microsoft antitrust testimony. A market is considered to have "tipped" when one product or standard has become dominant. A market is tipping when it is sliding toward the eventual domination by a single firm. It is generally claimed that tipping occurs when a product has generated sufficient momentum with regard to network effects that its domination is inevitable. Although there is considerable vagueness in the literature, the general idea seems to be that after a period of struggle, one firm breaks out from the pack and tipping ensues.

We assume that tipping has some meaning other than just market dominance. Because network effects only strengthen as market share increases, there should be a pattern to market share growth. First, when a firm is smaller than its competitors, growth should be slow because network effects should be working against the firm. Later, when consumers anticipate that a firm will become larger than its competitors, market share increases should come more easily, because network effects are self-reinforcing. This tipping point, or critical mass, should mark an acceleration in market share growth. In such instances, increases in market share for leading products would occur even without any advantages in product quality. As we will see, there is no evidence for markets tipping in this manner.

SOFTWARE MARKETS: BACKGROUND

We focus on a few key software application markets, particularly markets in which Microsoft has achieved or failed to achieve a dominant status. We examine spreadsheets and personal finance as two markets in which

Microsoft has had very different success, and Internet browsers because this market was so crucial to the case.

The Consumer's Choice

When a consumer is faced with software choices, whether changing to a completely different product, or just upgrading a current choice,[8] the logic of the choice is straightforward. First, the consumer must evaluate the increased value that would be brought about by using the new software relative to remaining with the current software. This extra value might come from new features, increased speed, better compatibility with other users, and so forth. On the other side of the ledger go the costs of purchasing the software, the costs of the transition (presumably users will be less productive as they learn to use the new software), and the costs of any file incompatibility with previous software (the cost of imperfect access to old data).

Software has several characteristics that make it appealing for consumers to remain with the same vendor. First and foremost is a concern with backward compatibility – compatibility with the learned skills associated with previous versions of a program and compatibility with file formats that were created with previous versions of the program. If the adoption of a new spreadsheet or word processor removed any ability to read the consumer's old files, it is very unlikely the consumer would make the change. That is why virtually all software producers try to provide some degree of backward compatibility with older versions. This cost is real. It is not an inefficient lock-in for the consumer to avoid changing software if the benefits to changing are less than this cost.

It is also common for software products to provide some ability to read files produced by other products so as to entice the users of other products to switch and to increase the value of the product to users who exchange files. Some software products lower the consumer's costs of switching by mimicking aspects of the user interface of other products.

There are, of course, numerous reasons why a user might have an interest in changing software applications. Even a user who is happy with the current product might need to move to a new operating system that doesn't run the old product (say from IBM-compatible to Mac). Or, as

---

[8] We use the term "upgrade" to imply that the product has been modified but is largely the same as before in the sense that the users do not have to learn very much new to use the product. Some market upgrades are really shifts to new products that happen to use the same name, or are owned by the same company. The text provides a few examples of upgrades that do not fit our definition, such as the introduction of WordStar 2000 as an upgrade of WordStar, and AmiPro's successor, WordPro.

is more commonly the case, the user might be looking for some additional features missing from his current product.

Another factor that influences consumers' choices and is likely to be related to large changes in market shares are paradigm changes, or market displacements. These are external changes in the markets that provide motivations for large numbers of current users to switch to a new product. These changes might be a design alteration in the nature of the product itself, or a change in the operating environment of the product. Examples would be the removal of copy protection, allowing the product to work in networked environments, the movement from 8- to 16-bit or 16- to 32-bit architectures, the growth of the Internet, the invention of macros, graphical systems, voice recognition, and so forth. If consumers find these changes compelling, they will be willing to switch products if necessary in order to take advantage of the new environment. Two such displacements were the movement from DOS programs to Windows programs and the creation of office suites.[9]

Measurement Issues

How does one go about measuring the quality of a software product? We leave the examination of the software quality to the experts writing for (mainly) computer magazines, and use a large number of product reviews as our quality measure. There are, however, still some issues that require judgment calls. First, many magazines do not give numerical scores to competing software products. In many instances, particularly during the 1980s, magazines compared features of various products without making judgments. When judgments were made, magazines often picked a "winner" or "editor's choice" without indicating the quality differential between winners and losers, and without differentiating among the losers.

To overcome some of these limitations, we used more than one method of comparison. The rankings generated with either of these methods are presented as timelines, which can then be compared with market shares.

Where magazines numerically rated individual software products, we used these ratings. Where numerical scores were given, we report these scores, normalized so that the highest rated product always receives a 10. In cases where reviewers rated software by qualitative categories such as "excellent," "good," and so forth, we converted these categories into numerical equivalents. In those cases where no overall rating was given, but only ratings for particular characteristics (ease of use, speed, and so forth), we take the average value of the characteristics ratings to get an

---

[9] In our book we analyze the impact of these displacements in more detail.

overall quality ranking for the software application relative to its competitors. In these cases we assigned numerical scores to these ratings (excellent = 10, good = 7.5, fair = 5, poor = 2.5) and summed the ratings across categories to arrive at a score for the package as a whole.[10]

For those reviews that provide clear winners, but no overall evaluation, we count the number of reviewers who state that a particular product is the best. We refer to the number of reviews making such judgments as the number of "wins." This latter measure, even though it provides no information about the remaining products, provides a relatively large number of data points.

To avoid clutter, we often remove from the subsequent figures products that were not important players. Occasionally, therefore, the winner in a particular review may be one of those packages that we have removed from the figure, but the reader can easily tell its presence from the fact that the highest score listed will be less than 10. In fact, this was a rare event. It typically involved a single review of a product that enjoyed only a momentary quality advantage.

Although both measures were constructed for each market, only the measure of wins is reported in this chapter. Interested readers will need to refer to our book for complete coverage (Liebowitz and Margolis 1999).

There are also choices regarding the measurement of market share. It can be measured either in units, or in revenues. Most of the time it makes little difference, but we report shares based on revenues unless otherwise specified. Because we usually report prices as well as market shares, readers can determine unit-based market shares for themselves.

Some computers come with a set of software products installed. Although the consumer may not use these preinstalled products, market share statistics treat these preinstalled products as though they represent actual purchase decisions and use.[11] In that sense, market share statistics might sometimes be misleading indicators of actual use. Fortunately, it appears that original equipment manufacturer (OEM) sales are not likely to influence our results too strongly. OEM sales, while increasingly important, are still a minority component of application markets. Office suites are among the more commonly included products, yet the importance of OEM sales is not high. Writing in 1996, IDC (International Data Corp.) analyst Mary Wardley stated that "OEM sales have suddenly

---

[10] This process picks winners consistent with magazine reviewers because, in every case we found, the product that produced the highest score on our constructed index also was the editor's choice.

[11] Revenues and quantities are reported based on sales of software vendors (producers) and include sales to OEMs, upgrades, and retail sales. Revenues are based on the price received by the vendor, and thus represent wholesale prices.

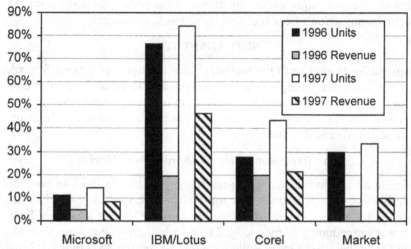

Figure 6.1. Original Equipment Manufacturer Sales as Share of Sales of Office Suites

grown to represent a significant percent of overall sales for office suites and thus spreadsheets. ... However, OEM sales have had little to no impact on Microsoft so far, and IDC believes their impact will remain negligible throughout the forecast period."[12]

The data on OEM sales of office suites in the two years for which they are available, 1996 and 1997, reveal OEM sales to have a limited impact, as illustrated in Figure 6.1. Although OEM sales are responsible for about 30 percent of unit sales in these two years, they are responsible for less than 10 percent of revenues. And for market leader Microsoft, they are responsible for only about 10 percent of sales and 7 percent of revenues. It is worth noting, in light of the role given to Microsoft's putative attempts to control OEMs in the government's case against Microsoft, the latter's limited use of OEM sales.

Finally, statistics on market shares and prices were generated using data collected by data collection companies Dataquest and IDC. We concluded after a brief examination that list prices don't seem to tell us very much. For one thing, they have not varied very much. Second, it must be remembered that list prices neglect the impact of office suites. Third, list prices do not allow us to control for the important role of upgrades, which are less expensive than first-time purchases. Also, the list prices fail to account for the units sold to OEMs, which have a far lower price.

---

[12] International Data Corp., "PC Spreadsheet Market Review and Forecast, 1996–2001," p. 10.

For all these reasons, we do not focus on list prices but instead on the actual transaction prices received by software producers.

SPREADSHEETS

Spreadsheets are one of the mainstays of computer applications. Spreadsheets allow the manipulation of numbers and formulas, and their conversion to charts. The leading spreadsheet is Excel, from Microsoft. It is one of the categories of applications where questions arise about the causes of Microsoft's success.

The Evolution of the PC Spreadsheet Market

Credit for the invention of the spreadsheet goes to Dan Bricklin and Bob Frankston, who created VisiCalc for the Apple II. VisiCalc had a list price of $250. Lotus 1-2-3 was introduced in January 1983 at a price of $495. It was immediately acknowledged to be a better product than VisiCalc. In December 1982 Gregg Williams wrote in *Byte* (p. 182) that 1-2-3 had "many more functions and commands than VisiCalc" and that 1-2-3 was "Revolutionary instead of evolutionary." *PC World* called it "state of the art."

In October 1983 *PC World* reported that 1-2-3 was outselling VisiCalc.[13] VisiCalc was removed from the market in 1985 after being purchased by Lotus. Users of VisiCalc were offered upgrades to 1-2-3.[14] In terms of market share, Lotus was to remain dominant for almost a decade. Unfortunately, we do not have detailed data on this early market. Still, from what we have pieced together, it is clear that a superior product, Lotus 1-2-3, was able to quickly wrest market share away from VisiCalc.

By 1985 most spreadsheets were meant to work with the IBM PC. Lotus 1-2-3 was the champ, leading other contenders such as Computer Associates (Easy Planner, $195), Ashton-Tate (Framework, $695), Software Publishing (PFS Plan, $140), and IBM (PlannerCalc, $80, and Multiplan 1.0, $250). Microsoft had Excel for the Mac (at $495) and Multiplan 2.0 ($195) for the PC.

Soon, many new spreadsheets arrived on the scene. Some were clones of 1-2-3 at lower prices (VP-Planner, The Twin, and VIP Professional). Other spreadsheets, such as Javelin and SuperCalc, tried to differentiate themselves by improving upon 1-2-3 in some manner, but although these alternatives received some praise, they did not receive universal acclaim and did not make much of a splash in the market.

Excel first appeared in 1985 but for the Macintosh only. Jerry Pournelle, a well-known columnist for *Byte* (and science fiction author), wrote

---

[13] *PC World*, October 1983, 120.   [14] *PC World*, December 1985, 221.

(incorrectly but nonetheless prophetically): "Excel will make the Mac into a serious business machine" (*Byte*, September 1985, 347).

In late 1987 Microsoft ported Excel to the PC (running under an early version of Windows) and Borland introduced Quattro for DOS. Microsoft's election not to produce a DOS version of the program was something of a gamble. The success of Microsoft Windows was far from assured until version 3.0, which became available in 1990. The fact that PC users did not flock to earlier versions of Windows most likely reduced the sales of Excel, because users would have had to load Windows to run the spreadsheet and then return to DOS for other applications. Also, many of the features of Excel worked best with a mouse, and it was rare at the time for PCs to have a mouse.

Thus began the market struggle between Microsoft, Borland, and Lotus. Reviews found Windows-based Excel to be superior to 1-2-3, with DOS-based Quattro in second place. The market share of 1-2-3 was unable to stand up to the assault of superior products. Excel's market share eventually surpassed that of 1-2-3, and it has been firmly in first place ever since.

Spreadsheet Quality

In the early and mid-1980s, the closest competitor to 1-2-3 in terms of reviews appears to be SuperCalc. David Stone, in *PC Magazine's* "Best of 1986" review (January 13, 1987, 115), had this to say: "If market dominance were based on rational criteria, Computer Associates' SuperCalc 4 would certainly replace 1-2-3 as the leading spreadsheet program. After all, it can do anything that 1-2-3 can do and adds some notable features of its own." But although various spreadsheets had attributes that were sometimes considered superior to 1-2-3's, there was no general consensus that any alternative was superior. For example, Michael Antonoff in *Personal Computing* (October 1987, 101) stated: "SuperCalc, VP-Planner, and Twin, lack the elegance of 1-2-3 in links to applications."

In late 1987, the quality of the competitors began to change. In a portentous statement, Jared Taylor in *PC Magazine* (November 10, 1987, 33) noted that "Microsoft Corp. has just unleashed a spreadsheet that makes 1-2-3 look like a rough draft." This reference was to Excel 1.0 for the PC, a port of its Macintosh program.

According to reviewers, Lotus appeared to fall behind its competitors in terms of functionality and usability. When comparing 1-2-3 to Excel, Michael Antonoff stated, "Excel offers a lot in the form of tantalizing features missing from the current version of 1-2-3" (*Personal Computing*, December 1987, 102). Mike Falkner called Quattro "a powerful spreadsheet with more features than 1-2-3 Release 2.01, yet fully compatible and a better price" (*PC Magazine*, December 12, 1987, 33).

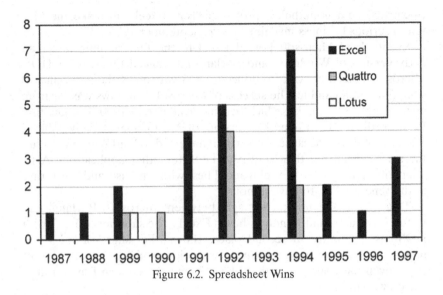

Figure 6.2. Spreadsheet Wins

These were not isolated opinions. Reviewers in general had a very high opinion of Excel in the late 1980s.[15] Clearly, Excel was thought to be the best spreadsheet.

The reason for Lotus's loss of prestige is illustrated better in Figure 6.2, which represents the number of times each spreadsheet won a comparison review in a year, or was identified in a magazine as the best product. Excel clearly was the winner over the ten-year period. Between 1989 and 1994, Quattro also managed a fair share of wins, although since 1994 Excel has monopolized the victories. The remarkable feature of this chart, however, is that over the entire ten-year period, Lotus 1-2-3 just barely avoids a shutout, managing but a single win out of the numerous instances where a magazine reviewer declared a winner.[16]

The message from these data is quite clear: Excel was clearly the leading spreadsheet in terms of capabilities. The main reservation about Excel was its need for powerful hardware. This last requirement was due to Excel's entirely graphical interface. As is the case with virtually all graphical software applications, Excel was slower to perform tasks than were DOS spreadsheets, even though it could show results that nongraphical (DOS) based applications could not. Once the hardware had caught up to the software (and Windows itself improved), there were no serious challengers to Excel's superiority.

---

[15] Excerpts from many reviews are provided in our book.
[16] We exclude the November 1993 issue of *InfoWorld* that gave Lotus the highest marks, because Excel was not included in the comparison.

The Role of Price

This brings us to another consideration: what about price? If we are interested in explaining changes in market share, we should expect both price and product quality to be important. If there are serious differences in the prices of competing products, a lower-quality but lower-priced product might have a larger market share than a higher-quality, higher-priced product.

The pattern of average prices received by the manufacturer is illustrated in Figure 6.3. Borland's price discount strategy is clearly revealed. Note also that Lotus kept its prices similar to Excel's even in the face of the latter's increasing market share (as we shall see shortly) and superior reviews. Lotus began clearly to undercut Microsoft's price only in 1996, well after it had fallen below Excel in terms of market share. But the big story is the stunning fall in prices. By 1997, the typical price (received by the vendor) for a spreadsheet had fallen to approximately $50, or a fall of over 80 percent, from the typical price in 1988.

Changes in Market Share: Analysis

The evidence indicates that if markets chose better products, Lotus should have lost market share and market dominance. After all, for a considerable period of time it was not the top-ranked product. The winner should have been Excel. Is this what happened? Absolutely. Figure 6.4 provides market share data (based on revenues) that reveals 1-2-3 losing its dominant position to Excel.

Other factors increased Excel's likelihood of success. Not only was it the best Windows spreadsheet, but it was the first Windows spreadsheet. It was also part of the first office suite, and it was part of the best office suite. Office suites and Windows were both strategic gambles by Microsoft that paid off handsomely. Given the superiority of Excel, this result should be viewed as support for the view that markets choose the better products.

These market share results do not provide any empirical confirmation for the idea of markets tipping. When a product has a small market share, network effects should work to hinder increases in market share, but beyond some breakout point network effects should work in favor of market share increases. This would tend to imply some form of bend or kink, where positively sloped market share curves are flatter to the left of the breakout point and steeper to the right. Instead, what we find is a fairly steady increase in Excel's market share and a fairly steady decrease in 1-2-3's. This may mean that network effects are just not a very important factor in this market, or that their impact on market share is more

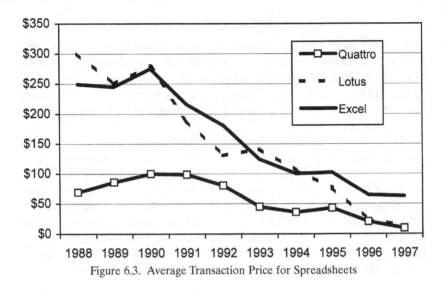

Figure 6.3. Average Transaction Price for Spreadsheets

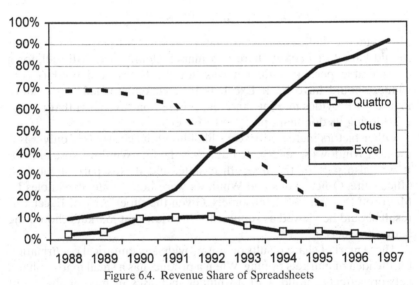

Figure 6.4. Revenue Share of Spreadsheets

complex than indicated in the concept of tipping. Either way, this does not bode well for the accuracy of the government's expert economists who discussed the concept of tipping with little or no skepticism.

There are some other issues worthy of examination. In a world of instant scalability, why did it take five years and not one, or two, for Lotus to be dethroned? We can offer some possible explanations. Users know that there is a tendency for software products to leapfrog each other in capabilities. It normally will not make sense for a consumer to switch products every time one product exceeds the capabilities of another, because of the costs of switching. Instead, it is rational for the consumer to expect that the next upgrade of a product that has fallen behind, but which has a history of technological innovation, to contain the features missing from the current version and perhaps even a few extra capabilities. Therefore, consumers will only switch when they cannot wait for the missing feature to appear in the next version of their current product, or when it becomes apparent that their current vendor has fallen behind the curve and will not be able to provide a product meeting their needs in the foreseeable future. It probably took two failed generations of products to convince the market that Lotus was not going to catch up to Excel anytime soon. Still, Excel averaged a gain of eight market share points a year, which by almost any other standard is quite amazing.

A second question that might arise in the mind of the reader is why Quattro never surpassed 1-2-3. It appears that we can categorize Quattro as a superior product to 1-2-3, even if it was inferior to Excel; however, Quattro might not have surpassed an inferior 1-2-3 for two reasons. First, if a 1-2-3 consumer was planning to switch, it would make more sense to switch to the number one product than to the number two product. Quattro's only advantage over Excel was its lower price.[17] Instant scalability gave Microsoft the chance to meet the demand of all defecting Lotus users without incurring increases in average cost. In markets without this feature, the number two firm likely would pick up some of the slack due to constraints in production for the leading firm. Second, between 1988 and 1995, when Quattro garnered superior reviews to Lotus, the gap with Lotus did diminish. It fell from a ratio of about 7:1 in sales to a ratio of 2:1. After that, however, Quattro no longer enjoyed clear superiority over 1-2-3.

Would the Lotus hegemony over spreadsheets have ended without the advent of Windows and office suites? Certainly some graphical user interface (GUI) was going to replace DOS, and spreadsheets were going to become graphical in nature. Given that Lotus was unable to produce a high-quality graphical spreadsheet, it would have lost the market to someone. Microsoft would have been a strong candidate to dethrone Lotus in any graphical environment because of Excel's total dominance in the Macintosh market.[18] If the market had gone to the Macintosh, where

---

[17] One finding that comes from examining the fuller set of products is that prices seem to play a very limited role, particularly for products sold to businesses. This might be due to the fact that training costs swamp software costs.

[18] Excel and Word had very dominant market positions in the Macintosh market long before their ascendance in the PC market.

Excel was clearly the dominant product, Lotus would have lost. If OS/2 had predominated, there is every reason to believe that the OS/2 version of Excel would have replaced 1-2-3. And if some third-party graphical operating system had prevailed on Intel based machines, there is every reason to suspect that Microsoft would have produced a better product than Lotus because of its familiarity with graphical products.

PERSONAL FINANCE SOFTWARE

Personal finance software allows individuals to balance their checkbooks, track their investments, and plan for the future. The software has become very easy to use and very inexpensive. The major players are Quicken by Intuit, Microsoft Money, and Managing Your Money by Meca. This market is particularly interesting because it is a market in which Microsoft is a major player but not the leader.

Network effects are probably smaller for these products than for many other software markets. Consumers generally are not interested in being able to exchange files with other individuals.[19] With the advent of the Internet, however, the possible compatibility of software with the offerings provided by one's banking institution has probably increased the level of network effects somewhat.

Personal finance products were introduced in the early to mid-1980s. "Andrew Tobias' Managing Your Money" was the original market leader, to be replaced by Quicken. Figure 6.5 shows the wins for the various products in the market. In the late 1980s Managing Your Money was initially considered the best and most powerful product in the category. When Quicken was introduced it received reviews that were less positive because it was not as powerful as Managing Your Money. It basically limited individuals to balancing their checkbooks and checking their budgets, but it did this quite well.[20] It also was less than one-third the price of Managing Your Money.[21]

Over time Intuit improved Quicken, adding more sophisticated features, and as Figure 6.5 reveals, by the early 1990s it was considered at least the equal of Managing Your Money. By the mid-1990s, Quicken was

---

[19] There is value for some individuals in being able to share these data with their accountants. There is an accepted file format for exchanging such information, however, that most products in the category follow.

[20] For example, in *PC Magazine*, September 1987, 482, we find the quote: "Quicken, the checkbook manager does one thing and does it well."

[21] The list price for Managing Your Money in the late 1980s was $220, and for Quicken was $60. According to Dataquest figures, the average price received by the vendor for Quicken in 1989 was $33 and for Managing Your Money was $110 (see tables 22 and 23 in the Dataquest data set: "Market Statistics 1994, Personal Computing Software Vendor Shipment and Revenue Data," June 6, 1994).

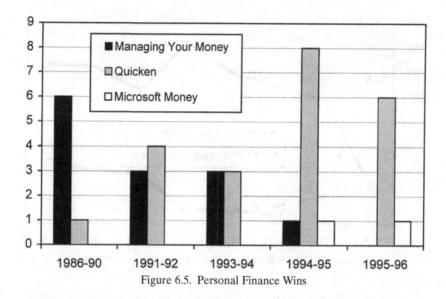

Figure 6.5. Personal Finance Wins

clearly considered the best product. Managing Your Money still appealed to those more interested in power – for example, tracking sophisticated investments as opposed to just ordinary stocks and bonds. Microsoft Money, which had recently appeared, appealed to those interested in simplicity.[22]

Figure 6.6 provides information on the market shares of the three leading products. This appears to be another case of one dominant firm followed by another dominant firm, what we have been calling serial monopoly. A market leader with 60 percent of the market is displaced within three years by another firm, which then achieves a market share of greater than 60 percent. The rapidity with which Quicken overtook Managing Your Money is astonishing, although the source of the data requires some caution on our part.[23] Still, market shares changed so

---

[22] For example: "But it's what Managing Your Money offers beyond basic banking that truly sets it apart from the rest. . . . The package provides the most comprehensive tax and financial planning and portfolio management of any product reviewed here. . . . This package is also the only real choice for active investors." *PC Magazine,* January 12, 1993, 258. Also: "If your needs are simple, you'll be especially happy with Money. Individuals who track investments or want to pay bills electronically should get one of the Quickens. . . . Those who want more than checkwriting – a total personal finance package – should consider Managing Your Money." *PC Magazine,* January 14, 1992, 42.

[23] Because of the large price differential, market shares based on revenues may give somewhat different results than those based on units sold, making is unclear exactly when Quicken began to dominate Managing Your Money. IDC has Quicken outselling

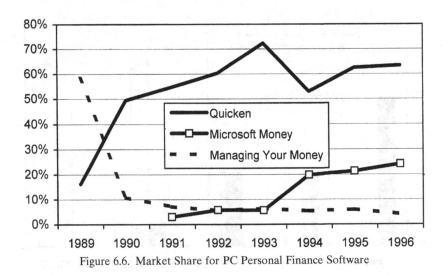

Figure 6.6. Market Share for PC Personal Finance Software

rapidly in this market that the concepts of inertia or lock-in seem entirely out of place. Also absent is any hint of tipping in this market.

There are some differences in the results found in this market from those found in other markets, however. It appears that Quicken became the leading product in the market when it had merely matched and before it had surpassed the quality of Managing Your Money. Figure 6.7, which represents the prices for the leading products, provides a possible explanation for Quicken's ascendancy before it surpassed the quality of Managing Your Money. The very high relative price of Managing Your Money is clearly apparent prior to 1992. Unlike many other software markets, this market caters to individuals as opposed to businesses. The retail price of Managing Your Money, being three times the price of Quicken, might well have deterred price-conscious individuals from choosing it when the two products were similar in quality and could well have led to the rapid demise of Managing Your Money.

By 1992, when the price of Managing Your Money was finally lowered to match the other programs in the personal-finance software category, it had lost its quality advantages. Also, Managing Your Money was hurt, as

Managing Your Money 8:1 in revenues and 25:1 in unit shipments by 1991. Dataquest reports almost identical unit sales for the two products in 1989 (a 10 percent edge to Managing Your Money), providing Managing Your Money a 3.5:1 edge in revenues. For 1990, however, Dataquest gives Quicken a 15:1 edge in sales and 4:1 edge in revenues in 1990. *Money Magazine*, November 1988, states that Quicken "does only check-writing and budgeting, but outsells the rest" (47). By 1990 Quicken was clearly ahead of Managing Your Money in unit sales and most likely in revenues.

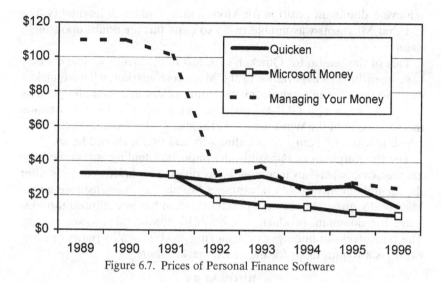

Figure 6.7. Prices of Personal Finance Software

were so many other products that we have examined in other markets, by the absence of a timely Windows version of the product; it was not until 1994 that a Windows version of Managing Your Money arrived.

We can conclude that consumers preferred Quicken's low price, simplicity, and checkbook handling to the sophisticated financial management and much higher price of Managing Your Money.

In 1991 Microsoft introduced its Money program for Windows. Unlike many of the market leaders in other applications markets, Intuit had a Windows product as early as Microsoft. In fact, Quicken's initial share of the Windows market was actually greater than its share of the DOS market. Quicken's market share in the Windows market ranged between 70 and 80 percent in the early 1990s, and was some 10 to 20 points higher than its overall market share.

Microsoft has gained market share throughout the decade, but not from Quicken. Instead, its Windows product has replaced products in the DOS market. Microsoft's share of the Windows market has remained virtually unchanged, having actually fallen slightly since 1991. Microsoft also has had a lower price than its competitors since 1992, perhaps taking its cue from some reviewers who argued that, because it was less powerful than its competitors, it should have a lower price.

Quicken's retention of its market leadership is not surprising given its high quality as indicated in successive reviews. According to those who argue that Microsoft's success is assured by leverage, Microsoft should have been able to leverage its ownership of the operating system to achieve a dominant position for Money, independent of its quality. The fact that Microsoft was unable to do so casts further doubt upon these claims.

Part of the reason for Quicken's success in the Windows market may have been Intuit's experience in the Macintosh market, where Quicken was also the leading program, giving Intuit a clear understanding in how to write a successful GUI application.[24] This appears to be a common theme: success in the Windows market is presaged by success in the Macintosh market. Of course, it is entirely logical that it should be so.

For the purposes of our study, the important finding is that we have another case where an incumbent was quickly replaced, but only after the incumbent lost quality advantages. We also have an instance where Microsoft's ownership of the operating system has not allowed it to dislodge the dominant product, in spite of its considerably lower pricing. This reinforces our findings that achieving product quality parity or superiority is a requirement for increased market share.

BROWSERS

Browsers are products that allow PC owners to access the World Wide Web (WWW). The software category is relatively new since the WWW is a relatively recent phenomenon. As late as October 1994, this market was largely unformed.

Mosaic (created by the University of Illinois's National Center for Supercomputing Applications) was the first successful browser. As *PC Magazine* reported in early 1995:

NCSA's Mosaic was the first Windows-based Web browser – the killer app that started the stampede to the Web. Today, largely as a result of its stellar success, the browser field is in furious ferment, with new products released weekly and existing ones updated sometimes hourly. Browsers are even making it into operating-systems: IBM includes a browser with OS/2 Warp, Version 3, and Microsoft plans one for Windows 95.[25]

The first magazine reviews of browsers that we found were in mid-1994. Netscape, which was formed by some former programmers of Mosaic, introduced Navigator in late 1994. As far as we can tell, magazine reviews considered Navigator to be better than Mosaic from the day of its introduction. Both products were free. Internet Explorer, Microsoft's entry in this market, makes its first (beta) appearance in our magazine reviews in September 1995.

---

[24] Intuit had the Macintosh program with the leading market share as early as 1988, when our data on this market begin.

[25] "Web Browsers: The Web untangled." *PC Magazine,* February 7, 1995, 192.

Because the browser "market" began as freeware, and largely continues as freeware, it is a somewhat unusual market in that there are no direct revenues. This is not, however, any different than the over-the-air television market, where stations do not generate any revenues from their viewers. Instead, television stations pay for their programming by selling advertising, and browser companies appear to have adopted a similar model. Revenues can come either from the sale of servers, which send out the information retrieved by browsers, or by selling advertising from the sites to which browsers initially go.[26] Although consumers can easily change the website that is the starting location for the browser, continued patronage of the original location (which is believed likely to occur) would provide considerable advertising revenues to the company that created the browser.[27]

The market for browsers is of great interest because of its role in the Department of Justice (DoJ) antitrust proceedings against Microsoft. The claims made by Justice are that Microsoft's inclusion of its browser with the operating system has foreclosed Netscape's ability to generate market share, independent of the quality of the browsers. The government is claiming that Microsoft's bundling of the browser into Windows 98 has caused the erosion of market share that has been Netscape's recent fate.

Given our findings in other software markets that market share is strongly related to product quality, we would expect a similar relationship to hold here. In fact, because all browsers have essentially the same price (zero), there are fewer other factors at work that might disturb this relationship.[28] In light of results from other markets, we can try to answer

---

[26] When a browser is first activated, it goes to a preordained location (e.g., Netscape's or Microsoft's home page), just as a television or radio tuner, when turned on, will be set for some frequency that may contain a station. The difference is that the browser is set to receive information from a web page that exists, whereas radio and television frequencies vary by city and thus may or may not be tuned to an actual station when first turned on.

[27] According to a survey in *Family PC Magazine,* "About 38 percent set their start-up page to a site they found surfing, while 15 percent made their own start page. Most people grow so accustomed to their start-up page they never change it." The survey also examined where readers obtained their browsers, an issue of some importance given the DoJ claim that inclusion on the opening screen was crucial: "When asked where they got their browser, 42 percent said they downloaded it, 32 percent got it from their ISP, and 12 percent said it came with their computer." "Browsers," *Family PC Magazine* (on line), October 1, 1998.

[28] Netscape originally gave its Navigator browser away but later, after it achieved a dominant market share, charged a positive price. After Microsoft's Internet Explorer, which was free, began making serious inroads into Netscape's market share, Netscape again began to give its browser away.

the following question: has Microsoft's browser achieved a market share incommensurate with the share that might be expected given the relative quality of its browser?

Figure 6.8 indicates the wins in the browser "market" since 1995. Because this market is so new, the time span is compressed, with intervals of six months as opposed to the one- or two-year intervals in prior charts. Still, the trend is very clear. Netscape Navigator was clearly considered the best product until the second half of 1996, after which Internet Explorer became the superior product.[29]

The time frame is compressed once again in Figure 6.9, which provides information on the market shares of the two products.[30] Market share here is measured differently than in other markets. Instead of measuring sales, which is the flow of new products into an already installed base, market share here reflects installed base. However, information on browser use also indicates that most browsers in use are of very recent vintage, so that stock and flow magnitudes are likely to be very similar.

The actual increase in Internet Explorer's market share has been a matter of some contention. Microsoft relied on a survey that indicated a relatively small increase in Internet Explorer's market share, and the government relied on browser usage data, which tend to reveal a considerably larger increase in Internet Explorer's market share. There are serious difficulties impeding an unambiguous measurement of browser usage, including the fact that many Internet service providers (ISPs) "cache" popular web sites and that some ISPs, such as AOL, put their own brand on someone else's browser. Nevertheless, it is clear that Internet Explorer has increased its market share. The Zona survey, on which Figure 6.9 is based, indicates one of the larger increases in Internet Explorer's market share as compared with other sources.

This increase in Internet Explorer's market share has occurred concomitantly with Internet Explorer's quality improvements relative to Netscape Navigator. Internet Explorer's market share barely grew at all, even though it was freely distributed with Windows and on the Internet, until after July 1996. This would be the same period of time where Internet Explorer first achieved parity with Netscape in product reviews. This is also the first time that Internet Explorer appears to have taken market share away from Netscape, which had previously experienced continued growth in market share.

---

[29] A similar document was entered into the court record in the direct testimony of Microsoft witness Richard Schmalensee.

[30] These data come from Zona Research, which conducts periodic surveys.

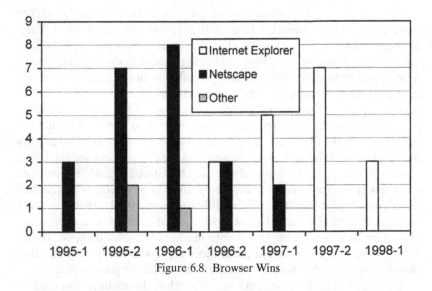

Figure 6.8. Browser Wins

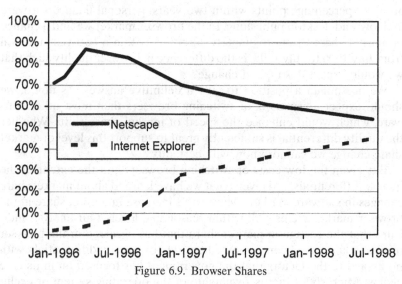

Figure 6.9. Browser Shares

The degree of superiority of Microsoft Internet Explorer after 1997, as indicated in the reviews summarized in Figure 6.8, has in our examinations of other markets always led to increased market share and even market dominance. Is there any reason to expect different results in this market?

There are several reasons that we might expect more rapid market share changes in this market than in the typical software market. First, network effects seem rather small in this market because there is little interactivity between users that might cause users to care who else uses their brand of browser. Second, compatibility with prior versions seems unimportant, since learning the idiosyncrasies of a particular browser takes far less time than learning a spreadsheet, word processor, or desktop publishing program. Further, there is less reason to worry about incompatibility with the files created by these programs since generally the only files that remain through multiple generations of browsers are the list of "favorite" sites, and these are fairly easily translated. Finally, the price of browsers is zero, and users presumably already have access to the free downloads available on the web, because browsers are of no value without Internet access. For these two reasons, instant scalability is even more important here than in other software markets. We should expect, therefore, that market shifts would occur more rapidly in the browser market than almost any other software market that we have encountered.

There are two other markets where market shares have changed by 50 or 60 percentage points within two years: personal finance software and low-end desktop publishing. In the browser market we find a change in market share of approximately 40 points within a two-year interval from July 1996 to July 1998. Is the difference in browser quality such that we would expect this type of change?

We are not in a position to give a definitive answer. As noted, we should expect lower costs of switching browsers than most other software, which would enhance the speed of market share shifts. Whether the quality differential is sufficiently great to support this level of market share change we cannot know with certainty.

But given the low costs of switching browsers and the extent of the quality differentials, and given what we have learned about market share changes in software markets, Microsoft's increase in market share in the browser market seems well within reasonable levels. Our analysis indicates that the change in market share that has occurred in the browser market could have been explained entirely by quality differentials, with no appeal to the factors that the government has focused on in its case against Microsoft – that is, ownership of the operating system or exclusionary contracts.

This is another market that does not seem to exhibit either inertia or tipping. Because network effects should be small in this market, however, it might not be a very strong test of lock-in or the tipping hypothesis.

Currently, Internet Explorer appears to have built up a considerable lead in market share, at least in terms of usage, although some data services do not agree.[31] As long as Internet Explorer retains its advantage in quality, our analysis of other markets indicates that Internet Explorer will continue to take share away from Netscape – whether or not it is included in the operating system.

MICROSOFT, MONOPOLY, AND CONSUMER HARM

Monopolists cause harm to consumers by reducing output and raising price. Although there has been much talk about Microsoft's impact on innovation, there is no clear relationship between monopoly and innovation, nor any data to test such assertions. The question of whether Microsoft acts like a monopolist and whether it causes harm to consumers in the traditional, well-tested context should be crucial to the current DoJ case. What is the evidence?

In the sections that follow we examine the price history in various software markets. Putting several disparate pieces of this pricing puzzle together makes, we believe, a persuasive case for concluding that Microsoft has not harmed consumers.

Word Processor and Spreadsheet Prices

Figure 6.10 reports average prices for the two largest markets, spreadsheets and word processors (in the PC, or IBM-compatible, market). The most relevant feature of this chart is the very large overall fall in prices, as already noted. This fall in prices is not constant throughout the period, however. From 1986 until 1992, prices were either constant or rising slightly in the word-processing market. From 1986 until 1990 prices were essentially constant in the spreadsheet market. Beginning in 1991 or 1992 prices fell in a very dramatic fashion. What is the proper interpretation of these price declines?

It will suffice for the moment to describe the early period as the Lotus era in spreadsheets and the WordPerfect era in word processing. Although any firm, including Microsoft, had considerable pricing latitude even when it had a small share of the market, it is likely the case that the profit-maximizing strategy was to follow the price set by the leader in the market. This conclusion is reinforced by our finding that, except in markets catering to individuals, price differentials were rather ineffective at generating additional market share.

---

[31] In November 1999 information from the Web Counter, based on approximately 450 million hits a month and 475,000 web pages (many pornographic, though), indicated that Internet Explorer had 76% of the market to Netscape's 19%. In March 1999, the same site reported that Internet Explorer had 68% of the usage market to Netscape's 31%. On the other hand, SuperStats, based on a smaller sample, found that Internet Explorer had 53% and Netscape had 42%, with AOL receiving 5%, but it is unclear what the AOL browser is.

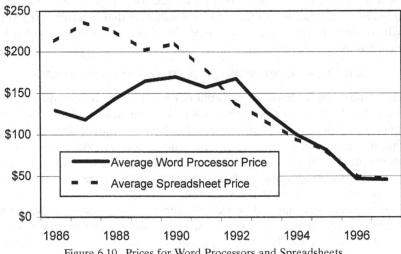

Figure 6.10. Prices for Word Processors and Spreadsheets

Figure 6.10 provides information on price changes. Monopoly and competition differ in the level of prices, but neither model implies persistent price changes. If the market were moving from a less competitive to a more competitive market equilibrium, however, prices would be expected to fall during the transition. If Lotus and WordPerfect tried to use their large market shares to generate short-run monopoly profits, and Microsoft did not, we would expect prices to fall as the markets stopped taking its cues from WordPerfect and Lotus and instead started to take their cues from Microsoft. Once the new regime was in place, prices should have stabilized at their new lower level, ceteris paribus.

If Microsoft believed that Lotus and WordPerfect lost their dominant positions because they failed to act competitively, it might have chosen a competitive price even after it achieved a dominant market share. That appears to be what has happened because there is no evidence of prices rising even after market shares above 99 percent are achieved, as in the Macintosh spreadsheet market. This pattern of Microsoft's behavior occurred in some other markets such as midrange desktop publishing that we do not cover in this chapter.

By itself, this evidence might be suggestive, but would fall short of a sufficient basis on which to draw conclusions. Combined with the evidence in the next two sections, however, there is a compelling case to be told in favor of Microsoft.

Microsoft's Overall Impact on Prices

One question that naturally arises in regard to pricing is how the markets examined in this study compare to markets overall. After all, it is possible that the pricing pattern in Figure 6.10 was reproduced in many other markets and had nothing to do with Microsoft's increased market share. We were able to perform a somewhat crude test of this claim. Dataquest provides consistent market definitions for fourteen software markets for the contiguous period 1988–95.[32] We calculated the average revenue for each category for each year. We assume that changes in category-wide average revenue moves in concert with individual product prices.[33]

Next, we categorized markets into three main groups: one group of markets where Microsoft has a product, one group where Microsoft has no product, and a third group where the products compete with some function of Microsoft's operating system.[34] All prices are normalized to their 1988 levels to simplify comparisons.[35] The results, shown in Figure 6.11, are rather striking. Although it appears that software prices in general have fallen over this period of time, some software prices have fallen far more than others. In particular, those categories where Microsoft participates, directly or indirectly, have had far more dramatic declines than in other markets, falling by approximately 60 percent compared with the relatively paltry 15 percent fall in prices for software in markets completely devoid of Microsoft's influence.

---

[32] The categories are: desktop publishing, accounting, draw and paint, forms, utilities/application, communication, personal finance, presentation graphics, spreadsheets, word processors, database, project management, integrated software. We proxied for separate desktop publishing categories by putting Microsoft into midrange and everyone else into high-end.

[33] Average "prices" calculated in this manner might not reflect actual prices. For example, shifts across products within a category might change the average price even if each price remained constant. We assume that such shifts are either minimal, or similar across product categories.

[34] The categories where Microsoft competes are midrange desktop publishing, personal finance, presentation graphics, spreadsheets, word processors, database, project management, and integrated software. The categories where Microsoft does not have an entrant are accounting, draw and paint, high-end desktop publishing, and forms. The categories that compete with the operating system are utilities/application and communication.

[35] Average prices are calculated as weighted averages, weighted by the revenues in each market. Unweighted average prices were also calculated and found to be almost identical.

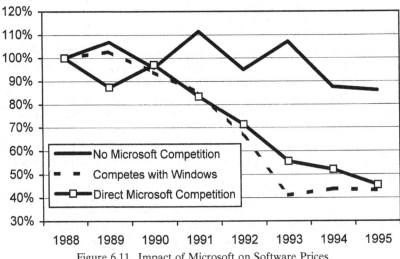

Figure 6.11. Impact of Microsoft on Software Prices

PC–Macintosh Price Comparison

The data allow one more interesting price comparison. We can compare prices for the same product in two markets with very different market shares. That is, we can compare Microsoft Word and Microsoft Excel in both the PC and the Macintosh markets.

Figure 6.12 provides market shares for these two products in the PC and Macintosh markets. Examination reveals that Microsoft achieved very high market shares in the Macintosh market even while it was still struggling in the PC market. On average, Microsoft's market share was about 40 to 60 percentage points higher in the Macintosh market than in the PC market in the 1988–90 period.[36] Not until 1996 was Microsoft able to equal in the PC market its success in the Macintosh market. These facts can be used to discredit a claim sometimes heard that Microsoft achieved success in applications only because it owned the operating system. Apple, not Microsoft, owned the Macintosh operating system and Microsoft actually competed with Apple products in these application markets.

Microsoft's market share in the late 1980s in the Macintosh market is generally higher than the market shares achieved by Lotus or WordPerfect in the PC market. Microsoft's market share by the mid-1990s in the

---

[36] This chart only examines Word for Windows, and ignores Word for DOS. The latter had a 13% and 16% market share in 1988 and 1989, respectively.

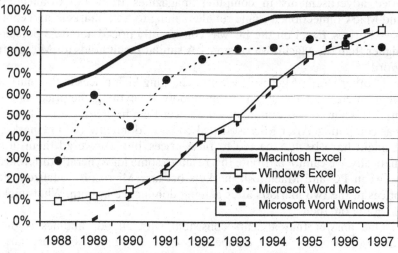

Figure 6.12. Excel and Word in Macintosh and PC Markets

Macintosh market was considerably higher than any leading firm in the DOS era. To a structuralist, Microsoft would appear to enjoy a monopoly in the Macintosh market. One might expect, therefore, that its prices in the Macintosh market to be at least as great as its prices in the PC market. Additionally, because it was trying to increase its market share in the PC market in the late 1980s, one might think that its prices there would be considerably lower than where it already had a "monopoly" market share.[37] Those holding a structural view of monopoly, therefore, might expect Microsoft to charge a higher price in the Macintosh market and a lower price in the PC market.[38]

Although there is some imprecision in the data,[39] the price comparisons suggest the exact opposite of this. PC Excel, far from being cheaper, in fact averages 13 percent higher prices than its Macintosh cousin during the period 1988–92. PC Word's price, on average, was more than 80 percent above the price for Macintosh Word prior to 1993. After that, the prices are virtually the same. To double check this result, we went to

[37] We have noted that low prices were not terribly effective at generating market share when the product was not the best, but they should be more effective when the product is the best.

[38] E.g., the followers of Joe Bain. See about half the papers in Goldschmid, Mann, and Weston (1974), which is largely a debate between followers of the Chicago School and Bain's disciples.

[39] We were forced to use Dataquest data for the late 1980s even though the price values are too variable to generate much confidence. That is why we looked for alternative sources.

price advertisements in computer magazines from PC Connection and Mac Connection, a single retailer selling to both markets, and compared prices. Excel on the PC was consistently priced about 33 percent higher than the Macintosh version.[40] A similar result holds for Microsoft Word.

In other words, Microsoft was not charging high prices in the market where it clearly has a structural monopoly. If anything, the prices in the market where it was dominant were lower than in the markets where it was competing. After Microsoft had come to dominate the PC market, it might have been expected to raise prices, but it lowered them dramatically. We cannot attribute this result to some idiosyncratic difference between PC and Macintosh markets because Microsoft equalized the prices in the two markets after gaining dominance in both. What might be going on, then?

One answer that appears consistent with all our findings is that Microsoft worries about competitors even when it has a very large market share. Such concern about potential entrants might explain why Microsoft has not lost any markets it has gained. The decline of DOS market leaders might have been partly due to an erroneous lack of such concern.

CONCLUSIONS

The concept of network effects has been a cudgel in the government's case against Microsoft and has been given a prominent place in Judge Jackson's finding of fact. The government's use of network effects requires that certain assumptions be true for the case to make economic sense. This chapter has opened a window into the workings of software markets. To our knowledge, ours is the first systematic examination of these markets. The results have run counter to much of the conventional wisdom.

The lack of evidence claims of market inertia and tipping should raise red flags to analysts of these markets who have treated these untested claims as established facts. The rapidity of market share changes should cause believers in market inertia to take pause. Also, the concept of tipping, which seems so reasonable in principle, seems to have no support if tipping is to mean that self-reinforcing mechanisms accelerate rates of change.

The rapid changes in market share and the close relationship between these changes and product quality that was demonstrated in this chapter

---

[40] In June 1990 Excel and Microsoft Word for Windows were both $329 while both products for the Macintosh were $245. In 1989 Macintosh Word and Excel were both $255 while Excel for Windows was $319. In 1988 both products were $249 in the Macintosh market, but Excel was $319 in the PC market.

for three markets was repeatedly found in our other work. The large and rapid changes in market shares are counter to the claim that dominant firms become locked in. In this chapter we have seen instances of a once-dominant firm that faded into obscurity, including Managing Your Money and Lotus 1-2-3 (and, elsewhere, WordPerfect, PageMaker, Ventura, First Publisher, and Prodigy). In some instances, the product that replaced these onetime leaders was a product from Microsoft; in other instances, it was from some other company. In each instance, however, the product that replaced the incumbent was of higher quality and often cheaper.

The evidence makes clear that the most important factor for replacing an incumbent firm is to produce a better product. Other factors are undoubtedly also important, but just getting a product to the starting line of a new race was unlikely to be successful if the product was not of high quality. Sometimes price played a role, although it appeared to have a surprisingly small role (perhaps because price changes were often mimicked by other firms). Also of interest was the finding that being number two was of little value. Virtually all the shift in market share seemed to go to the number one product as measured by quality.

The other important finding is the remarkable track record of Microsoft in terms of producing better products at low prices. Although it has been suggested that Microsoft did not earn its large market shares in applications, we have found the evidence to be at complete variance with this suggestion. In those instances where Microsoft moved from a low to a high market share, its products were clearly better than the previous market leader's. When its products were not superior, Microsoft did not make inroads against the market leader.

It has been suggested that Microsoft has used it monopoly position to refrain from lowering prices. Any claim that Microsoft harms consumers through monopolistic pricing is wholly at odds with the evidence we have uncovered. Microsoft appears to have a regime of low prices in markets it has come to dominate. Naturally, Microsoft also had to hurt its competitors by these actions.

It is true that the government has focused on the operating system and not on applications, although the states involved in the case had attempted to bring the application market into the case and seemed only to lack sufficient time to do so. Evidence on Microsoft's pricing of the operating system, although largely given behind closed doors, does not seem to be contrary to our findings in applications markets and does not seem capable of answering the basic question of monopoly power. As we have stated before, monopoly does not imply rising prices, only high prices.

We conclude that the use of network effects in antitrust cases appears to be unwarranted in the software industry. We also believe that Judge

Jackson was mistaken in his findings of fact, which clearly signal that he is going to find Microsoft guilty of monopoly behavior. (As we go to press, Judge Jackson has so ruled.) Because there is no evidence in any other industry indicating that network effects have the pernicious effects that have been so often attributed them, we believe that it is unwise for network effects to be granted any role in antitrust whatsoever.

REFERENCES

Brynjolfsson, Erik, and Chris F. Kemerer. 1996. Network Externalities in Micro-computer Software: An Econometric Analysis of the Spreadsheet Market. *Management Science* 42: 1627–47.

Byte. Various issues.

David, Paul A. 1985. Clio and the Economics of QWERTY. *American Economic Review* 75: 332–37.

Family PC Magazine. Various issues.

Farrell, J., and G. Saloner. 1985. Standardization, Compatibility, and Innovation. *Rand Journal of Economics* 16: 70–83.

Gandal, N. 1994. Hedonic Price Indexes for Spreadsheets: An Empirical Test for Network Externalities. *Rand Journal of Economics* 25: 160–70.

Goldschmid, H. J., H. M. Mann, and J. F. Weston. 1974. *Industrial Concentration: The New Learning.* Boston: Little, Brown.

Info World. Various issues.

International Data Corp. "PC Spreadsheet Market Review and Forecast, 1996–2001."

Kobayashi, B., and L. Ribstein. 1996. Evolutions of Spontaneous Uniformity: Evidence from the Evolution of the Limited Liability Company. *Economic Inquiry* 34: 464–83.

Liebowitz, S. J., and S. E. Margolis. 1990. The Fable of the Keys. *Journal of Law and Economics* 33: 1–26.

    1995. Path Dependence, Lock-In and History. *Journal of Law, Economics, and Organization* 11: 205–26.

    1999. *Winners, Losers, and Microsoft: Competition and Antitrust in High Technology.* Oakland, CA: Independent Institute.

Money Magazine. Various issues.

PC Magazine. Various issues.

PC World. Various issues.

Personal Computing. Various issues.

Reback, Gary, Susan Creighton, David Killam, and Neil Nathanson, with the assistance of Garth Saloner and W. Brian Arthur. 1995. Technological, Economic and Legal Perspectives Regarding Microsoft's Business Strategy in Light of the Proposed Acquisition of Intuit, Inc. *Upside Magazine,* February.

7

Technological Standards, Innovation, and Essential Facilities

Toward a Schumpeterian Post-Chicago Approach

Richard N. Langlois

> Political controversy to one side, new technology should not
> be allowed to obscure an old truth. The basic problem is
> a rerun of the issues for rails and telecommunications: can
> outsiders connect to the network?
>
> Richard Epstein (1998)

Economics is a conservative discipline. Even its revolutions do not stray far from basic accepted principles, and sometimes they merely reassert basic accepted principles. The Chicago School of antitrust analysis scored victory after victory over the Harvard School by an assiduous application of static neoclassical price theory.[1] A new challenger, the so-called post-Chicago approach, accepts the same basic principles, even as it dresses them up in the elegant if improbable clothes of mathematical game theory.[2] What unites these approaches is a devotion to a concept of competition oriented fundamentally around price and quantity. Other dimensions of competition may sneak in, such as competition for "quality" in the abstract. But price theory deals poorly with what is arguably the central impulse of actually existing competition: technological change. "In capitalist reality as distinguished from the textbook picture," wrote Joseph Schumpeter (1950), the most important form of competition arises not from competition "within a rigid pattern of invariant conditions, methods of production and forms of industrial organization," but rather from "the new commodity, the new technology, the new source of supply, the new type of organization . . . competition which commands a decisive cost or quality advantage and which strikes not at the margins of the profits and the outputs of existing firms but at their foundations and their very lives."

---

[1] See note 23, and surrounding text.
[2] See note 28, and surrounding text.

In this chapter, I attempt to take Schumpeter's perspective seriously. Drawing on literatures that concern themselves centrally with the patterns and processes of technological change, I focus on a set of issues very much on the present-day agenda: antitrust policy toward network industries in which technological standards are important. As both scholars and legal cases have suggested, one might logically view a set of standards as an "essential facility" – a technological bottleneck – for those who wish to connect to the network.

Scholars have for the most part displayed skepticism if not hostility to the essential facility doctrine on both legal and economic grounds.[3] The doctrine adds nothing new to the legal arsenal, critics have claimed, nor does the idea draw on any economic insights not gained from a traditional analysis of monopoly behavior. It is a central contention of this chapter that there is a distinctive logic to a doctrine of essential facilities. But that logic becomes clear only by moving beyond standard price-theoretic accounts of the behavior of firms to consider head-on the phenomenon of innovation. The pace and direction of innovation may not be the central issue in all "bottleneck" cases. But when technological standards are involved, we can presume that the dimension of technological change will typically be at least as important as those of price and quantity.

In what follows I attempt to define the limits of the standard price-theoretic account for understanding the problem of essential facilities and offer instead a perspective drawing on the theory of property rights in a regime of innovation. Contrary to what is suggested by traditional economic analysis, I argue that, as a logical matter, refusals to deal by essential facility monopolists are not always equivalent to the exercise of existing monopoly power through price, and there are good theoretical reasons for an essential facility doctrine to concern itself with refusals to deal even when it fails to touch other exercises of market power by a legally acquired monopoly. I introduce the concept of the *scope* of an essential facility, understood in analogy with a similar concept in the economics of patents, and suggest that the degree to which antitrust policy should concern itself with the ownership or control of a technical standard ought to be proportional to the scope of the standard.

At the same time, however, a Schumpeterian perspective reminds us that, in a world of dynamic technological competition, even possession of a standard with wide scope may afford only temporary protection, and the winds of Schumpeterian creative destruction may be a better bulwark against monopoly than the cumbersome and interest-laden processes of antitrust law and policy. Nonetheless, the notion of the scope

---

[3] See, e.g., Areeda (1990), Ratner (1988), Reiffen and Kleit (1990), and Gerber (1988).

of a standard may prove useful in many cases, including those involving regulated (or formerly regulated) industries or involving tradeoffs in intellectual property rights.

BACKGROUND

Since the early 1980s, a doctrine of "essential facilities" has gained popularity in legal argument and judicial decision making. Broadly speaking, the doctrine is this: "an owner of a crucial input cannot deny access if a firm seeking access cannot practicably obtain the input elsewhere" (Ratner 1988: 330).[4] Most accounts trace the idea to the 1912 case of *United States v. Terminal Railroad Association*, in which a consortium that included financier Jay Gould controlled railroad facilities for crossing the Mississippi at St. Louis.[5] The doctrine has also surfaced in cases involving such "bottleneck" inputs as a professional sports stadium, warehouse space in Providence, Rhode Island, and a joint marketing arrangement for Colorado ski slopes.[6]

Recently, however, a number of cases have emerged in which the facility claimed essential is in the nature of technological knowledge and in which the access desired is in the nature of connection to a network.[7] This category includes a number of cases involving physical networks like electricity or telecommunications, where there are clear elements of natural monopoly and the presence of explicit regulation.[8] More interestingly, perhaps, there have also been cases in which plaintiffs have desired access to what is in effect a "virtual" network – that is, a network in which participants are linked together by their economic complementarity and adherence to common technological standards rather than by physical interconnection. Two examples have involved the Eastman

---

[4] Epstein (1998: 302) cites a more expansive formulation: "The essential facilities doctrine requires a firm with monopoly power in one market to deal equitably with competing firms operating in adjacent markets that depend on it for essential inputs." See also Kellogg, Thornes, and Huber (1992). The distinction between merely granting access and "dealing equitably" is an important one to which I return.

[5] 224 U.S. 383 (1912). For an analysis of this case, see Reiffen and Kleit (1990).

[6] *Hecht v. Pro-Football, Inc.*, 570 F.2d 982 (D.C. Cir. 1977), *cert. denied*, 436 U.S. 956 (1978); *Gamco, Inc. v. Providence Fruit and Produce Bldg., Inc.*, 194 F.2d 484 (1st Cir.), *cert. denied*, 344 U.S. 817 (1952); and *Aspen Skiing Co. v. Aspen Highlands Skiing Corp.*, 472 U.S. 585 (1985).

[7] See *BellSouth Advertising v. Donnelley Information Publishing*, 719 F.Supp. 1551, 1566 (S.D. Fla. 1988). ("Although the doctrine of essential facilities has been applied predominantly to tangible assets, there is no reason why it could not apply . . . to information wrongfully withheld. The effect in both situations is the same: a party is prevented from sharing in something essential to compete.")

[8] *Otter Tail Power Co. v. United States*, 410 U.S. 366 (1973); *MCI Communications Corp. v. Am. Tel. & Tel. Co.*, 708 F.2d 1081 (7th Cir. 1983), *cert. denied*, 464 U.S. 891 (1983).

Kodak Company. In one case, a competitor in the production of film sued for access to the technical specifications for a new camera Kodak was developing, arguing that Kodak's dominance in film conferred on it the ability to set a universal standard for film and that conformance to such a standard was essential for any competitor.[9] More recently, the Supreme Court considered a case involving Kodak's refusal to sell replacement parts for its photocopiers to customers who purchased repair services from firms other than Kodak itself.[10] Because parts are standardized to a particular brand of copier, competing repair organizations are "locked in" to Kodak's standards for parts, plaintiffs argued, which standards then become an essential facility.

There is reason to think that cases involving technical standards as essential facilities are likely to rise in prominence with the continued advance of microelectronics and the Internet. One can clearly read many aspects of the ongoing cases against Microsoft as involving implicit (and sometimes explicit) claims that the technical standards of a computer operating system constitute an essential facility. And a federal district court recently granted a preliminary injunction to a maker of computer workstations that had claimed (among other things) that Intel's refusal to provide timely information on the specifications of its newest microprocessors amounted to foreclosure of an essential facility.[11]

Richard Epstein (1998) has recently given attention to the doctrine of essential facilities within a broader discussion of the law and economics of common carriers. In general, he argues, rights of private property and freedom of contract constitute an institutional structure superior to that of government regulation, because (among other reasons) competition can usually be counted on to limit the arbitrary or exploitive exercise of private property rights. But in situations of impacted monopoly, notably those in which one contracting party controls facilities with the character of a public good, an exception to the general rule arises. Epstein argues that Anglo-American common law has always been sensitive to this exception, and that one of its important responses has been the law of common carriers. Broadly speaking, that body of law requires owners of bottleneck facilities to grant access on reasonable and nondiscrimi-

---

[9] *Berkey Photo Inc. v. Eastman Kodak Co.*, 603 F.2d 263 (2d Cir. 1979), *cert. denied*, 444 U.S. 1093 (1980).

[10] *Image Technical Serv., Inc. v. Eastman Kodak Co.*, 903 F.2d 612, 616 n.3 (9th Cir. 1990), *aff'd*, 112 S. Ct. 2072 (1992). A district court had issued a summary judgment in favor of Kodak, which was overturned on appeal. The Supreme Court upheld the reversal.

[11] *Intergraph Corp. v. Intel Corp.*, CV 97-N-3023-NE (N. D. Ala.) 1998. The Federal Circuit vacated the injunction on November 5, 1999. See *Intergraph Corp. v. Intel Corp.*, 98–1308, Fed. Cir.

natory terms.[12] Historic examples included coaches and inns; modern examples include railroads and oil pipelines.

The doctrine of essential facilities thus constitutes a kind of special case of the logic of common carriers. As such, it has an intellectual heritage that stretches back before *Terminal Railroad*. Epstein points to the 1810 English case of *Allnut v. Inglis*.[13] Here the plaintiff, a wine importer, refused to pay the fee asked by a London customs warehouse that had the exclusive right to store wine from overseas. Finding for the plaintiff, Lord Ellenborough held that, although in general "every man may fix what price he pleases upon his own property or the use of it," the possessor of a monopoly, "if he will take the benefit of the monopoly, . . . must as an equivalent perform the duty attached to it on reasonable terms."[14]

Such a duty is especially clear in the case of a statutory monopoly like the customs warehouse in *Allnut*. Here the duty of a common carrier arises in essence out of contract: as part of the acceptance of a monopoly from the government, one agrees to serve all comers on reasonable and nondiscriminatory terms.[15] Nonetheless, the law following *Allnut* viewed de facto as well as de jure monopoly as potentially falling under the principles of common carriers, even though the de facto case raises difficult issues both of practice and of concept. In the words of a seventeenth-century treatise cited in *Allnut*, even private monopoly can sometimes be "affected with the public interest."[16]

The problem of de facto monopoly arises also in present-day application of an essential facility doctrine. Although the doctrine has featured in cases with a clear regulatory contract,[17] in most cases the facility claimed essential has been under strictly private control. From the perspective of antitrust law, it is not so much the private character of the monopoly that is the issue as it is the extent to which the bottle-. neck monopoly was legally acquired. It is a well-established principle,

---

[12] Reinterpreting this in economic terms, a common carrier cannot refuse to deal, cannot price discriminate, and (depending on one's interpretation) cannot charge a full monopoly price.

[13] 12 East 525, 104 Eng. Rep. 206 (K. B. 1810).

[14] Ibid. at 538, 104 Eng. Rep. at 210–11, cited in Epstein (1998: 283).

[15] The idea of a "regulatory contract" has lately come into policy discourse in the context of the widespread deregulation of industries once thought of (and regulated) as natural monopolies. To the extent that such deregulation involves a repudiation by the government of its end of the deal (the statutory monopoly), deregulation may involve a taking under the meaning of the Constitution. See, e.g., Sidak and Spulber (1996).

[16] Lord Matthew Hale (1609–76), De Portibus Mari (posthumously published in the 1780s), cited in Epstein (1998: 282–83).

[17] See cases cited in note 8. Moreover, the essential facility in *Terminal Railroad* was part of a system under federal regulation.

encapsulated in a famous dictum of Learned Hand in the *Alcoa* case, that antitrust liability should not fall on a firm that gained market dominance through its own "superior skill, foresight, and industry." In such a case, wrote Hand, "a strong argument can be made that, although the result may expose the public to the evils of monopoly, the [Sherman] Act does not mean to condemn the resultant of those very forces which is its prime objective to foster: finis opus coronat. The successful competitor, having been urged to compete, must not be turned upon when he wins."[18]

The problem of private de facto monopoly affects the essential facility quite directly. The doctrine envisages *refusals to deal* by a monopolist, not the charging of a monopoly price. To put it differently, the issue is primarily access, not the terms of access.[19] Thus the doctrine does not in principle attempt to regulate the pricing behavior of a legally acquired monopoly. But why then insist on open access? The answer at some level must be that denying access is somehow worse than merely exploiting an existing monopoly through price. Exclusion must somehow extend or go beyond the legitimate exploitation of the legally acquired monopoly. This proposition is a fulcrum on which the doctrine of essential facilities turns.

THE ECONOMICS OF VERTICAL RESTRAINTS

The issues here fall into the broad area of vertical restraints, on which there is a large literature. The central question has long been this: can a firm with monopoly power in one market "leverage" that power into another market by some kind of vertical relationship (including the refusal to engage in a vertical relationship)?[20] It originally seemed obvious to many that this was so, a view given intellectual veneer (if not necessarily substance) by the writings of Joe Bain and the so-called Harvard School in the 1950s.[21] Indeed, Williamson (1979) describes the coalescence of these intuitions into an "inhospitability tradition" in antitrust policy: whenever a (vertical) contract appears nonstandard – that is, whenever it involves anything other than the selling of goods at

[18] *United States v. Aluminum Co. of America*, 148 F.2d 416, 430 (2d Cir. 1945).

[19] Of course, charging an exorbitant price can be a *means* of denying access, and courts have sometimes seen high pricing as a refusal to deal. Sullivan and Jones (1992), citing *United States v. Western Electric*, 846 F.2d 1422, 1428 (D.C. Cir. 1988).

[20] By "vertical" one means a relationship between entities in successive locations in the chain of production – for example, the relationship of a manufacturer with an input supplier or of a wholesaler with a retailer. This is in contrast to "horizontal" relationships involving competitors at the same level in the chain.

[21] Meese (1997) refers to this as the "populist" view.

a linear spot price[22] – one must presume the contract has an anticompetitive motivation.

In what is certainly the central drama in the recent intellectual history of antitrust, the package of intuitions and traditions represented by the Harvard School came under successful attack by a Chicago School wielding the bright sword of neoclassical price theory (Posner 1979).[23] Chicago's logic here may be distilled into what is called the "chain-link" or "fixed-sum" theory of monopoly.[24] A firm that has monopoly power at one level in a chain of production can at best transmit that monopoly to other levels; it cannot create more monopoly power than it already has.[25]

Consider tying arrangements, a classic form of vertical restraint. Suppose that a firm with monopoly power ties the purchase of the good over which it has power to the purchase of another (usually, but not necessarily, complementary) good. For concreteness, consider the tying of the purchase of a copying machine to the purchase of toner and paper. The monopolist can extract the maximum amount of surplus by charging the optimal monopoly price for copiers. But the monopolist cannot increase that surplus by raising the price of the tied paper and toner over competitive levels, because to do so would be to raise above the optimal level the effective price to consumers of the copying machine. Why then engage in tying? The answer may involve either a desire to "meter" output in order to price discriminate or perhaps to protect brand-name assets by preventing the user from employing inferior complements that would degrade the quality of service.[26] Both of these increase economic efficiency, at least so long as the complementary inputs are used in fixed

---

[22] "Linear" pricing is when the buyer's expenditure on a good is exactly proportional to the amount purchased, with the constant of proportionality being the price. In far less opaque terms, it is the simple per-unit pricing we are all familiar with. This stands in contrast to multipart tariffs and other "nonlinear" pricing schemes, which I touch on later. On this terminology, see Tirole (1988).

[23] In fact, however, one could argue that the Chicago School was actually going beyond traditional price theory into what is now called the New Institutional Economics. Indeed, it is arguably the inhospitability tradition that, in seeing the nonstandard as anticompetitive, drew on neoclassical price theory. On this point, see Langlois (1989) and Meese (1997).

[24] For the chain-link metaphor, see Gerber (1988: 1085), citing Hovenkamp (1985a). For the fixed-sum terminology, see, e.g., Kaplow (1985).

[25] See generally Bork (1978: 225–45), Posner (1979: 926–27), Scherer and Ross (1990: 522), and Tirole (1988: 170).

[26] Price discrimination as an explanation of tying was first offered by Director and Levi (1956) and Bowman (1957). On quality control and other possible efficiency justifications for tying, see Shughart (1997: 478–79).

proportions (Scherer and Ross 1990: 566).[27] The Chicago result general-
izes to other kinds of vertical arrangements, including vertical integration. These cannot (under Chicago assumptions) increase existing
monopoly power; and most have plausible efficiency explanations, such
as the resolution of efficiency-impeding free-rider externalities (Tesler
1960; Marvel 1982).

The Chicago School's victory quickly invited attack from so-called
post-Chicago critics, some of whom claim to have established a post-
Chicago synthesis.[28] These critics largely accept that vertical arrangements can have efficiency rationales and that there is a fundamental truth
to the fixed-sum-monopoly logic. Yet, they claim, there exist circumstances under which, and perspectives from which, vertical arrangements
can have anticompetitive effects as well.[29] The principal criticism of the
Chicago approach has been that, in relying on conventional price theory,
Chicago has taken an excessively static view. Price theory assumes a particular structure of the economic problem the monopoly faces. Within
such a given structure, the monopoly can do no more than make the most
of its existing monopoly. But often, as Louis Kaplow (1985: 524) suggests,
the "firm's motivation is to *change the structural conditions it faces* in the
future in order that it may receive greater profits in the future." And by
changing those underlying structural conditions, the monopoly may well
be able to "leverage" itself into a position even more powerful than the
one from which it started.

To the extent, however, that the post-Chicago critics have added a
dynamic element to the static analysis of Chicago, they have done so
along one very particular and narrow dimension, namely, that of strategic analysis.[30] And, just as Chicago prevailed with the superior fire power
of price theory, the critics – who have indeed established themselves now
as the dominant mainstream – forged an even more high-tech weapon:
mathematical game theory. Rather than confine attention to a single
period, such strategic analysis looks at the behavior of firms in multiple

---

[27] When substitution is possible among inputs, vertical restraints can sometimes lead to
allocative inefficiency, but the models are complex and the results ambiguous. See
Scherer and Ross (1990: 522–26, 566–67) and Kaserman and Mayo (1995: 307–10). See
also Reiffen and Vita (1995).

[28] See generally Hovenkamp (1985b), Baker (1988), and Riordan and Salop (1995).

[29] That is, the post-Chicago position is only that vertical restraints should be treated under
a rule of reason rather than as preemptively or per se legal. There is essentially no
support among economists for the position that vertical arrangements of any kind should
be per se illegal – as some still are under the law.

[30] For the characterization of the limits of the Chicago position as a failure to include
strategic considerations (rather than as a more general inattention to dynamics and
change), see Williamson (1983) as well as references cited in note 28.

periods and asks whether behavior in the short run might be explained not by advantages to be gained immediately but by advantages to be gained in a future period. These models tend to be highly stylized, and they normally portray firms as possessing cognitive and maximizing abilities even more formidable than those on which the Chicago School insisted. Nonetheless, strategic behavior (even in the narrow sense) is surely important to some extent in business practice, even if that extent may be much less than is suggested by the superabundance of game-theoretic models in the economics literature.

At the risk of only a little oversimplification, let me characterize the essence of the strategic criticism of Chicago in a way that will prove useful for understanding the issues of essential facilities and will also help make clear the limits of a strategic perspective – or at least the limits of a strategic perspective blinkered in by game theory. The core of the fixed-sum-monopoly argument is that it construes the firm's problem as that of short-run profit maximization. Vertical arrangements without independent efficiency rationales only impede that goal, and therefore are not "rational" in the short run. But if the firm is looking to a longer-run position, it may be rational to earn less than full monopoly profits in the short run in hope of greater future gain. But this reduces to a claim that the strategic firm is engaging in *predatory behavior* in order to disadvantage its rivals. Such behavior would include not only predatory pricing but also nonprice actions that might (at some short-run cost) serve to eliminate or simply disadvantage rivals in the long run (Kaplow 1985; Comanor and Frech 1984; Ordover and Willig 1981).

The logic of strategic vertical restraints thus mimics that of predatory pricing. Pre-Chicago analysis took it for granted that firms with deep pockets would want to lower prices below short-run costs to drive rivals out of business, which would then allow such firms to recoup their short-run losses and more. Indeed, charges of predatory pricing go back to some of the earliest antitrust cases, including *Standard Oil*.[31] The Chicago School has been critical of the possibility of predatory pricing, which it views as typically an irrational (i.e., nonoptimal) strategy (Tesler 1966). Post-Chicago critics would cast this as another instance of Chicago's myopic attention to the short run (in which predation is costly) to the neglect of the long run (in which predation might pay off) (Kaplow 1985: 527–28). But I think it is possible to paint the Chicago criticism in a slightly different light, one that raises some serious issues for game theory: it is not so much that the critics of predatory pricing focus on that strategy's short-run costs but rather that they highlight the often ephemeral character of the long-run benefits. In the game-theoretic

---

[31] *Standard Oil Co. v. United States*, 221 U.S. 1 (1911), on which see McGee (1958).

approach to strategic behavior, the future structural conditions (to use Kaplow's term) that firms try to influence today appear every bit as clearly and sharply as do the conditions today.[32] To those who actually make the decisions, however, these possible future conditions appear far more hazy – they are but guesses. And firms do not try to execute closed-form optimal strategies but rather try to position themselves in ways they hope will prove favorable. The more uncertain the world, the harder to tell predation from dynamic competition.

Another question that arises in analyzing predatory behavior is to what extent there are structural barriers to prevent (re)entry once a rival has been eliminated or severely disadvantaged.[33] In many cases, for example, causing a rival to exit does not destroy the physical assets the rival once used to compete, leaving those assets available to new competitors. As Areeda and Hovenkamp put it, "any price is lawful once it appears that the prerequisites for successful predation – especially the ability to maintain monopoly prices after rivals are destroyed – are absent. In that event, predation is not likely to be present and, even if it were, there would be no 'dangerous probability' that monopoly would result" (Areeda and Hovenkamp 1992: 631). The question of barriers to entry returns us very near the problem of essential facilities. For, as Harold Demsetz (1982) has argued in an important article, barriers to entry always boil down to property rights, whether de jure or de facto. And the ownership of an asset essential to production may well constitute such a barrier.

THE ECONOMICS OF ESSENTIAL FACILITIES

As a particular kind of vertical restraint, the denial of access to an essential facility raises both static and dynamic issues. From the static (or short-run) point of view, the issues revolve around whether *denying* access is rational behavior for a monopolist that could have extracted maximum surplus simply by *charging a monopoly price* for access (Reiffen and Kleit 1990; Gerber 1988).

The logic here is the same as for tying. Suppose (to use the paradigm example) that a private monopolist controls the only possible access across a river, and that the monopolist secured its position legally. Suppose in addition that the monopolist also owns one of many competitors that must cross the river; for example, suppose the monopoly owner of a railroad bridge also owns one of several railroads that wish

---

[32] Indeed, far from being highly uncertain, predators in most game-theoretic models have information superior to that of other players. See Ordover and Saloner (1989).

[33] This is the basis for the "structural" test for predation advocated by Joskow and Klevorick (1979). See also Elzinga and Mills (1994).

to cross the bridge. The monopolist does not need to exclude competing railroads in order to maximize its rents; it only need charge all railroads a monopoly price to cross. Charging the competitors high prices will certainly advantage the railroad owned by the monopolist, but that will not increase the monopolist's total take. Even if the monopolist excluded all competing railroads, it would still be limited to the total rents available because of its ownership of the bottleneck. Indeed, the monopolist would want to charge its (now monopoly) railroad division an internal transfer price equal to what would have been the competitive price to cross the river, thus avoiding the problem of "double marginalization" that occurs if successive stages of production are both separately monopolized (Spengler 1950).

Why then would an essential facility owner ever want to refuse to deal with rivals? One answer is that a simple linear price to cross the river might not fully capture all the rents to be had from the bridge monopoly. Indeed, consumer surplus in the train example arises not because anyone values the passage of the trains themselves but rather because consumers ultimately value the passage of the goods (widgets, let us say) those trains carry. To the extent that a per-train fee appears to shippers as a fixed cost, the fee won't enter into the railroad's marginal cost per widget and therefore (under competitive conditions) will not figure into the per-widget price the railroad charges widget shippers. This may mean that the railroads operate at a loss, which may in turn imply that the bridge owner will have to reduce its fee to retain customers. But it certainly means that the bridge owner will not be able to capture all the surplus of the widget shippers. In such a case, the bottleneck monopolist may prefer to refuse to deal with competitors of its railroad so that it can earn all its profits from its (now monopoly) railroad rather than from the bridge.[34]

Before saying that refusals to deal can therefore be anticompetitive, one has to deal with two very different issues. The first is that there may well be pricing alternatives that could extract the full amount of surplus. One can avoid the problem described here by using a "nonlinear" price,

---

[34] Notice that this strategy requires that there be barriers to reentry, which arise by hypothesis in this case from the "essential" – not easily duplicated – character of the bottleneck stage. The possession of the bottleneck asset is thus the exclusionary property right alluded to earlier. In a case in which there is no such barrier, the anticompetitive character of the vertical integration is less clear. At worst, competitors are disadvantaged because they would have to enter simultaneously at both stages. But if we assume that there are capabilities for entry already available at both stages, then what makes entry more difficult in the integrated case is only the cost of coordinating those existing capabilities into a unified entry by vertical partners, through a joint venture, for example.

that is, a two-part (or in general a multipart) tariff. Instead of asking a fee per train, the bridge owner could ask a crossing fee (which does not depend on the number of widgets that cross) plus a per-widget "royalty."[35] Such a two-part tariff can approximate perfect price discrimination and is normally efficiency enhancing (Tirole 1988: 146).[36] Herein may lie the difficulty, however, as price discrimination is illegal under the Robinson-Patman Act (Gerber 1988: 1084).

The more difficult issue is this. If a refusal to deal is a method of extracting monopoly rent in situations in which appropriate pricing is either impossible or illegal, why should such refusals be treated any differently from the setting of a monopoly price? If the monopoly was acquired through "superior skill, foresight, and industry," then why should one method of exploiting the monopoly be any more anticompetitive than another? Indeed, a doctrine that permits the charging of a monopoly price but penalizes refusals to deal (or other nonprice mechanisms of extracting monopoly rents) may encourage firms to evade sanction by inefficiently transforming facilities into forms that allow low-cost metering and pricing (Gerber 1988: 1093).

There are two possible directions of response. One would be to reopen the question of whether an essential facility doctrine should consider price as well as access. This direction would return the essential facility doctrine to its common-carrier roots and transform it into an alternative mechanism for the regulation of privately owned public goods. But taking this path immediately leads to two barriers. The first is the matter of practicability: it may be far easier for antitrust policy to affect access than to regulate price, because the latter implies both a far greater information requirement and some kind of ongoing surveillance. Traditionally, price regulation in such cases has taken the form of administrative oversight, a procedure that, although not without costs of its own, may be better suited to ongoing surveillance than are judicial processes.[37] The second barrier is the one implied in the Learned Hand dictum, namely the issue of incentives.[38] Using a logic similar to that lying behind the

[35] I use this term deliberately to highlight that pricing problems of this sort abound in knowledge-based industries. For example, a book author who receives an advance plus royalties on copies sold is being compensated by a two-part tariff.

[36] The two-part tariff is also preferable to a per-widget charge alone, because "the monopolist can reduce the marginal price below the monopoly price and recoup lost profits through the fixed fee. The fixed fee thus induces the monopolist to lower prices, which is good for welfare." Tirole (1988: 146).

[37] Goldberg (1976) has argued that one should view administrative regulation of this sort as a mechanism for carrying out an ongoing "administered contract" between the owner of the essential facility and its customers.

[38] *United States v. Aluminum Co. of America*, 148 F.2d 416, 430 (2d Cir. 1945).

standard economic defense of patents, one could argue that to prohibit a firm from exploiting the benefits of a legally acquired monopoly is to discourage the very sort of briskly competitive behavior that is fundamental to economic efficiency.[39] (I return to this point later in the context of innovation.)

A second direction of response would be to limit the essential facility doctrine to situations in which the firm's behavior serves not to exploit a given monopoly position but somehow to extend that position – to create "more" monopoly power than was envisaged in the original (legally acquired) monopoly.[40] And, as Kaplow (1985: 524) suggests, this can occur only when the firm's behavior somehow allows it to affect the structural conditions it faces rather than merely allowing it to maximize a fixed pie of profit. In this situation, however, game theory has not provided a satisfactory strategic account of a situation in which the owner of a genuinely essential facility can benefit from attempting to monopolize a downstream market, because the owner of such a facility always benefits from greater competition in the downstream market through its monopoly upstream. It is only when the owner of an input is not fully a monopolist that vertical restraints can be anticompetitive, because those restraints can help increase the input owner's market power (Ordover and Willig 1981; Whinston 1990). The owner of an input that is truly essential already has all the market power possible.[41]

ESSENTIAL FACILITIES AND INNOVATION

Fortunately, the strategic account from game theory does not circumscribe the possible ways in which a firm might attempt to change the structural conditions it faces today in the hope of future gain. For example, a firm may try to change structural conditions by controlling the rate and direction of innovation in the system of which the essential

---

[39] One may want to encourage the private creation of essential facilities because, even though the charging of a monopoly price is inefficient relative to the charging of a competitive price, a situation in which the facility exists (even if monopolized) is preferable to the situation in which no facility exists. As in the patent case, the deadweight loss of monopoly is the price for whatever remaining social surplus the facility's existence generates.

[40] In economic terms, this would presumably mean reducing welfare below what would have been implied in the exploitation of the legally acquired monopoly. It is logically possible that extending a monopoly could generate an *increase* in social surplus, for the same reason that the creation of the original monopoly might have done so. (Cf. note 39.)

[41] Of course, in many real-world essential facility cases, the facility claimed essential may not be literally the only alternative. For example, an operating system with more than 90% of the market is an essential facility for most users, but it still has competitors. I return to this point later.

facility is a part. Although such behavior is clearly "strategic" in some
sense, it does not always take place in a world in which the possibilities
of action fall neatly into the form of a game whose detailed contours and
potential stakes are easily knowable in advance.[42]

As a useful entry point to this argument, consider the analogy with
the law and economics of patents suggested earlier. The dominant
account of the economics of patents stresses the role of patents in inducing innovation. By creating a property right and thus a barrier to entry,
a patent holds up to a would-be inventor the carrot of economic rents.
According to this account, such a lure is necessary because of the peculiar nature of inventive knowledge: although its creation entails a fixed
investment, the marginal cost of transmitting the knowledge is zero.
Knowledge is also nonrivalrous, in that one person's consumption of it
does not diminish the ability of others to consume it; and knowledge may
also be difficult to exclude others from or to charge for.[43] Invention, in
short, is a public good much like a bridge. Without the right to exclude
people (and thereby receive economic rents), no one would expend the
resources necessary to create the invention (or bridge) in the first place,
because marginal revenues would never cover costs.[44] The deadweight
loss of monopoly during the life of the patent is thus the price of having
the invention at all, just as the costs of a monopoly gained through "superior skill, foresight, and industry" may be the price of having some essential facility at all.[45]

However, recent scholarship has cast doubt on – or at least greatly
reduced the reach of – this traditional model. For one thing, empirical
studies have suggested that the unadorned model fits few industries
(Levin et al. 1987). In pharmaceuticals, for example, the model fits well
enough: firms must expend large sums up front in the search for new
molecules with therapeutic value. Once discovered, such molecules can
be quickly described to other scientists and easily copied by other firms.
Without patents, there would be little incentive for the necessary up-

---

[42] For a relevant attempt to cast innovation in such a form, however, see Ordover and
Willig (1981).

[43] The canonical source of this description of inventive knowledge is Arrow (1962).

[44] A more technical way to state the proposition is that the social return to the invention
would exceed the private return, leading to an underinvestment in invention relative to
the hypothetical social optimum. Cf. Arrow (1962).

[45] Gerber (1988: 1103–10) has suggested using the logic of the patent law to determine
whether the returns from an essential facility constitute a reward for the generation of
net economic value. Citing *Hecht* (see note 6), Sullivan and Jones (1992: 183) detect "a
shared perception in many opinions that for many essential facilities, the defendant
was less an innovator and more the lucky beneficiary of having entered a thin market
first."

front research and development. But in many – perhaps most – other industries, often called "cumulative technology" industries, the model fits poorly. In these industries, inventions are not discrete and self-contained; instead, technology advances through a succession of incremental improvements. Moreover, innovations in these industries reflect knowledge that is not easy to codify and transmit but is instead sticky and "tacit" (Polanyi 1958). As a result, invention in cumulative-technology industries is less of a public good – and thus less in need of the lure of monopoly rents – than the traditional model suggests.

One implication is that the costs of patenting may outweigh the benefits in cumulative-technology industries. The traditional literature would suggest that such an imbalance could always be redressed by shortening the life of patents. The most interesting recent scholarship, however, has focused instead on the problem not of optimal patent length but of patent *scope* (Merges and Nelson 1990; Mazzoleni and Nelson 1998). Scope (or breadth) refers to the generality of the claims a patent asserts. For example, the infamous Selden patent in the early American automobile industry claimed the very idea of a gasoline-powered internal-combustion car.[46] The difficulty with such broad claims in a cumulative-technology industry is not merely that they may create deadweight losses in excess of benefits but rather that they foreclose avenues of future improvement and innovation.

Most cumulative technologies are in the nature of *system products*, that is, products that permit or require the simultaneous functioning of a number of complementary components. The next section takes up the theory of such products in more detail. For the moment, two observations from the theory of innovation are in order. First, improvement in system products is likely to take place differentially among the components, often focusing on those components that are bottlenecks in the system (Rosenberg 1976).[47] Second, innovation normally proceeds fastest when a large number of distinct participants are trying multiple approaches simultaneously. Because of the complexity that system products normally exhibit, and because of the qualitative uncertainty inherent in the process of innovation,[48] multiple approaches and numerous participants provide greater genetic variety than would a single innovator (or small number of innovators), which leads to more-rapid trial-and-error learning (Nelson and Winter 1977). The evolution

---

[46] U. S. Patent No. 549,160, issued November 5, 1895. The patent covered the carriage, the drive mechanism, and the engine.

[47] Hughes (1992) calls such bottlenecks "reverse salients."

[48] On the idea that, especially in the context of innovation, uncertainty is of a more fundamental or "structural" sort than is usually represented in economic models, see Langlois (1984) and Langlois and Cosgel (1993).

of improvement in a system product typically results in the emergence of new bottlenecks, in surprising and often major changes in the relative importance of existing components, and in the introduction of wholly new components (Langlois and Robertson 1992; Hughes 1992).

A broad patent is one that locates control of multiple components in the hands of a single party. In so doing, a broad patent limits the number of approaches to and participants in the improvement of the system. Moreover, the patent holder can use the (often vague) scope of the grant to block or delay through litigation innovations elsewhere in the system that threaten the long-run value (and therefore the rent stream) of the package of components the patent holder controls (Merges 1994). Notice that blocking by patent is a form of exclusion whose effects are not an indirect way of extracting an optimal rent from an existing monopoly. The intent and effect of blocking is to shape the future contours of the system product and its ownership, which can mean either (1) an attempt to maintain a monopoly position that might otherwise evaporate with the evolution of improvement in the system or perhaps (2) an effort to enhance an existing monopoly position by nudging innovation in directions that magnify the value of the components under the patent holder's control.[49]

Clearly, there is an analogy here with essential facilities. Because essential facility cases involve vertical relationships, the facility owner necessarily controls one component of what is at least minimally a "system." In many cases, of course, innovation may not be the central issue: *Terminal Railroad* was not about technological change and the future pattern of rents in the national rail system. But if we restrict our attention to cases in which the essential facility consists in intellectual property (of which technical standards are an important special case), then the analogy with patents is almost perfect. As the empirical literature on intellectual property suggests, there are ways other than patents in which a firm can protect its distinctive technological knowledge (Levin et al. 1987). The firm may closely guard its trade secrets instead of patenting, or it may simply possess knowledge that is tacit and inherently costly to acquire. Moreover, as I suggest presently, owners of technical standards (or the products that define and embody technical standards) can experience patentlike protection because of the phenomenon of network effects. An essential facility consisting of non-

---

[49] Others have noticed that protecting an existing monopoly (rather than "leveraging" that monopoly) can be a motive for exclusion. See, e.g., Baseman, Warren-Boulton, and Woroch (1995). Also, the literature on "predatory product innovation" may be seen as a narrow variant of the possibility that an existing monopolist can attempt to enhance its position by influencing the direction of technical change. See Ordover and Willig (1981). I return to these issues in more detail later.

patented (but, by definition, protected) intellectual property can thus be analyzed along the lines marked out previously.

Indeed, there may be a close analogy between the scope of a patent and the *scope of an essential facility*. A facility whose control by a single party encompasses several components of a system product would be broader than one whose control implicates fewer components. And the scope of the essential facility may well be a key consideration in antitrust policy.

INNOVATION IN SYSTEM PRODUCTS

In order to proceed further, we need to look more carefully at the concept of a system product. In general, a system product is one in which several components must work together simultaneously to produce the desired output. The components thus must be compatible with one another or, to put it another way, must be held together by a common architecture. Figure 7.1 depicts such a system. Here the four components all connect to a common "compatibility module," which specifies the system's architecture.[50] If one party were the only feasible supplier of, say, component 1, then component 1 would be a bottleneck, and the means to produce it an essential facility. In this case, the scope of the bottleneck would clearly be narrower than if the compatibility module had only one feasible supplier, because to control the compatibility module (the architecture) implicates all components in the system.

In general, systems are hierarchical: each of the components may itself be a system (or, if you prefer, a subsystem). Automobiles are system products, but they are also parts of a larger transportation system that includes, for example, roads, gas stations, repair shops, parking facilities, and traffic courts. Within any system, then, there are potential bottlenecks of varying scope. Notice also that what is essential is relative to a particular system (or subsystem), a point to which I return.

Systems vary in the degree to which they are modular (Langlois and Robertson 1992). Modularity refers both to the structure of the system's design and to its standards – that is, it refers to the degree to which the

---

[50] Many important systems do in fact take the form of components plugged into a central unit like an automobile chassis, a computer bus, or a stereo amplifier. Nonetheless, it is possible in principle for the components to connect to one another directly without first connecting to a common module. In the language of computers, we can think of such a case as reflecting a peer-to-peer architecture. Even in the peer-to-peer case, however, there is still a "compatibility module," namely, the "virtual" architecture that connects the components together. Such a virtual architecture would then be in the nature of pure intellectual property not instantiated in a physical device. It would be the abstract set of standards on which the architecture is based. I return to the issue of standards presently.

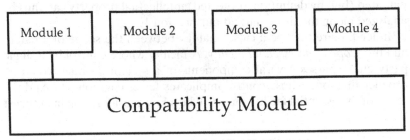

Figure 7.1. A Modular Systems Product

system is in fact decomposable into modules and to the degree to which the interfaces among the modules are fixed and invariant.[51] If a system possesses at least some degree of modularity – as most do – we can talk about whether the system is *open* or *closed.* An open system is one in which information about the "interfaces" or connections among the components is publicly shared and available. A closed system is one in which the information is tightly guarded. Open systems are generally nonproprietary, in that the standard (the information about connections) is either unowned or owned by a collective body or by a nonprofit organization like a trade association. A closed system is necessarily proprietary, at least de facto, and proprietary systems are ultimately closed at some level: although the owner of a proprietary system can choose to divulge relevant technical specifications to others, in the end that owner can always change the underlying standards unilaterally. In many real-world cases, systems will have a mix of proprietary and open elements.

Of course, ownership, and the structure of competition among owners, is at the heart of a concern with essential facilities. In the case of system products, competition can take two forms: *inter*system competition and *intra*system competition. The former is in many ways the more familiar case. Here competition takes place at the level of the systems as a whole. For example, each automobile is a system of complementary components. But the choice we find in the market is among complete prepackaged systems, and most components from one automobile do not fit on a different model.[52]

By contrast, intrasystem competition refers to competition at the level of components within a particular system. Such competition requires at

---

[51] On modularity as a design principle, see Simon (1981), Alexander (1964), and Clark (1985).

[52] Langlois and Robertson (1992) refer to such prepackaged systems as "entities." David (1987) talks about "system variants."

least some degree of openness and modularity. Similar modules compete as substitutes while remaining complementary to the other modules in the system. For example, one can choose among many different brands of computer monitors or modems that are compatible with a personal computer. As we will see, modularity requires a (relatively) fixed architecture, so that compatibility modules typically do not compete against one another – or, rather, competition among compatibility modules is necessarily intersystem competition.[53]

It is possible, indeed even typical, for intrasystem competition and intersystem competition to go on simultaneously. For example, two relatively open modular systems could compete in a classic "battle of the systems." Historical examples would include AC versus DC power before the turn of the century (David 1991; David and Bunn 1990), the 33⅓-RPM versus the 45-RPM phonograph record (Robertson and Langlois 1992), and the VHS system versus the Beta system for videocassette recorders (Cusumano, Mylonadis, and Rosenbloom 1992). It is also possible to have intersystem competition among systems with different degrees of intrasystem competition. In the limit, one could have an open modular standard (with intense intrasystem competition) pitted against one or more closed proprietary systems. For example, certain relatively closed and proprietary systems of machinery for fabricating semiconductor chips supplied by Applied Material, Inc., compete with systems from multiple vendors adhering to an open public standard (Langlois 2000). The relatively more closed architecture of the Apple Macintosh computer continues to compete with a personal computer architecture (once called the IBM architecture and now called the "Wintel" architecture) that is relatively more open and benefits from relatively more intrasystem competition (Langlois 1992). And the recent litigation between the Discover Card and the Visa credit card network turned importantly on the relative merits of intrasystem versus intersystem competition.[54]

---

[53] In the case of a system with open public standards, there can, of course, be competition among *physical* compatibility modules. But there remains only one "real" source of compatibility, namely, the standard. For example, the amplifier (technically, the preamplifier) is the principal physical compatibility module in a stereo system; but, because the connection among components is an open public standard, there are many competing producers of amplifiers. To coin a phrase, we might say that the open and nonproprietary character of the standard has "commoditized" the physical compatibility module. On stereos as modular systems, see Langlois and Robertson (1992); for a more detailed account, see Robertson and Langlois (1992).

[54] *SCFC ILC, Inc. v. Visa U.S.A., Inc.*, 819 F.Supp. 956, 963 and n.2 (D. Utah 1993), *aff'd in part and rev'd in part*, 36 F.3d 958 (10th Cir. 1994). Visa is an open system in which a consortium of financial institutions jointly manages the functions of clearing transactions, establishing brand image, and conducting research and development. Within this

The mix of intersystem and intrasystem competition in an industry is influenced – but, as I argue, not completely determined – by several economic factors: the extent of economies of scale relative to the extent of the market, the diversity of consumer tastes, and the possibilities for innovation. In general, innovation can come three ways: from changes in the components, from changes in the way the components are interconnected, or both. A system lends itself to *architectural* innovation when the parts are standardized but the connections among the parts are not, thus encouraging innovative recombinations of standardized parts (Henderson and Clark 1990). By contrast, a system lends itself to *modular* innovation when the interfaces among the parts are standardized, thus encouraging improvement in the performance of the parts without changing the way in which they are hooked together (Langlois and Robertson 1992). And a system lends itself to *systemic* innovation when both the parts and the architecture of connection can easily change simultaneously (Teece 1986).

Consider automobiles as an example. There are significant economies of scale in the assembly of automobiles; but, relative to the size of the market for cars, those economies are exhausted early enough that many different firms can profitably offer consumers many different models, each a distinct system product. Although there may be some competition among parts suppliers for the custom of the assembler, the primary mode of competition is intersystem. Why? Because economies of scale in assembly are exhausted early, there are no great benefits to consumers in having a single system – one kind of car.

Now, we could imagine a world in which manufacturers were all required to produce identical generic "people's cars," the parts for which were all standardized and interchangeable. This would create a regime of intense intrasystem competition among assemblers and parts suppliers, leading to modular innovation in the parts. But the benefits of this competition would likely be outweighed by the costs. Consumers have a wide variety of different tastes for system packages, and many people thus might prefer a more expensive vehicle tailored to specific tastes over

framework, the member institutions issue cards that compete with one another as well as with cards not in the Visa system. Like American Express and a few others, Discover is a closed proprietary system that manages all necessary functions internally. Dean Witter, then a division of Sears, Roebuck and the owner of the Discover Card, had purchased a Visa member bank from the Resolution Trust Corporation and sought to issue Visa cards. When Visa prohibited the issue, and then passed a bylaw against the issuance of Visa cards by owners of cards that compete with Visa, Dean Witter sued, charging a violation of section 1 of the Sherman Act. The court found in favor of Visa. For contrasting discussions of the relative merits of intersystem and intrasystem competition in this case – by the economists who served as expert witnesses for the litigants – see Evan and Schmalensee (1995) and Carlton and Frankel (1995). See also Balto (1997).

a less expensive generic car.[55] Of course, saying that parts are inter-changeable does not mean that they are all identical, as there can be competition – including competition for quality and for innovation – within the constraint that the parts connect to standardized interfaces. Thus cars could be differentiated by the parts they use rather than by the overall design. To take a trivial example, one could plug in a high-quality car stereo system as easily as a low-quality one. But, in the case of cars, this enforced modular system is not likely to be optimal despite the benefits of modular innovation it would produce. Architectural and systemic innovations can also benefit consumers, especially when tastes are diverse. And economies of scale in this case are insufficiently large to outweigh those benefits.

In the automobile example, the benefits of standardization come entirely from the economies of scale in production they enable. But, in other cases, standardization can have additional benefits that come not from the supply side but from the demand side. These benefits arise from the much discussed phenomenon of *network effects*: the benefits to any individual of a would-be standard depend on how many other individuals already adhere (or are likely to adhere) to that alternative.[56] As more and more users commit to a standard, that standard becomes increasingly attractive to others; the commitment of those others makes the standard even more attractive – and so on in a cumulative fashion that is often described as "positive feedback" (Arthur 1990). These are called network effects because, in the first instance, they arise in the case of physical connection networks like telephone systems. The value to me of a phone system increases with the number of other people who are on the system. But the concept has been applied to "virtual networks" in which the connections are not physical but rather in the nature of economic complementarity (Katz and Shapiro 1985; Arthur 1990). For example, the benefit to consumers of a new digital television standard is proportional to the amount of programming they expect to be available on that standard, which is in turn dependent of the number of

[55] Of course, if manufacturers could lower the price sufficiently, more and more consumers would be willing to forgo differentiation. See Lancaster (1971). This was arguably what drove sales of Henry Ford's generic Model T – any color you want as long as it's black – in the early auto industry. By standardizing the design, he could take advantage of economies of scale and learning economies to reduce price so dramatically that it offset for many people the disbenefits of the car's generic style. This strategy began to fail, however, as the market for inexpensive but more-differentiated used cars thickened by the 1920s. See Langlois and Robertson (1989).

[56] The works most often cited on the subject are probably David (1985), Katz and Shapiro (1985), and Farrell and Saloner (1985). For recent surveys, see David and Greenstein (1990) and Economides (1996).

people who adopt the standard. Technological standards can generate economies of scale on both the demand side and the supply side simultaneously. For example, users of a computer operating system may benefit from a large installed base that generates lots of software and other complementary goods and services, while that same installed base allows software developers to reduce costs by focusing their efforts on a single standard platform.

As in the case of production economies of scale, network effects may be exhausted at scales smaller than the entire market. When this is the case, competition can take place between rival systems much as in the automobile case. Sometimes, however, the benefits of compatibility are so great that the network effects are not exhausted at any scale smaller than the entire market. In such a case an entire market can "tip" when a candidate standard has gathered a critical mass of adherents, leaving that candidate as *the* standard. It is this possibility that Paul David (1985) popularized in his now-famous account of the QWERTY typewriter keyboard.

TECHNOLOGICAL STANDARDS AS ESSENTIAL FACILITIES

As we saw, the "essential" character of an input is always relative to the system of which it forms a part. To put it another way, "essentialness" is always an issue that speaks to *intra*system competition. As a result, the analysis of an essential facility will depend crucially on the degree of *inter*system competition in the industry. An input that is crucial to a system that is one of many alternatives has a status different from that of an equally crucial input to a system that is the only alternative.

The case of *Image Technical Services v. Kodak* raises the multisystem issues in a clear way.[57] Here there are many brands of copier, each brand, along with its complementary "aftermarket" for parts and service, representing a distinct system product. To put it another way, each maker of copiers supplies what is in effect a distinct compatibility module on which its aftermarket inputs depend. In refusing others access to the aftermarket (by tying the purchase of copiers to the use of Kodak's own parts and service), Kodak has foreclosed an essential facility. I do not wish to analyze the case in great detail. But the economic issues turn on the extent to which competition among copier makers disciplines Kodak's ability to engage in "installed-base opportunism."[58] If consumers have perfect information, or if reputation effects work well, consumers ought to take into account the

---

[57] See note 10.
[58] A firm engages in installed-base opportunism when it raises the price of complementary products after buyers have been "locked in" to a standard by the purchase of the compatibility module the firm sells.

effect of aftermarket lock-in when they make their initial purchasing decisions; and if there are many alternatives available, no copier maker should be able to engage in such behavior unless there are independent efficiency reasons for it (Shapiro and Teece 1994; Shapiro 1995).

From the point of view of innovation, the issues appear somewhat different. Now our concern turns to the ways in which the pattern of ownership of the supply of modules influences the pace and direction of technical change. The facts of *Kodak* may not illustrate these points well, so consider instead the personal computer industry.[59]

When personal computers first emerged in the late 1970s, there were a number of incompatible platforms in active competition, many of them proprietary (like the Apple II) but many grouped around a mostly open standard (Intel-compatible microprocessor, the S-100 bus, and the CP/M operating system).[60] The nature of the market began to change in 1981 when IBM introduced its personal computer (PC). Because IBM wanted to develop its personal computer quickly, it relied almost exclusively on outside suppliers, including Intel for the microprocessor and Microsoft for the operating system. Because of this outsourcing strategy and the standards it necessitated, others could easily imitate the IBM hardware platform, which effectively became an open system at the component level – that is, any would-be maker of computers could obtain industry-standard components and compete with IBM. However, crucial parts of the overall standard (namely, the microprocessor and the operating system) remained largely under proprietary control. Because of the strength of the IBM name in generating network effects – principally because it created the expectation among users that the key vendor would continue to provide services long into the future and that a wide array of complementary devices and software would rapidly become available – the IBM standard became the dominant hardware platform, largely driving out competing alternatives during the decade of the 1980s.

In the case of the personal computer, the rise of a single dominant – but largely open and nonproprietary – standard focused innovation in modular directions. And it is the ensuing rapid improvement in components, including not only the chips but various peripheral devices like hard disks and modems, as well as the proliferation of applications software, that has led to the rapid fall in the quality-adjusted price of the total personal computer system (Langlois 1992).

---

[59] The following paragraphs draw on Langlois (1992).
[60] A "bus" is a system of interconnection among components in the computer. The S-100 bus was an open public standard. The microprocessor architecture was a proprietary standard, but in fact the Intel 8080 faced competition from the Zilog Z80, a "clone" chip. CP/M was the property of Digital Research, Inc., but its technical details were widely available.

Was this result inevitable? As I suggested earlier, such economic factors as economies of scale and diversity of tastes influence the pattern of competition among systems. But they do not fully determine it. The evolution of any industry is determined not only by economic forces existing at any time but also by a historical legacy of technological possibilities and of organizational and institutional structures.[61] By the time IBM developed its PC, the "dominant design"[62] of the computer as an open modular system had already been established and a network of capabilities already existed around that design. This legacy influenced IBM's design decisions. But consider the case of Japan, where the idea of the PC fell on very different ground. There the computer was taken up by a handful of vertically integrated systems houses more accustomed to architectural than to modular innovation. Each firm designed its own proprietary system incompatible with the systems of others even to the level of applications programs. The result was a vibrant intersystem rivalry, but, in the absence of a dominant standard, a much retarded development of the industry in comparison with that of the United States (Cottrell 1994).

One way to couch the problem of optimal intersystem versus intrasystem rivalry is in terms of the tradeoff between the benefits of differentiated products and the benefits of the economies of scale (whether supply side or demand side) that come from standardization. This point has not been lost on the formal literature of standard setting (Farrell and Saloner 1986). What seems not to have been noticed, however, is that the nature of this tradeoff is a function of whether variety must be provided through distinct systems with competing standards (which the literature assumes) or whether variety can be provided largely through recombinations of compatible modules. This in turn depends on the economies of scale in packaging the entire system. Where there are significant economies of scale, as in automobiles and probably copiers, we would expect that variety must be provided by competing systems. But where there are attenuated economies of scale in packaging the entire system, as in personal computers, it becomes cheaper to provide variety through the modules. As a rough approximation, we might say that there is less of a tradeoff between variety and standardization the greater the extent to which variety is a matter of "software" rather than "hardware."[63]

---

[61] For an elaboration of this argument, see Langlois and Robertson (1995).

[62] On the concept of a dominant design, see Tushman and Murmann (1998).

[63] In part, this is a matter of our perspective within the hierarchy of systems. Even if there are economies of scale in assembling major components of the system, there may not be economies of scale in offering variety in the system as a whole. For example, there are economies of scale in assembling televisions and videocassette recorders. But there are no such economies to hooking those components together and playing one of a wide

The implications of this analysis for the doctrine of essential facilities are far from clear. For one thing, antitrust is not an institution well suited to intervening in the evolution of industries at this level. Indeed, in view of the tremendous information requirements involved, it is not clear that any sort of industrial policy is suited to the task. Moreover, there may be reason to think that, although structures may be path-dependent in the short run, there exist long-run forces that may help to correct a nonoptimal tradeoff between intersystem and intrasystem competition. Suppose that a system-product industry were organized as a rivalry among competing incompatible systems when a single standard would have been superior (in that it would have unleashed greater innovation and improved welfare). The existing players may be earning rents and may thus have an incentive to keep the structure intact. But if a move to a single standard would improve welfare, then there are unexploited gains from trade to be had by an entrant (or existing player) who champions such a standard.[64] Something very much along these lines occurred in the market for technical workstations. Here Sun Microsystems successfully championed an open-system strategy in the face of competition from systems that were far more closed and proprietary.[65]

Another way to see this issue is to note that, when there is vibrant intersystem competition, there are more possible entry points for innovation. Multiple competing systems provide a way not only of providing variety but also of experimenting with organizational and design alternatives.[66] The interesting question, then, is when and to what extent property rights can create barriers to experimentation. And this suggests

---

variety of available tapes. Similarly, there are economies of scale in packaging variety in cars, but lower economies in packing variety in the wider transportation system, because travel to different destinations using complementary modular assets like roads is a source of variety. Notice that, in both cases, it is the software rather than hardware – the tapes in one case and the destinations in the other – that creates much of the variety in the larger system. Of course, cars and (perhaps a lesser extent) video hardware nonetheless continue to provide some element of the variety, because different hardware can interact with the software to produce slightly different experiences. Driving through the Berkshires in a Porsche is not the same as driving there in a Chevy; watching *Star Wars* on a wide-screen television is not the same as watching it on a nineteen-inch screen. In the case of personal computers, however, even the hardware can be varied by recombining modules.

[64] A similar point is made in a slightly different context by Liebowitz and Margolis (1994: 141).

[65] See generally Garud and Kumaraswamy (1993), Khazam and Mowery (1996), and Baldwin and Clark (1997).

[66] Indeed, the process of providing variety (searching the product space, in the lingo of economists) and the process of experimenting with organizational and technological alternatives are really the same process. On this point, see Lachmann (1986: 15–16).

that we pick up the other end of the stick and begin with the case of pure intrasystem competition.

In many technological systems, extreme modularity is an important design alternative, making possible the provision of variety at the component level. In such systems, the scale benefits of compatibility may not be exhausted by the extent of the market, leading to the eventual dominance of a single set of compatibility standards. The structure of property rights in such cases is crucial to the evolution of the product and of competition. In analogy with the law and economics of patents, we can think about how the structure of ownership may channel future innovative efforts.

In the first instance, proprietary ownership of a standard can be a property right that creates a barrier to entry. The logic is as follows. Products compete with one another along many (price-adjusted) dimensions of merit. Consumers choose those products that are superior along some or all dimensions. When there are many competing packages (intersystem competition), consumer choice typically fragments among differentiated products, and competing standards can coexist. In other cases, however, network effects may force all consumers into the same standard. But standards do still compete. If a contending standard offers a great enough improvement along enough dimensions of merit, a critical mass of adherents may switch to the alternative, thus establishing it as the new dominant standard.

Apart from the punctuated character of the switching among alternatives, standards competition does not differ fundamentally from competition among other sorts of products, except in the following respect. In standards competition, one crucial dimension is the fact of universal compatibility itself. In thinking about the choice between vinyl records and compact discs (CDs) when the latter first appeared, one would have considered (on a price-adjusted basis) the sound quality and other technical and aesthetic aspects of the two alternatives. But one would also have had to consider any existing sunk investment in vinyl disks and the fact that relatively few titles were then available on CD. Compatibility with an existing stock of complementary assets is one dimension of merit. But it is not, in a sense, a dimension of merit intrinsic to the product in the same way that sound quality is. Rather, it is a source of merit conferred on the standard by history.[67]

Standards are barriers to entry in the precise sense that competing products cannot gain advantage without *significant* superiority along

---

[67] This is, of course, the source of the claim, hotly debated in the literature, that the existence of network effects can easily lead to the emergence of technically inferior and economically inefficient standards. Cf., e.g., Arthur (1989) and Liebowitz and Margolis (1995).

noncompatibility dimensions of merit – as was in fact the case with CDs (Teece and Coleman 1998).[68] Ownership of this barrier to entry is very much akin to the possession of a patent. The nature of such ownership will vary. In some cases, as when the standard is imbedded in the production of physical compatibility modules, the property right is protected in effect by trade secrecy or the inherent difficulty of copying. In other cases, the standard may actually be protected by copyright.

In a well-known article, Edmund Kitch (1977) argued that patents serve a "prospect function" (Merges and Nelson 1990; Mazzoleni and Nelson 1998). When patents are sufficiently broad, he claimed, they offer their holder a secure opportunity to orchestrate in an orderly fashion the subsequent development of the original idea. One could tell a somewhat analogous story in the case of proprietary rights to standards. Because standards are complex, there may be benefits when the development of the standard is under control of a single firm, since that firm can think through the standardization issues synoptically without the tug of competing interests and that firm has the necessary incentive to champion a superior standard even to the extent of subsidizing its early adoption.

It is certainly true that, by reducing the transaction costs of redeploying assets and coordinating among contracting parties, centralized ownership and control can have advantages in situations of truly systemic innovation (Langlois and Robertson 1995). And perhaps one could argue that wide proprietary control of a newly emerging standard might be such a situation. But the countervailing considerations weigh even more heavily. Precisely to the extent that a standard is complex and reflects an underlying cumulative technology, centralized control may actually limit the development of a standard. To work properly, complex standards require collaboration with users and with suppliers of the various components of the system. Indeed, as Hayek has argued, such complex standard sets as human languages or the common law could only have evolved as "spontaneous orders."[69] Even the proprietary developer of a standard needs to access the knowledge of a wide variety of collaborators, and even a proprietary standard is often something of a spontaneous order. Moreover, wide scope is not obviously necessary to motivate a potential "champion" for a standard. Any party with a

---

[68] "The firm can earn a rent equal to its advantage in switching costs. The size of this rent is constrained by the size of the switching costs and the extent to which other suppliers can provide products that ease the transition of complementary goods to new platforms; or such an increase in performance to justify investment in new complementary goods."

[69] See, e.g., Hayek (1973). The idea of spontaneous order as an approach to standard setting has gained considerable attention in the field of software. See Raymond (1999).

long position in assets likely to appreciate if the standard is adopted
has the incentive to expend resources to try to bring about that
outcome.[70] For example, with Sun Microsystems, its incentive to champion a largely open system for technical workstations lay in its possession of distinctive knowledge and innovative ability complementary to
the standard.[71]

Another important consideration, of course, is the extent to which the
owner of a standard can manipulate that standard in ways that convey
private advantage at the expense of more rapid development of the
technology. For example, an owner can alter a standard strategically
or can simply make the system less standard by deliberately reducing
the degree of modularity in the components under its control.[72] Why
might a standards owner do this? The literature offers two contrasting
theories.

One set of theoretical stories falls under the rubric of "predatory
product innovation" (Ordover and Willig 1981). The idea here is that a
firm with market power that provides more than one complementary
module for a system product may try to leverage its power by creating
a new "generation" of the system that is incompatible with the old
system. Even if this new system is superior in the eyes of consumers,
economic welfare can suffer because the incompatibility freezes out
independent suppliers of the previous generation of components, thus
raising the market power of the innovating firm. The innovating firm
raises its costs in the short run (in spending resources on research and
development) in order to gain advantage in the future. What makes the
behavior predatory in this account is that the future gain is not (all) the
result of creating new value but comes in part from increased market
power.

There are several problems with the idea of predatory innovation.
Apart from the possibility that the bundling of components by a single
manufacturer may have efficiency benefits in addition to the benefits of
the innovation, the theory raises disturbing practical issues, because it

---

[70] It has long been noticed that the ownership of complementary assets can be a substitute for patent protection. See, e.g., Hirshleifer (1971), Casson (1982: 206–8), and Teece
(1986).

[71] Sun evidently believed that the rents to these distinctive capabilities would be greater
with the large market that an open standard offered than they would in the smaller
market of intersystem rivalry among closed proprietary systems.

[72] The latter is of course related to the phenomenon of technological bundling, although
demodularization is a stronger form of this phenomenon than is simply packaging
modular components together. I do not wish to summarize the large literature on
bundling here, except to suggest that there may be efficiency motives, having to do with
systemic innovation or with the saving of transaction costs, that can be relevant in some
cases.

asks courts to distinguish "good" innovation from "bad" innovation, a decision with which unsuccessful competitors will be all too happy to assist.[73] Even in the clean and neat world of game theory, predatory product innovation is a logical possibility of almost Scholastic quality. It is yet more worrisome an idea in the uncertain world of innovation, where even the innovators cannot always reliably predict the effects of their innovation.[74]

The other brand of story one finds in the literature appears to take a diametrically opposite tack. Here the problem is not one of too much innovation but of too little. This possibility has not received the same theoretical (i.e., mathematical) attention as predatory innovation, probably because it is a story that lends itself less easily to game theory. But the underlying theory seems to be the following (Baseman et al. 1995). As we saw, a standard may be displaced by a competitor offering significantly higher functionality. To the extent that the existing standard is open, this hurdle is lower, because a competitor can offer improvements in functionality while maintaining backward compatibility. The owner of a dominant standard may thus want to manipulate the standard in ways that close off the possibilities for a competitor to achieve compatibility. This has a tendency to retard the generational advance of the system.

Here the idea of the "scope" of the standard becomes important. The owner of a standard that controls the compatibility of a large fraction of the components of a system is in a much better position to close off avenues of innovation that threaten the rent-earning potential of the standard. The owner of a standard with relatively smaller scope is always in danger of being "invented around" or made obsolete if it closes off access or otherwise exercises its market power unduly.

TECHNOLOGICAL STANDARDS ANTITRUST POLICY

What, then, are the policy implications of this analysis? At the prima facie level, they are these:

- Antitrust policy should err on the side of openness of standards, all other things equal.

---

[73] This first concern, and to some extent the second as well, are raised in Sidak (1983). For a response, see Ordover, Sykes, and Willig (1983).

[74] The practical problems of the Ordover-Willig analysis are compounded in my view by being tied to a test for predatory conduct that looks to the "front end" of predation, namely the incurring of short-run costs and predatory intent. As I have argued, a test that looks to the "back end" – the property rights that may allow recoupment – makes far more sense in the uncertain world of innovation.

- The attention that policy pays to a case ought to be proportional to the *scope* of the standard over which owner of the essential facility has de facto or de jure control.

Arrayed against these proposals are two sets of objections or qualifications. The first set arises from the analogy with patent policy itself, whereas the second arises from dynamic or Schumpeterian considerations more broadly.

A policy that requires a party to open to others the standard it controls is effectively a taking of intellectual property rights. Viewed strictly from the standpoint of economic efficiency, such a taking is desirable only when the benefits outweigh the costs. As I have suggested, and as the case of personal computer hardware illustrates, there can be considerable benefits to an open system. The analogy with patent policy suggests two possible costs, however. The first is the potential benefit to inducing future innovation that comes from guaranteeing the innovator's prospective monopoly returns. But, in the case of a broad patent – or a broad standard – the remuneration that monopoly rights confer far outstrip the risk-discounted ex ante costs of innovation. Moreover, in the case of a broad patent or standard, the ability of the patent holder to block future innovation will do more to diminish the incentive for technological progress than will any weakening of intellectual property rights.

The second cost would arise if, as Kitch (1977) suggests in the case of patents, unified ownership would allow for a speedier and more coherent development of the standard. As I suggested earlier, however, this benefit would be more likely in the very early stages of the development of a broad technical standard. Once a standard becomes mature, development of the standard increasingly takes on the character of a spontaneous order, even when the standard is under proprietary control. Moreover, there are mechanisms other than unified ownership – including not only formal standard-setting bodies but also informal mechanisms involving lead users and dominant players – to provide a more synoptic view and to effect relatively more systemic changes.

The larger dynamic or Schumpeterian issues are more difficult to deal with. At one level, I have argued that attention to the shapes and patterns of innovation does tend to give credence to the post-Chicago view that a competitor in control of a standard can "leverage" its current position by manipulating the standard in ways that channel future innovation in directions beneficial to the standard owner but not necessarily as beneficial to society as possible. But what Schumpeter giveth to activist policy he may just as quickly taketh away.

I have suggested that ownership of a technological standard is a property right that creates a barrier to entry and confers Ricardian scarcity rents on its possessor. In Schumpeter's famous image, however, competition is a "perennial gale of creative destruction" (Schumpeter 1950). And, as David Teece and others have insisted, the rents we observe in this windswept kind of competition are at best quasi rents (i.e., temporary scarcity rents) and are more likely "Schumpeterian" rents (i.e., temporary returns to entrepreneurship and innovation) (Teece and Coleman 1998). Clearly, the narrower the scope of a technological standard, the more temporary – the more "Schumpeterian" – the rents are likely to be. For example, major personal computer applications programs like word processors and spreadsheets involve technical standards, and competition among such programs involves network effects. This has led to dominant applications in the various program categories, and the owners of those dominant programs have presumably enjoyed rents during the period of dominance. But those periods have historically been relatively brief, as new dominant programs (embodying a new standard) came to displace their predecessors in a process of "serial monopoly" (Liebowitz and Margolis 1999).

Clearly, there can be standards – like, perhaps, those embodied in an operating system – with greater scope than those of major applications programs. One would expect the duration of the "serial monopoly" in such cases to be longer, and the rents earned to approach something more like the Ricardian type. Nonetheless, it may well be that such rents are an inevitable part of the competitive process, and the gale of creative destruction can better deal with even such cases than can a hamhanded and politically motivated government: surgical antitrust policy is an illusion (Teece and Coleman 1998).

If this is true, then the approach suggested here – like most other approaches to antitrust policy – is of little relevance, especially in cases of ordinary private monopoly under Sherman 2 and related statutes. In many cases involving standards as essential facilities, however, the issues revolve either around regulated (or formerly regulated) enterprises with a government-granted franchise or around tradeoffs in government-granted intellectual property protection. In such cases, the winds of competition blow through what are already government-created canyons. Here at least the concept of the scope of a standard, and the analysis presented here more generally, may be of not inconsequential value.

REFERENCES

Alexander, C. 1964. *Notes on the Synthesis of Form*. Cambridge, MA: Harvard University Press.

Areeda, P. 1990. Essential Facilities: An Epithet in Need of Limiting Principles. *Antitrust Law Journal* 58: 841–53.

Areeda, P., and H. Hovenkamp. 1992. *Antitrust Law: An Analysis of Antitrust Principles and Their Application.* 1992 Supplement. Boston: Little Brown.

Arrow, K. 1962. Economic Welfare and the Allocation of Resources to Invention. In R. Nelson, ed., *The Rate and Direction of Inventive Activity: Economic and Social Factors,* 609–26. Princeton: Princeton University Press.

Arthur, W. B. 1989. Competing Technologies, Increasing Returns, and Lock-In by Historical Events. *Economic Journal* 99: 116–31.

1990. Positive Feedbacks in the Economy. *Scientific American* 262: 92–99.

Baker, J. 1989. Recent Developments in Economics that Challenge Chicago School Views. *Antitrust Law Journal* 58: 645–57.

Baldwin, C., and K. Clark. 1997. Sun Wars: Competition within a Modular Cluster, 1985–1990. In D. Yoffie, ed., *Competing in the Age of Digital Convergence,* 123–57. Boston: Harvard Business School Press.

Balto, D. 1997. The Murky World of Network Mergers: Searching for the Opportunities for Network Competition. *Antitrust Bulletin* 42: 793–850.

Baseman, K., F. Warren-Boulton, and G. Woroch. 1995. Microsoft Plays Hardball: The Use of Exclusionary Pricing and Technical Incompatibility to Maintain Monopoly Power in Markets for Operating System Software. *Antitrust Bulletin* 40: 265–315.

Bork, R. 1978. *The Antitrust Paradox: A Policy at War with Itself.* New York: Basic Books.

Bowman, W. S. 1957. Tying Arrangements and the Leverage Problem. *Yale Law Journal* 67: 19–36.

Carlton, D., and A. Frankel. 1995. The Antitrust Economics of Credit Card Networks. *Antitrust Law Journal* 63: 643–68.

Casson, M. 1982. *The Entrepreneur: An Economic Theory.* Totowa, NJ: Barnes and Noble Books.

Clark, K. 1985. The Interaction of Design Hierarchies and Market Concepts in Technological Evolution. *Research Policy* 14: 235.

Comanor, W., and H. Frech. 1984. Strategic Behavior and Antitrust Analysis. *American Economic Review* 74: 372–76.

Cottrell, T. 1994. Fragmented Standards and the Development of Japan's Microcomputer Software Industry. *Research Policy* 23: 143–74.

Cusumano, M., Y. Mylonadis, and R. Rosenbloom. 1992. Strategic Maneuvering and Mass-Market Dynamics: The Triumph of VHS over Beta. *Business History Review* 66: 51–94.

David, P. 1985. Clio and the Economics of QWERTY. *American Economic Review* 75: 332–37.

1987. Some New Standards for the Economics of Standardization in the Information Age. In P. Dasgupta and P. Stoneman, eds., *Economic Policy and Technological Performance,* 206–39. Cambridge: Cambridge University Press.

1991. The Hero and the Herd in Technological History: Reflections on Thomas Edison and the Battle of the Systems. In P. Higonnet, D. Landes, and H. Rosovsky, eds., *Favorites of Fortune: Technology, Growth, and Development in the Industrial Revolution,* 72–119. Cambridge, MA: Harvard University Press.

David, P., and J. Bunn. 1990. Gateway Technologies and Network Industries. In A. Heertje and M. Perlman, eds., *Evolving Technology and Market Structure*, 121–56. Ann Arbor: University of Michigan Press.

David, P., and S. Greenstein. 1990. The Economics of Compatibility Standards: An Introduction to Recent Research. *Economic Innovation and New Technology* 1: 3–41.

Demsetz, H. 1982. Barriers to Entry. *American Economic Review* 72: 47–57.

Director, A., and E. Levi. 1956. Law and the Future: Trade Regulation. *Northwestern University Law Review* 51: 281–317.

Economides, N. 1996. The Economics of Networks. *International Journal of Industrial Organization* 17: 673–99.

Elzinga, K., and D. Mills. 1994. Trumping the Areeda-Turner Test: The Recoupment Standard in Brooke Group. *Antitrust Law Journal* 62: 559–84.

Epstein, R. 1998. *Principles for a Free Society: Reconciling Individual Liberty with the Common Good*. Reading, MA: Perseus Books.

Evan, D., and R. Schmalensee. 1995. Economic Aspects of Payment Card Systems and Antitrust Policy toward Joint Ventures. *Antitrust Law Journal* 63: 861–901.

Farrell, J., and G. Saloner. 1985. Standardization, Compatibility, and Innovation. *Rand Journal of Economics* 16: 70–83.

1986. Standardization and Variety. *Economic Letters* 20: 71–74.

Garud, R., and A. Kumaraswamy. 1993. Changing Competitive Dynamics in Network Industries: An Exploration of Sun Microsystems' Open Systems Strategy. *Strategic Management Journal* 14: 351–69.

Gerber, D. 1988. Rethinking the Monopolist's Duty to Deal: A Legal and Economic Critique of the Doctrine of "Essential Facilities." *Virginia Law Review* 74: 1069–113.

Goldberg, V. 1976. Regulation and Administered Contracts. *Bell Journal of Economics* 7: 426–48.

Hayek, F. A. 1973. *Law, Legislation, and Liberty*. Chicago: University of Chicago Press.

Henderson, R., and K. Clark. 1990. Architectural Innovation: The Reconfiguration of Existing Product Technologies and the Failure of Established Firms. *Administrative Science Quarterly* 35: 9–30.

Hirshleifer, J. 1971. The Private and Social Value of Information and the Reward to Inventive Activity. *American Economic Review* 61: 561–74.

Hovenkamp, H. 1985a. *Economics and Federal Antitrust Law*. St. Paul, MN: West.

1985b. Antitrust Policy after Chicago. *Michigan Law Review* 84: 213–84.

Hughes, T. 1992. The Dynamics of Technological Change: Salients, Critical Problems, and Industrial Revolutions. In G. Dosi, R. Giannetti, and P. A. Toninelli, eds., *Technology and Enterprise in a Historical Perspective*, 97–118. New York: Oxford University Press.

Joskow, P., and A. Klevorick. 1979. A Framework for Analyzing Predatory Pricing Policy. *Yale Law Journal* 89: 213–70.

Kaplow, L. 1985. Extension of Monopoly Power through Leveraging. *Columbia Law Review* 85: 515–56.

Kaserman, D. L., and J. W. Mayo. 1995. *Government and Business: The Economics of Antitrust and Regulation*. Fort Worth, TX: Dryden Press.

Katz, M., and C. Shapiro. 1985. Network Externalities, Competition, and Compatibility. *American Economic Review* 75: 424–40.

Kellogg, M. K., J. Thorne, and P. W. Huber. 1992. *Federal Communications Law*. St. Paul, MN: West.

Khazam, J., and D. Mowery. 1996. Tails That Wag Dogs: The Influence of Software-Based "Network Externalities" on the Creation of Dominant Designs in RISC Technologies. In D. Mowery, ed., *The International Computer Software Industry: A Comparative Study of Industrial Evolution and Structure*, 86–103. New York: Oxford University Press.

Kitch, E. 1977. The Nature and Function of the Patent System. *Journal of Law and Economics* 20: 265–90.

Lachmann, L. M. 1986. *The Market as an Economic Process*. Oxford: Blackwell.

Lancaster, K. 1971. *Consumer Demand: A New Approach*. New York: Columbia University Press.

Langlois, R. 1984. Internal Organization in a Dynamic Context: Some Theoretical Considerations. In M. Jussawalla and H. Ebenfield, eds., *Communication and Information Economics: New Perspectives*, 23–49. New York: Elsevier.

1989. Contract, Competition, and Efficiency. *Brooklyn Law Review* 55: 831–45.

1992. External Economies and Economic Progress: The Case of the Microcomputer Industry. *Business History Review* 66: 1–50.

2000. Capabilities and Vertical Disintegration in Process Technology: The Case of Semiconductor Fabrication Equipment. In N. Foss and P. Robertson, eds., *Resources, Technology, and Strategy*, 199–226. London: Routledge.

Langlois, R., and M. Cosgel. 1993. Frank Knight on Risk, Uncertainty, and the Firm: A New Interpretation. *Economic Inquiry* 31: 456–65.

Langlois, R., and P. Robertson. 1989. Explaining Vertical Integration: Lessons from the American Automobile Industry. *Journal of Economic History* 49: 361–75.

1992. Networks and Innovation in a Modular System: Lessons from the Microcomputer and Stereo Component Industries. *Research Policy* 21: 297–313.

1995. *Firms, Markets, and Economic Change: A Dynamic Theory of Business Institutions*. London: Routledge.

Lerner, J. 1995. Patenting in the Shadow of Competitors. *Journal of Law and Economics* 38: 463–95.

Levin, R., A. Klevorick, R. Nelson, and S. Winter. 1987. Appropriating the Returns from Industrial R&D. *Brookings Papers on Economic Activity* 3: 783–820.

Liebowitz, S. J., and S. Margolis. 1994. Network Externality: An Uncommon Tragedy. *Journal of Economic Perspectives* 8: 133–50.

1995. Path-Dependence, Lock-In, and History. *Journal of the Law, Economics, and Organization* 11: 205–26.

1999. *Winners, Losers, and Microsoft*. Oakland, CA: Independent Institute.

Marvel, H. P. 1982. Exclusive Dealing. *Journal of Law and Economics* 25: 1–25.

Mazzoleni, R., and R. Nelson. 1998. The Benefits and Costs of Strong Patent Protection: A Contribution to the Current Debate. *Research Policy* 27: 275–86.

McGee, J. S. 1958. Predatory Price Cutting: The Standard Oil (N.J.) Case. *Journal of Law and Economics* 1: 137–69.

Meese, Alan J. 1997. Price Theory and Vertical Restraints – a Misunderstood Relation. *UCLA Law Review* 45: 143–204.

Merges, R. 1994. Intellectual Property Rights and Bargaining Breakdown: The Case of Blocking Patents. *Tennessee Law Review* 62: 75–106.

Merges, R., and R. Nelson. 1990. On the Complex Economics of Patent Scope. *Columbia Law Review* 90: 839–916.

Nelson, R., and S. Winter. 1977. In Search of More Useful Theory of Innovation. *Research Policy* 5: 36–76.

Ordover, J., and G. Saloner. 1989. Predation, Monopolization, and Antitrust. In R. Schmalensee and R. Willig, eds., *Handbook of Industrial Organization*, 573–96. New York: Elsevier.

Ordover, J., A. Sykes, and R. Willig. 1983. Predatory Systems Rivalry: A Reply. *Columbia Law Review* 83: 1150–66.

Ordover, J., and R. Willig. 1981. An Economic Definition of Predation: Pricing and Product Innovation. *Yale Law Journal* 91: 8–53.

Polanyi, M. 1958. *Personal Knowledge*. New York: Harper and Row.

Posner, R. 1979. The Chicago School of Antitrust Analysis. *University of Pennsylvania Law Review* 127: 925–48.

Ratner, J. 1988. Should There Be an Essential Facilities Doctrine? *University of California Davis Law Review* 21: 327–82.

Raymond, E. 1999. *The Cathedral and the Bazaar*. Sebastopol, CA: O'Reilly and Associates.

Reiffen, D., and A. Kleit. 1990. *Terminal Railroad* Revisited: Foreclosure of an Essential Facility or Simple Horizontal Monopoly? *Journal of Law and Economics* 33: 419–38.

Reiffen, D., and M. Vita. 1995. Comment: Is There New Thinking on Vertical Mergers? *Antitrust Law Journal* 63: 917–41.

Riordan, M., and S. Salop. 1995. Evaluating Vertical Mergers: A Post-Chicago Approach. *Antitrust Law Journal* 63: 513–68.

Robertson, P., and R. Langlois. 1992. Modularity, Innovation, and the Firm: The Case of Audio Components. In F. M. Scherer and M. Perlman, eds., *Entrepreneurship, Technological Innovation, and Economic Growth: Studies in the Schumpeterian Tradition*, 321–42. Ann Arbor: University of Michigan Press.

Rosenberg, N. 1976. *Perspectives on Technology*. Cambridge: Cambridge University Press.

Scherer, F., and D. Ross. 1990. *Industrial Market Structure and Economic Performance*. Chicago: Rand McNally.

Schumpeter, J. 1950. *Capitalism, Socialism, and Democracy*. New York: Harper and Brothers.

Shapiro, C. 1995. Aftermarkets and Consumer Welfare: Making Sense of *Kodak*. *Antitrust Law Journal* 63: 483–511.

Shapiro, C., and D. Teece. 1994. Systems Competition and Aftermarkets: An Economic Analysis of *Kodak*. *Antitrust Bulletin* 39: 135–62.

Shughart, W. 1997. *The Organization of Industry*. Homewood, IL: BPI/Irwin.

Sidak, J. 1983. Debunking Predatory Innovation. *Columbia Law Review* 83: 1121–49.

Sidak, J., and D. Spulber. 1996. Deregulatory Takings and Breach of the Regulatory Contract. *New York University Law Review* 71: 851–999.

Simon, H. 1981. *The Architecture of Complexity*, in The Sciences of the Artificial. Cambridge, MA: MIT Press.

Spengler, J. 1950. Vertical Integration and Antitrust Policy. *Journal of Political Economy* 58: 347–52.

Sullivan, L., and A. Jones. 1992. Monopoly Conduct, Especially Leveraging Power from One Product or Market to Another. In T. Jorde and D. Teece, eds., *Antitrust, Innovation, and Competitiveness*, 165–84. New York: Oxford University Press.

Teece, D. 1986. Profiting from Technological Innovation: Implications for Integration, Collaboration, Licensing, and Public Policy. *Research Policy* 15: 285–305.

Teece, D., and M. Coleman. 1998. The Meaning of Monopoly: Antitrust Analysis in High-Technology Industries. *Antitrust Bulletin* 63: 801–54.

Telser, L. G. 1960. Why Should Manufacturers Want Fair Trade? *Journal of Law and Economics* 3: 86–105.

——— 1966. Cutthroat Competition and the Long Purse. *Journal of Law and Economics* 9: 259–67.

Tirole, J. 1988. *The Theory of Industrial Organization*. Cambridge, MA: MIT Press.

Tushman, M., and J. P. Murmann. 1998. Dominant Designs, Technology Cycles, and Organizational Outcomes. *Research in Organizational Behavior* 20: 231–66.

Whinston, M. 1990. Tying, Foreclosure, and Exclusion. *American Economic Review* 80: 837–59.

Williamson, O. E. 1979. Assessing Vertical Market Restrictions: Antitrust Ramifications of the Transaction Cost Approach. *University of Pennsylvania Law Review* 127: 953–93.

——— 1983. Antitrust Enforcement: Where It's Been, Where It's Going. *St. Louis University Law Journal* 27: 289–314.

8

Intellectual Property and Antitrust Limitations on Contract

Michelle M. Burtis and Bruce H. Kobayashi

The existence of a tradeoff between the use of ideas and the incentives for their creation is both a central and recurring theme in the legal and economic analysis of intellectual property rights. It is the primary issue in legal and economic analyses that attempt to define the proper scope of legal protection for intellectual property (Arrow 1962; Easterbrook 1982).

This inquiry is not limited to the scope of property rights contained in federal or state statutory or common law. An integral part of the inquiry into the proper scope of intellectual property laws is how related contracts affect the use-creation tradeoff. Contracts based on use of intellectual property rights are an indispensable complement to intellectual property (Nimmer 1998; Kobayashi and Ribstein 1999; Ginsburg 1997). However, the scope of contracting over intellectual property rights is limited by law in important ways.

First, the intellectual property laws impose limits on contracts. Contracts can be held unenforceable because they are preempted by the federal intellectual property laws. The primary inquiry is one of use versus creation, with preemption resulting if the contract upsets the system of "uniform federal standards" that are "carefully used to promote invention while at the same time preserving free competition."[1] Second, provisions of the copyright law, such as the first-sale and fair-use doctrines, directly limit copyright holders' ability to control use of their works.

Enforcement of contracts that do not conflict with federal intellectual property laws can be limited by other policy concerns. For example,

We acknowledge helpful comments from Luke Froeb, Bruce Johnsen, Robert Raben, Greg Werden, and participants at the Mercatus Center Symposium on Dynamic Competition and Public Policy. Kobayashi would like to thank the Law and Economics Center at George Mason University for generous support. Any remaining errors are the authors'.
[1] *Sears Roebuck & Co. v. Stiffel Co.*, 376 U.S. 225 (1964).

general contract principles can lead to invalidation of contracts. And use of valid contracts judged to be anticompetitive can be curtailed through application of the antitrust or intellectual property misuse laws.

Arguments for limitations on contracts are frequently based on the assumption that they alter the carefully considered optimal tradeoff between use and creation reflected in the federal intellectual property statutes (Lemley 1995, 1999). However, if the statutory regime in fact does not resemble an optimal balancing of use and creation, restrictions on contract may instead serve to prevent welfare enhancing alterations to imperfect intellectual property laws.

Not surprisingly, some of the most acute problems in defining legal rights have occurred in areas where technological progress has challenged or moved ahead of existing legal doctrine. The protection of intellectual property embodied in computer software is a prime example of the challenge new technologies pose for existing intellectual property protection. Computer software unquestionably embodies useful ideas and is a good candidate for some type of intellectual property protection. Indeed, after much consideration, Congress modified the copyright laws specifically to provide protection to software.[2] In practice, however, the use of the copyright laws to protect intellectual property embodied in computer software has not fit comfortably within existing legal doctrine, and courts have struggled to fit the proverbial "square peg in the round hole."[3] As a consequence, intellectual property protection for computer software has severe practical and legal limitations. Costly litigation over the scope of both copyright and patent protection for software continues to be both vigorous and unsettling to software developers. As a result, the scope of the legal right possessed by the intellectual property owner has yet to be clearly defined (Baird 1984; Galler 1995; Menell 1987; Dam 1995: 367–71).

Given these limitations, software developers have frequently relied on secrecy or privately negotiated contractual restrictions on the use of their products as an alternative to imperfect statutory intellectual property protection (Palmer 1986; Kitch 1980). These privately negotiated contractual restrictions have raised concerns that have resulted in both private and public litigation. If the primary reason that parties agree to such restrictions is to ensure that software developers are able to appro-

---

[2] The 1980 amendments implemented the recommendations contained in the Final Report of the National Commission on New Technological Uses of Copyrighted Works (CONTU) (July 31, 1978), which recommended that the Copyright Act "be amended ... to make it explicit that computer programs, to the extent that they embody the author's original creation, are proper subject matter for copyright." See Copyright Act, 17 U.S.C. 101 (defining the term "computer program").

[3] *Computer Associates International v. Altai*, 982 F.2d 693, 712 (2nd Cir. 1992).

priate a sufficient return on their creative investments in writing software, then refusal to enforce restrictive contracts – or vigorous and unpredictable antitrust litigation – will generate uncertainty, limit the software developer's ability to appropriate the returns to its activity, and reduce investment (Hall 1986).

Nowhere is this issue more central than in examining whether the application of the antitrust laws to intellectual property industries is likely to increase or decrease social welfare. As Bowman (1973) noted in his seminal work on patent and antitrust law, much attention has been paid to the supposed conflict between antitrust and intellectual property law. "Antitrust law and patent law are frequently viewed as standing in diametric opposition. How can there be compatibility between antitrust law, which promotes competition, and patent law, which promotes monopoly?"

Bowman concluded that this supposed conflict is largely illusory. Indeed, the conflict arises only when one attempts to analyze one aspect of the use-creation tradeoff without simultaneously considering the other. Once both aspects are considered, intellectual property and antitrust law are clearly compatible:

Both antitrust law and patent law have a common central economic goal: *to maximize wealth by producing what consumers want at the lowest cost.* ... Antitrust law does not demand competition under all circumstances. Quite properly, it permits monopoly when monopoly makes for greater output than would the alternative of an artificially fragmented [inefficient] industry. The patent ... is designed to provide something which consumers value and which they could not have at all or have as abundantly were no patent protection afforded.

This chapter argues that the failure by the courts and the antitrust agencies to consider adequately both aspects of the use-creation tradeoff has led to a confused and uncertain policy with respect to contract enforcement, antitrust, and intellectual property laws. The failure to recognize the compatible goals of contracts, intellectual property law, and antitrust law has resulted in an ex post economic and legal antitrust analysis that treats the licensing and sale of intellectual property as a static monopoly pricing problem. Further, similar competition policy arguments have been put forth and accepted by some courts in narrowing the scope of intellectual property rights to computer software.

We argue that this inappropriate ex post analysis can severely weaken intellectual property protection for software and has resulted in the abrogation of procompetitive contracts and practices. The two-pronged attack on the incentives for investment in the production of software will drive software developers to inefficient secrecy and deter socially efficient investment in the production of original ideas. Moreover, continuing the use of this inappropriate ex post analysis will lead antitrust agencies disproportionately to select innovative software developers for review, cause the courts to further weaken the intellectual property right system, and cripple the incentive for investments in the development and production of software.

A MODEL OF COMPETITION IN COMPUTER SOFTWARE MARKETS

In this section, we present a model of competition in the development, production, and sale of software. Although the model is highly stylized, we use it to illustrate the competitive effect of changes in both the scope and breadth of copyright protection, and how private contracting, which serves as an alternative to copyright protection, positively affects the market equilibrium and social welfare.

To illustrate the primary issues, we assume software developers are divided into two distinct types, original developers and imitators. Original developers expend resources in designing and developing the source code used in a software program.[4] Imitators expend resources copying the source code of an original developer. We also assume that the relative cost of original development and the cost of imitation can be altered by changes in the level of copyright protection and by contracts between developers and downstream users of the software.[5] Finally, we assume that the strength of copyright protection can be indexed by a single dimensional variable, z, and that the strength of contractual protection can be indexed by a single variable, k.

Let F_O denote the original developer's cost of "developing" the software, and let F_I denote the costs of imitating. We assume that imitation requires at least one original version of source code and that, in the absence of either copyright or contractual protection, imitation versions of the source code cost less to produce than an original.

A well-designed copyright law will disproportionately restrict those activities that come closest to outright copying of protected expression. Thus, we assume that the cost of developing an original version of software falls relative to the cost of imitation as z is increased. However, the existence of copyright protection also tends to raise the cost of "original" authorship (Landes and Posner 1989). Thus, we assume that the costs of

---

[4] The use of the term original here is consistent with its accepted meaning in copyright law under the Copyright Act, 17 U.S.C. 101.

[5] These contracts could include, for example, nondisclosure agreements with employees or even licensees of the software, or organizational arrangements such as vertical or horizontal integration to limit the amount of interfirm dissemination of information (Kitch 1980).

producing either an original or an imitation version of source code increase with the strength of copyright protection, z. In reality, even "original" software will borrow from the existing stock of ideas not protected by patents or copyrights. Thus, by reducing the existing stock of ideas that can be legally embodied in new software, increases in the strength of intellectual property right protection for software will increase the costs of producing even an "original" version of the source code.[6]

Once an original developer has successfully developed a copy of the source code, copies of the software embodying the source code can be produced and distributed to consumers at a constant cost equal to a_O by the original developer and a_I by an imitator. Thus, the costs of original development, F_O, and imitation, F_I, are treated as fixed costs that do not vary with the number of original and imitation software units sold, q_O and q_I respectively. We assume that marginal costs, a_O and a_I, can be affected by the contractual restrictions, indexed by k, adopted by original software developers. Specifically, increases in k increase imitators' costs of distribution, so that a_I is increasing in k. The effect of increases in k on a_O, however, are ambiguous. For example, imposition of contractual restrictions such as the use of a blanket license can simultaneously increase imitators' costs while decreasing the developer's production and distribution costs. It is also possible that contracts that increase imitators' costs have little effect or even increase costs for the firm imposing the restrictions (Salop and Scheffman 1987).

To model the competitive interaction between competing software products, we assume, for simplicity, that with N_O original and N_I imitation source code versions, the equilibrium price, P^*, and quantities of original ($N_O q_O^*$) and imitation ($N_I q_I^*$) software is determined by a Cournot interaction of these competing firms (Willig 1990; Kwoka 1979; Tirole 1988; Shapiro 1989). Our use of this assumption is not an endorsement of the Cournot model as a valid or accurate description of behavior in software markets. Rather, our intent is to highlight the shortcomings of the static Cournot model in markets in which intellectual property protection is crucial.

Under Cournot assumptions about software market firm behavior, the equilibrium market price and quantity will be completely determined by

---

[6] Increases in contractual (or organizational) restrictions aimed at preventing imitation can have a similar effect on F_O and F_I. For example, vertical integration, contractual secrecy requirements, or trade secrecy would make it more costly for imitators to obtain a copy of the source code. However, such devices are both privately and socially costly to implement and enforce. Thus, contractual restrictions or secrecy may raise the costs of producing both original and imitation versions of the source code. Because of the similarity of these effects and the effect of increasing z, we do not model them separately here.

the equilibrium number of original (N_O) and imitation (N_I) versions of the source code. The equilibrium number of source code versions are, in turn, determined by the equilibrium profitability of producing either an original or imitation version of the source code.

We use simulations based on this standard model of competition to illustrate market outcomes with varying levels of copyright and contractual protection. The specific assumptions used and the derivations of the results are contained in the appendix to this chapter.

Table 8.1 lists the simulated market equilibrium based on the specific functional forms described in the appendix. The table lists whether an equilibrium exists and, if one does, the number of each type of firm (N_O, N_I), the equilibrium price, P, and quantity, Q, and both gross welfare (GW) and welfare net of F_O and F_I (NW). The far left column of Table 8.1 lists the situation where the cost of imitation is relatively low ($F_I = .1$ and $F_O = .4$) and corresponds to the conditions that would exist with a weak copyright regime. Weak copyright protection allows imitators to copy and enables them to produce a version of the source code at relatively low cost. Moving to the right in Table 8.1 corresponds to increases in the strength of copyright protection, z, which results in an increase in the cost of producing a noninfringing imitation relative to the cost of producing a noninfringing original version.

The first row in Table 8.1 corresponds to the absence of strong contractual restrictions that serve to disadvantage imitator firms and reflects equal marginal costs of distributing original and imitation software. Moving down the rows in Table 8.1 reflects increased contractual restrictions used by original developers that significantly increase the relative costs faced by imitators for distributing and selling their products. In the example, we assume the contracts decrease the costs of distributing original software and increase the costs of distributing imitation software.

Table 8.1 shows that the existence of copyright protection and contractual restrictions that increase the relative costs of producing and distributing imitation software are necessary to produce an equilibrium. In all of the cases where an equilibrium exists, original firms can rely on the existence of some copyright protection and the use of contractual restrictions. In all but one of the cases where an equilibrium exists, the equilibrium outcome results in three original versions of the source code being produced[7] and the complete deterrence of imitator entry. The remaining case has two original firms and one imitator firm competing in equilibrium.

---

[7] The equilibrium existence of multiple original versions of the source code is consistent with current copyright law doctrine, which does not protect copyrightable material from independent creation. See Landes and Posner (1989: 344–46), Dam (1995: 337).

Table 8.1. Simulation Results

	A. ($z = 0$) $F_I = .10$ $F_O = .40$	B. ($z = 1$) $F_I = .20$ $F_O = .45$	C ($z = 2$) $F_I = .30$ $F_O = .50$	D. ($z = 3$) $F_I = .40$ $F_O = .55$	E. ($z = 4$) $F_I = .50$ $F_O = .60$
I. (k = 0) $a_I = .010$ $a_O = .010$	No equilibrium	No equilibrium	No equilibrium	No equilibrium	No equilibrium
II. (k = 1) $a_I = .020$ $a_O = .0095$	No equilibrium	No equilibrium	No equilibrium	No equilibrium	No equilibrium*
III. (k = 3) $a_I = .030$ $a_O = .0090$	No equilibrium	No equilibrium	No equilibrium	No equilibrium*	No equilibrium*
IV. (k = 4) $a_I = .040$ $a_O = .0085$	No equilibrium	No equilibrium	No equilibrium*	No equilibrium*	$N_O,N_I = 3,0$ $P = .256, Q = .74$ $GW = .46$ $NW = .28$
V. (k = 5) $a_I = .050$ $a_O = .0080$	No equilibrium	No equilibrium	No equilibrium*	$N_O,N_I = 2,1$ $P = .267, Q = .73$ $GW = .45$ $NW = .30$	$N_O,N_I = 3,0$ $P = .256, Q = .74$ $GW = .46$ $NW = .28$
VI. (k = 6) $a_I = .060$ $a_O = .0075$	No equilibrium	No equilibrium*	No equilibrium*	$N_O,N_I = 3,0$ $P = .256, Q = .74$ $GW = .46$ $NW = .30$	$N_O,N_I = 3,0$ $P = 256, Q = .74$ $GW = .46$ $NW = .28$
VII. (k = 7) $a_I = .070$ $a_O = .0070$	No equilibrium	No equilibrium*	$N_O,N_I = 3,0$ $P = .255, Q = .74$ $GW = .46$ $NW = .31$	$N_O,N_I = 3,0$ $P = .255 Q = .74$ $GW = .46$ $NW = .30$	$N_O,N_I = 3,0$ $P = .256, Q = .74$ $GW = .46$ $NW = .28$
VIII. (k = 8) $a_I = .080$ $a_O = .0065$	No equilibrium	No equilibrium*	$N_O,N_I = 3,0$ $P = .255, Q = .75$ $GW = .46$ $NW = .31$	$N_O,N_I = 3,0$ $P = .255, Q = .75$ $GW = .46$ $NW = .30$	$N_O,N_I = 3,0$ $P = .255, Q = .75$ $GW = .46$ $NW = .28$
IX. (k = 9) $a_I = .090$ $a_O = .0060$	No equilibrium	$N_O,N_I = 3,0$ $P = .255, Q = .75$ $GW = .46$ $NW = .33$	$N_O,N_I = 3,0$ $P = .255, Q = .75$ $GW = .46$ $NW = .31$	$N_O,N_I = 3,0$ $P = .255, Q = .75$ $GW = .46$ $NW = .30$	$N_O,N_I = 3,0$ $P = .255, Q = .75$ $GW = .46$ $NW = .28$

Note: For definition of terms, see related discussion in text and notes.

Table 8.1 also allows a comparison of the use of restrictive contracts versus stronger copyright laws to deter imitation. The highest net welfare level is achieved when there is "moderate" copyright protection ($z = 1$) and strong contractual restrictions ($k = 9$). Because increases in the strength of copyright protection are assumed to increase the costs of all expression, even original expression, increases in the level of copyright protection beyond those necessary to induce the production of original versions of the source code will begin to reduce welfare. Thus, contractual restrictions that raise the costs of distributing imitation software without increasing the cost of distributing original software will be more efficient and will result in higher levels of net welfare.

Conversely, the absence of either strong copyright protection or strong contractual restrictions results in the nonexistence of a market equilibrium. The absence of an equilibrium is a manifestation of the familiar appropriability/free-rider problem that differentiates intellectual property and other public-good markets from private markets. Absent intellectual property or contractual protection, imitation will be cheaper than coming up with an original innovation, idea, or expression. And when it is cheaper and more profitable to imitate than it is to come up with an original product, firms will choose to imitate, and will appropriate the returns from the original firm's investment. Given this, no firm will want to invest in producing an original version of the source code.

To see this, consider the case where the costs of distributing original and imitation software are the same, and where copyright law is weakened so that $F_I = .1$ and $F_O = .4$. Under these conditions, it is not surprising that *imitation entry* is relatively attractive, as the cost of imitation is one-fourth the cost of producing an original version of the software. This large-scale imitator entry reduces the present value of the gross profits from selling an original version of software below the cost of developing an original version of the source code.

Clearly, no firm that anticipates this outcome would rationally invest in producing an original version of the source code. And the lack of an original version precludes the existence of an imitation version. While large-scale imitation entry makes a policy of weak copyright laws attractive from a static welfare point of view, it also prevents development of an original version of the source code from being an equilibrium decision.[8]

The results from Table 8.1 also can be used to illustrate the fallacy of using an ex post analysis that considers only the price of software or some index of concentration to evaluate the appropriate limits of copyright protection or to justify an antitrust investigation into restrictive licensing practices. An analysis seeking to minimize market concentration and/or to lower the equilibrium price would suggest that the

---

[8] In the cases marked with an asterisk in Table 8.1, cases exist where imitator entry would not drive original profits below zero. However, these cases are not equilibria, as the marginal original firm would rather be an imitator firm.

removal of "barriers to entry," such as contractual and copyright restrictions on imitators, would improve welfare. Indeed, under Cournot assumptions, if both copyright protection and contractual protection are removed from firms that have already incurred F_O, the number of firms will rise, the total quantity will rise, and the market price will fall.

For example, suppose initially that an equilibrium exists with three original firms in the market, and that all barriers to imitation are removed so that $a_O = a_I = .01$ and $F_I = .1$. Under these conditions, five imitation firms will choose to enter the market. Because at this point the original firms' entry and investment decisions are sunk, the three existing firms will make positive gross profits after imitation entry occurs and thus will continue to produce and sell software. The Hirshmann-Herfindahl Index (HHI) will fall from a "highly concentrated" 3,333 to a "moderately concentrated" 1,250.[9] The market price will equal .12 (approximately half the level of any equilibrium in Table 8.1). The market quantity will rise to .88, and static welfare will rise to .484. Thus, *if we assume the existence of one or more original firms*, both copyright protection and restrictive contracts that increase the costs of producing and distributing imitation software lead to more concentrated markets, higher equilibrium prices, and lower static welfare. This outcome is the standard grounds for condemnation of "barriers to entry" under a traditional static antitrust analysis.

This outcome can be generated only if the original firms were somehow mistakenly induced to develop the software in the first place. Such an outcome could be achieved, for example, by an unanticipated weakening of the copyright laws or an unanticipated antitrust attack on contractual restrictions that increase imitators' costs of distributing software that occurred *after* the investment in the production of an original version of the source code had occurred. If firms are not systematically fooled, however, anticipation that such a policy will be continued will deter *future* investments in the production of original software. And unless the onetime gain from the increased use of existing ideas is more important that the continued maintenance of incentives for future innovation, such a myopic policy would decrease dynamic welfare.

The simulations demonstrate Bowman's (1973) general welfare point quoted in the introduction of this chapter. To the extent that the copyright and antitrust laws are viewed as having the same goal, the maximization of dynamic welfare, some tolerance for a more concentrated market structure, higher prices, and greater profits for existing software

[9] The U.S. Department of Justice and Federal Trade Commission *Horizontal Merger Guidelines* (April 2, 1992), reprinted in *Trade Reg. Rep.* (CCH) at 13,104 (April 7, 1992), contain specific numerical thresholds associated with the HHI.

firms may be necessary. And when compared with increasing the strength and scope of intellectual property rights under copyright laws, practices that have been condemned as anticompetitive, such as contracts that disadvantage rival firms producing imitation software, and horizontal and vertical mergers, can be a more efficient way to provide incentives for the production of original software.

LEGAL PROTECTION FOR SOFTWARE AND DATABASES

Intellectual property laws do not protect costly-to-produce but nonoriginal works, such as databases, against free riding. In *Feist v. Rural Telephone Services*, the Supreme Court rejected the "sweat of the brow" theory of copyright.[10] The Court held that the contents of a factual work that required great effort to compile (in this case, a telephone directory) were not protectable under copyright if they did not meet a threshold standard of originality.

Protection of noncopyrightable factual works could in theory be protected under state misappropriation laws (Karjala 1994; Paepke 1987); however, application of state misappropriation laws has been severely limited by federal preemption (Merges et al. 1997: 750; Epstein 1992; Baird 1983). It has long been considered legal to copy a competitor's nonpatentable product or noncopyrightable expression as long as it has been disclosed to the public. Protection of publicly disclosed ideas under state unfair competition laws is limited to protection against source confusion and does not extend protection more generally against misappropriation by an imitator (Wiley 1989; Lichtman 1997).

Thus, for ideas and information found to lie outside of the patent and copyright laws, protection of ideas against misappropriation is generally limited to those areas where special sui generis federal legislation has been enacted (Menell 1987; Dam 1995), to *successfully* hidden trade secrets (Friedman, Landes, and Posner 1991), and to nonpreempted and otherwise enforceable contracts (Kobayashi and Ribstein 1999). Where trade secrecy is not an option, and no federal sui generis protection is available, contract may be the only option. For example, noncopyrightable databases must rely on contractual restrictions to protect them from misappropriation.[11]

For those works that can be copyrighted, both legal and practical considerations have resulted in copyright being used as the primary means

---

[10] 499 U.S. 340 (1991).

[11] *ProCD v. Zeidenberg*, 86 F.3d 1447 (7th Cir 1996). Sui generis intellectual property protection for noncopyrightable compilations (such as computer databases or the directory in *Feist*) was eliminated from the final version of the Digital Millennium Act. See 56 BNA Pat. Tr. & Copy. J. 691 (10/15/98).

to protect computer software through a system of statutory intellectual property rights.[12] However, the scope of the legal right granted to computer software has not been clearly resolved.

The primary way in which courts have attempted to define the limits of copyright protection is through application of the idea-expression dichotomy. It is well established in law that the scope of the right given under the copyright laws covers only the form of expression and does not protect ideas.[13] Determining exactly what constitutes copyrightable "expression" and what constitutes noncopyrightable "ideas," however, has proved to be a difficult task to carry out in practice. Courts' inability to adequately deal with this issue has lead to much uncertainty over the scope of the protection afforded by copyright law.

Two primary economic approaches determine the scope of copyright protection. The first emphasizes the effect that broadening the scope of copyright to include the protection of ideas would have on the cost of developing copyrighted materials generally (Landes and Posner 1989: 348). This approach adopts a traditional intellectual property right approach that focuses on the effect changes in the level of protection has on the supply of copyrighted ideas. The second approach adopts a standard competition-antitrust analysis to determine the proper scope of the copyright laws. This approach largely ignores the standard intellectual property issues and emphasizes the effect that protecting ideas would have on increasing the danger of welfare losses from monopoly (Warren-Boulton, Baseman, and Woroch 1995).

This dichotomy does not imply that the two approaches are always or even largely inconsistent. For example, consider the classic merger doctrine in copyright law, which denies protection when idea and expression merge (Landes and Posner 1989). Under a competition-antitrust analysis, copyright would be denied because allowing a de facto copyright over an idea would increase the deadweight losses from monopoly. Under an intellectual property right approach, copyright would be denied because the de facto expansion of copyright protection to ideas would increase the cost of producing subsequent original ideas. In either case, the scope of copyright is similarly limited.

In other cases, however, the two approaches have very different implications for where the line between idea and expression should be drawn.

[12] CONTU recommended in 1978 use of copyright protection for computer software. This recommendation was included as part of the 1980 amendments to the copyright statute. See Copyright Act 17 U.S.C. 102. For a more detailed discussion of this issue, see Dam (1995: 338–39). Our analysis does not explicitly address the issue of software patents. For a general discussion of the issue of software patents and their limitations, see Dam (1995: 367–71), Galler (1995: 21).

[13] *Baker v. Selden*, 101 U.S. 99 (1879).

For example, consider the case where, out of many ex ante identical ways to express an idea, one clearly evolves as the industry standard. According to the intellectual property approach that focuses on the cost of expression, the existence of many ex ante alternatives suggests that property right protection would have little effect on the cost of producing original expressions. Thus, copyright protection would be granted to the expression in this case. However, analyses based on the competition-antitrust theory of copyright focus on the costs of noncompatibility and suggest that, from an ex post viewpoint, expressions that have become de facto standards have merged with ideas. In this case, application of an ex post merger doctrine suggests no copyright protection should be enforced.[14]

An examination of copyright doctrine confirms that it is largely consistent with a focus on free riding. For example, the copyright laws do not protect a copyright holder from the existence of an identical but independent creation, and thus do not seek to grant in any relevant sense "copyright monopolies."[15] Indeed, this is consistent with the results of our simulations, as all of the equilibrium outcomes consisted of multiple firms developing and selling original software based on their own version of the original source code.

Likewise, our approach is consistent with the prohibition against copyrighting works copied from the public domain,[16] from predecessor programs,[17] or from industry conventions.[18] In all of these cases, the ideas preexist in a form that is presumably equally accessible to all who wish to use them. Because no free riding of the type highlighted in our model can occur, copyright protection in these cases is not warranted. Finally,

---

[14] Dam (1995) notes that these arguments incorporate competition policy arguments to interpret intellectual property laws and suggests that such a policy may be unwise, as it "might well . . . undermine the coherence of both fields of law, since the antitrust laws remain available to attack true market monopolies and restraints of trade in software markets." Further, standard competition arguments have been advanced primarily to support "me-too" copying, where market power in the antitrust sense did not exist. "Thus, to deny protection on competitive grounds is to introduce a kind of mini-antitrust law for intellectual property cases that we would be unwilling to apply in other areas of law."

[15] Dam (1995: 359). Landes and Posner (1989: 344–47) also explain the nonactionability of accidental infringement based on the effect that avoidance of such duplication would have on the production of originals. In contrast, competition analyses do not generally consider or differentiate between the case where the copying was accidental or not.

[16] *Computer Associates.*

[17] *Apple Computer, Inc. v. Microsoft Corporation and Hewlett-Packard Co.*, 35 F.3d 1435 (1994).

[18] Ibid. Note that a prohibition against copyright protection for works copied from or based on industry conventions does not imply that the industry convention or other types of standards should not be copyrightable.

our analysis suggests there are areas where intellectual property right protection would address free-riding behavior but would also increase the costs of original expression. In these cases, enforcement of contracts that prevent misappropriation may be superior to granting broad intellectual property rights (Ginsburg 1997).

Many important areas of the idea-expression dichotomy remain far from settled, however. A review of the existing case law concerning the scope of copyright for computer software clearly illustrates the tension between the two standard theories and the uncertainty underlying the scope of the legal right held by a software owner. A large number of litigated cases have involved a situation similar to the one contained in the model – a dispute between the developer of a first-to-market product and an imitator with a directly competitive follow-on "me-too" product. Not only are the competing software programs close substitutes, but the primary issue being litigated often is whether the imitating producer's me-too software program can be made as close as possible, from the buyers' perspective, to the original product (Dam 1995). And the courts' choice of which one of the two approaches to use in resolving the idea-expression dichotomy has been far from consistent and has often resulted in decisions that severely limit the use of copyright as a predictable or effective tool to protect computer software (Nimmer and Krauthaus 1995).

The absence of a coherent approach is clearly illustrated by the Second Circuit's influential "filtration approach" set out in *Computer Associates v. Altai*.[19] The opinion clearly signals hostility toward Congress's decision to use copyright to protect computer software.[20] Quite separate from the underlying philosophical issue, the approach set out in *Computer Associates* seems flawed as a means to separate rationally idea and expression. Under the *Computer Associates* approach, an original program is first broken down into component parts at a number of levels (abstraction). The component parts of the program are then put through a "filtration" process where unprotectable ideas and protectable expression are separated. Finally, the allegedly infringing program is compared with the portion of the original program that remains after all of the elements that have been found to be either "ideas or are dictated by efficiency or external factors, or taken from the public domain" have been removed.

If the purpose of this approach is to *reduce* the original program to a "core" level of expression, such an approach seems inconsistent with the

---

[19] *Computer Associates.*
[20] The judge in the case explicitly acknowledges that his decision will provide a disincentive for future computer program research and development. Ibid., 712.

doctrine set out in *Feist* that original compilations are copyrightable even though the individual elements of the compilation are not.[21] Alternatively, one could argue that one plausible "level" of abstraction would include subsets of the original compilation, or the compilation as a whole. Such an approach, however, would require consideration of an infinite number of levels of abstraction and is unlikely to help in clarifying the bounds of nonliteral infringement.

The lack of a coherent approach to copyright protection for computer software has led to inconsistent holdings by the lower courts (Dam 1995) and to the deadlock reached by the Supreme Court in the *Lotus v. Borland* case.[22] In *Lotus v. Borland*, the district court, in a series of opinions, held that parts of Lotus's 1-2-3 spreadsheet program's user interface, including its menu tree, were copyrightable and infringed by Borland in its competing Quattro Pro spreadsheet.[23]

The district court's decision, written by Judge Keeton, was consistent with his earlier ruling in *Lotus v. Paperback*.[24] In *Paperback*, Judge Keeton found that the Lotus 1-2-3 menu structures were protected expression covered by Lotus copyrights and infringed by similar structures contained in Paperback's competing VP-Planner software. Judge Keeton explicitly adopted an intellectual property approach by rejecting the defendant's arguments that there was an ex post merger of expression and idea because the Lotus menu had become a de facto standard:

> By arguing that 1-2-3 was so innovative that it occupied the field and set a *de facto* industry standard, and that therefore, defendants were free to copy plaintiff's expression, defendants have flipped copyright on its head. Copyright protection would be perverse if it only protected mundane increments while leaving unprotected as part of the public domain those advancements that are more strikingly innovative.

Similarly, in the Borland Litigation, Keeton found that the 1-2-3 menu structures were copyrightable expression.[25] Keeton explicitly rejected the notion of ex post merger being put forth by the defendants in the case: "[a] very satisfactory spreadsheet menu tree can be constructed using different menu commands and a different command structure from those of Lotus 1-2-3. . . . it is possible to generate literally millions of satisfactory menu trees by varying the menu commands employed."

---

[21] 499 U.S. 340 (1991).

[22] 516 U.S. 233 (1996) (summary affirmance due to deadlocked Court).

[23] 831 F.Supp. 223 (1983) (holding that Lotus 1-2-3 menu was copyrightable expression and infringed).

[24] 740 F.Supp. 37 (1980).   [25] See *Borland* II, 799 F.Supp. at 216.

The Court of Appeals reversed, holding that the menu tree was not copyrightable expression and that the Lotus menu tree was an uncopyrightable "method of operation." The court analogized the Lotus 1-2-3 menu to the buttons on a video cassette recorder (VCR), and argued that "if specific words are essential to operating something, then they are a part of a "method of operation" and, as such, are unprotectable."[26]

Arguing over whether the Lotus 1-2-3 menu tree is akin to the buttons on a VCR seems an unlikely way to determine in a rational or principled fashion the proper scope of copyright for computer software. Nor does attempting to figure out what is "essential" or "nonessential" seem more helpful – it is unclear what, if any, expression contained in a software program would be found to be "unessential." Both of the court's suggestions seem to degenerate quickly to futile semantic exercises, an approach criticized by Landes and Posner (1989): "We hope that the debate will be resolved not by the semantics of the words 'idea' and 'expression' but by the economics of the problem and, specifically, by comparing the deadweight costs of allowing a firm to appropriate what has become an industry standard with the disincentive effects on originators if such appropriation is forbidden."

The court's consideration of "program compatibility" issues and the argument that a program's attainment of the status as a "de facto standard" should cut against copyrightability suggests a better articulated economic principle on which the line between idea and expression should be drawn. In this case, the unique social cost identified by those wishing to condemn copyright protection is that users of original software programs will face switching costs if software is not allowed to be compatible or if follow-on firms are not allowed zero-priced access to "de facto" industry standards. In addition, those who would condemn copyright protection in these cases posit that the existence of switching costs can lead to customer lock-in, where these customers can remain "captives" of the current program even when a superior alternative comes along.[27] Thus, minimization of these costs requires that follow-on programs should be permitted to borrow freely elements of the de facto standard.

There are several problems with these arguments when applied to defining the scope of copyright protection. First, and foremost, application of what are essentially competition policy arguments to the problem of whether something is copyrightable will be costly in terms of lost

---

[26] 49 F.3d 807 (1st Cir. 1995).
[27] The example of the persistence of the QWERTY keyboard and the VHS video recorder are often given as manifestations of this problem. See ibid., 817.

incentives for investments in software. Because the arguments are being used to condemn copyright protection, acceptance of these arguments suggests a move to the system that Judge Keeton pejoratively referred to as one that "stands copyright on its head." That is, as soon as a program attains the status of a de facto standard, copyright protection for those portions of the program become uncopyrightable and part of the public domain – open to copying by all, including those who wish to free-ride on the investments of the original author by simply "cloning" the now unprotected elements of the original program.[28] Applying the results of our model, such an outcome will, on the margin, result in a loss of incentives for and lower amounts of investment in the production of original software.

Further, it is not at all clear why the mere existence of switching costs yields a compelling reason for the elimination of property right protection through copyright for software. As Dam (1995: 351) points out, the existence of switching costs is ubiquitous in all economic decisions, and it is unclear that the failure to switch to a slightly more efficient standard constitutes a market failure or a social loss. Nor, is it clear, as an empirical matter, that the problems of lock-in and the perpetuation of inefficient standards is an empirically relevant issue. As Liebowitz and Margolis have shown in a series of articles, the existence of inefficient standards perpetuated by switching costs and lock-in is an empirical myth.[29]

Finally, even if one accepts that Borland should be able to use the Lotus 1-2-3 menu, it is unclear that the complete condemnation of copyright protection is warranted under these circumstances. As Judge Boudin noted in his concurrence, "a different approach" to that set out by the majority would be to base copyrightability decisions on traditional intellectual property law precedents that are independent of these competition policy arguments. To the extent that access to "de facto standards" is warranted, such access can be granted according to the existing copyright doctrine of "fair use." The advantage of this approach is that it would fall short of punishing success by preserving rather than elimi-

---

[28] It is unclear what market share is required to become a de facto standard. Dam (1995: 356) reports that Lotus market share was 37%, trailing Microsoft's Excel program, which had a share of 52.7% of the spreadsheet market.

[29] The prime example of inefficient standards, the QWERTY keyboard, is based on an assertion that is demonstrably false. See Liebowitz and Margolis (1990, 1994). In addition, the fact pattern in the Beta/VHS video recorder competition, also cited as evidence of inefficient path dependence, and in many of the software application markets, are simply inconsistent with the conditions that the theoretical model suggests are necessary for the perpetuation of inefficient standards. See, e.g., Liebowitz and Margolis (1995a,b, 1999), Levinson (1996a, 1996b).

nating the copyright holders' property right, while permitting limited and specific exceptions to infringement through the well-developed doctrine of fair use.[30]

LIMITATIONS ON CONTRACT

Throughout this chapter, the primary problem faced by the developer of an original computer software program is free riding or misappropriation by imitators caused by the lack of impediments to low-cost entry. To the extent that statutory protection under the federal copyright laws yields inadequate or uncertain protection against misappropriation, the developer must turn to alternative means of protecting his investment. Yet the developer selling or licensing software to the public on a large scale may find his noncontractual alternatives severely limited and/or uncertain. Thus, the use of restrictive contracts may be a *necessary* condition for the production of ideas, including original versions of the source code for a computer program or a costly database. Under these circumstances, restrictive contracts that discourage entry into intellectual property industries by imitators can improve incentives for production of these useful programs and databases.

Contractual protection of ideas can be limited through the nonenforcement of restrictive contract terms (Kitch 1980: 685–88). Restrictive terms can be preempted by the federal laws. For example, in *Lear v. Adkins*, contractual provisions that stopped the licensee from challenging the validity of the patent were voided. For computer software, the practical effect of contract preemption may be limited. States can pass laws that provide remedies that are not "equivalent" to copyright. Courts have generally enforced contracts under state contract law under both section 301 of the Copyright Act and the common law.[31]

---

[30] The fair-use doctrine is consistent with our efficiency analysis based on the prevention of free riding. Specifically, the doctrine of fair use distinguishes generally between productive or transformative uses and reproductive uses. For a detailed discussion of the fair-use doctrine, see Landes and Posner (1989), Posner (1992), and Landes (1992). In applying a fair-use analysis to the Lotus-Borland litigation, Judge Keeton found Borland's use to have been reproductive, and that the facts failed to support a finding of fair use. See *Lotus v. Borland*, 831 F.Supp. 223, 241 (1993). In contrast, courts that have used the fair-use analysis where the use has been transformative have found fair use. For example, in cases where the software attached to, rather than replaced, the original program, the courts have accepted the defense of fair use. See, e.g., *Sega Enterprises v. Accolade*, Inc., 977 F.2d 1510 (9th Cir. 1992), and *Atari Games Corp. v. Nintendo of America, Inc.*, 975 F.2d 832 (Fed. Cir. 1992).

[31] Under section 301 of the Copyright Act, a state law can survive if there is proof of an extra element in addition to those required for copyright infringement claim. For contract law, this extra element is the agreement of the parties. See Merges et al. (1997: 821).

Nonenforcement of restrictive terms would be generally limited to those terms that would be held unenforceable based on general contract principles, such as defective formation and unconscionability (Lemley 1999; Kobayashi and Ribstein 1999).

Some have suggested that properly formed contracts should be preempted by the first-sale doctrine, which provides that the copyright holder cannot restrict what a purchaser of copy does with *that* copy.[32] Thus application of the first-sale doctrine would render restrictive contractual terms attached to a sale unenforceable. However, to the extent that the distribution of computer software and databases can be legally characterized as a license, the producers of information, by licensing rather than selling their software, can choose to opt out of the first-sale doctrine.[33] Although some courts have characterized such licenses as sales, and have invalidated restrictive contract terms under the first-sale doctrine, contracting around the first-sale doctrine was anticipated by Congress.[34] In addition, the recently passed Uniform Computer Information Transaction Act broadly characterizes transactions as licenses, and supports enforcement of contractual restrictions (Kobayashi and Ribstein 1999).

Even if contract law allows broad enforcement of restrictive terms in contracts, such contracts are subject to scrutiny under the patent and copyright misuse and the antitrust laws. Standard antitrust analyses, as practiced by federal regulatory agencies and as implemented by the courts, assess the different circumstances faced by original developers and imitators based on the concept of "barriers to entry." Rather than focusing on the benefits of "barriers to entry," which mitigate the advantages the imitators obtain by free riding on the original developer's work,

---

[32] See Merges et al. (1997: 439). Thus, the purchaser may not make additional copies. However, attempts by the copyright holder to limit the way in which the particular copy is used would be barred.

[33] The ability of copyright holders to make portions of the intellectual property laws default rather than mandatory rules is controversial (Lemley 1999; Kobayashi and Ribstein 1999). In the case of the first-sale doctrine, allowing parties to opt out can be efficient. In effect, the first-sale doctrine forces the copyright holder to capitalize any potential for multiple uses into the original purchase price. Allowing the parties to contract for the level of use can allow a more refined level of price discrimination (e.g., by allowing a potential licensee to agree to limit use in exchange for a lower price), which can in turn be welfare increasing (*ProCD*; Liebowitz 1985; Bakos, Brynjolfsson, and Lichtman 1999; Besen and Kirby 1989; and Meurer 1997; Hausman and Mackie-Mason 1988).

[34] The committee report to section 109(a) of the Copyright Act of 1976 indicates that Congress anticipated that parties might contract out of a first-sale right. See Lemley (1995) citing the Committee on the Judiciary, H.R. Rep. No. 94-1476. Thus, it does not seem that enforcement of a contract that waives the first-sale right would directly conflict with the law or impede accomplishment of Congress's objectives.

conventional antitrust analyses focus on entrants' disadvantages vis-à-vis the existing "incumbent" firm (Gilbert and Newbery 1982). The implication of these analyses is that consumers will be best served by encouraging entrants into industries where profits are "high" by eliminating or mitigating the effects of such barriers. The role of the entrant is to stimulate competition, drive prices down, reduce industry profits, and increase consumer welfare. Schumpeter (1942) suggested the misguided nature of this approach:

In analyzing ... business strategy ex-visu of a given point of time, the investigating economist or government agent sees price policies that seem to him predatory and restrictions of output that seem to him synonymous with loss of opportunities to produce. He does not see that restrictions of this type are, in the conditions of the perennial gale, incidents, often unavoidable incidents, of a long-run process of expansion which they protect rather than impede. There is no more of a paradox in this than there is in saying that motorcars are traveling faster than they otherwise would because they are provided with brakes.

The static viewpoint Schumpeter warned against has led to antitrust and misuse attacks on contractual and licensing practices in intellectual property industries. The courts and agencies have used such analyses, for example, to question whether the use of trademarks are anticompetitive because they cause entrants to invest in advertising to promote their product and overcome the brand loyalty associated with the mark.[35] They have also used them to scrutinize whether certain contracts that place limits on licensees, such as tie-ins and restrictions on use beyond the first sale, constitute misuse of patents[36] and copyrights.[37] The history of antitrust law contains many examples where intellectual property,[38]

---

[35] See *Borden, Inc. v. Federal Trade Commission*, 674 F.2d 498 (6th Cir. 1982) (although not implemented, the commission found compulsory trademark licensing "within the range of remedies it had the power to impose"). See also Krouse (1984), Posner (1970).

[36] In *Morton Salt Co. v. G. S. Suppiger Co.*, the Court held that patent misuse does not require proof of an antitrust violation. For movement away from this doctrine, see *Mallinckrodt Inc. v. Medipart Inc.*, 24 U.S.P.Q. 1173 (Fed. Cir. 1992), and the 1988 amendments to section 27(d) of the Patent Code (harmonizing tying under misuse and antitrust analyses).

[37] Copyright misuse has been sparingly applied by the courts as a defense to infringement. But see *Lasercomb America, Inc. v. Reynolds*, 911 F.2d 970 (4th Cir. 1990). For an analysis suggesting the expanded use of copyright misuse, see Lemley (1999).

[38] The Supreme Court's hostility to intellectual property in the mid-twentieth century led Justice Jackson to complain that "the only patent that is valid is one which this Court has not been able to get its hands on." See *Jurgensen v. Ostby & Barton Co.*, 335 U.S. 560, 572 (1949). And just twenty-five years after the Court's decision in *Int'l News Service v. Associated Press*, 248 U.S. 215 (1918) (granting the AP a quasi property in news against its competitors), the government successfully challenged the AP's bylaws on antitrust grounds, *United States v. Associated Press*, 326 U.S. 1 (1945). The majority opinion upheld

related contracts, licenses, organizations,[39] and combinations[40] have been the targets of antitrust enforcement. Perhaps the height of this trend was the definition of the "nine no-no's" of patent licensing, which included a laundry list of many contracting arrangements that have since been found to be efficiency-enhancing in many contexts.[41]

While subsequent administrations have backed away from the nine no-no's[42] and the creation of the Federal Circuit Court of Appeals has reduced the judiciary's antiintellectual property stance,[43] recent developments suggest at least a partial return to attacks on licensing contracts in intellectual property industries.

With respect to computer software, the federal antitrust agencies recently have adopted the view that "network externalities" and "installed user bases" constitute welfare decreasing barriers to entry. As

the government's successful challenge of AP's bylaws, which prohibited all AP members from selling news to nonmembers and granted each member powers to block its non-member competitors from membership. The majority's opinion led Justice Murphy to suggest that requiring the Associated Press to share its products with competitors would "discourage competitive enterprise and would carry the anti-trust laws to absurd lengths." For a more complete discussion of the Court's hostility to intellectual property, see Dam (1994), Hall (1986: 72).

[39] Fisher, McGowan and Greenwood (1983) (discussion of the antitrust case against IBM in the 1970s).

[40] Bittlingmayer (1988) (discussing the aircraft patent pool).

[41] The nine no-no's include prohibitions against (1) tying of unpatented materials; (2) licensing of future patents; (3) restrictions on resale; (4) restrictions on licensee's activities falling outside the scope of the patent; (5) agreements that the patentee will not grant, without the licensee's consent, further licenses to any other person; (6) an extension of the patent grant to permit mandatory package licensing; (7) basing royalties on an amount not reasonably related to the licensee's sales of products covered by the patent; (8) for the owner of a process patent to attempt to place restrictions on the licensee's sales made by the use of the patented process; (9) for a patentee to require a license to adhere to any specified or minimum price. See Remarks by the Deputy Assistant Attorney General Bruce Wilson before the Michigan State Bar Association, *Trade Reg. Rep.* (CCH) at 50,146 (September 21, 1972). For an analysis of patent licenses as cartel arrangements, see Priest (1977). For economic analysis suggesting the efficiency of such practices, see McGee (1966), Bowman (1973), and Yu (1981).

[42] Remarks of the Assistant Attorney General for Antitrust Rule, The Antitrust Implications of International Licensing: After the Nine No-Nos, 33 BNA *Trademark and Copyright Journal* (November 6, 1986), 18–23.

[43] For example, in *Abbott Laboratories v. Brennan*, 952 F.2d 1346 (Fed. Cir. 1991), the Federal Circuit has not followed the Supreme Court's ruling in *United States v. Lowes*, 371 U.S. 38 (1962), and *Jefferson Parish Hospital District No. 2 v. Hyde*, 466 U.S. 2 (1984), which suggested the existence of intellectual property implied the existence of market power. The Sixth Circuit has also held that market power may not be presumed from the fact that a computer program is protected by copyright. See *A.I. Root v. Computer Dynamics Inc.*, 806 F.2d 673 (6th Cir. 1986). For a recent case, see *C.R. Bard v. M3 Systems, Inc.*, 157 F.3d 1340 (1998).

we noted earlier, the phenomenon of network externalities is either simply a recognition of the existence of scale economies in the production of ideas, or an empirically unsupported assertion about the propensity of markets to choose inefficient standards. Neither the existence of scale economies nor the unproven existence of inefficient path dependence suggests a compelling reason to submit software markets to heightened antitrust scrutiny, especially when such scrutiny can result in the destruction of contracts used to encourage the production of intellectual property.[44]

The most prominent examples have been the recent actions of the antitrust agencies against Microsoft and Intel for various licensing practices.[45] The investigation into Microsoft's licensing practices was initiated by the Federal Trade Commission in 1990 and was subsequently taken over by the Department of Justice (DoJ) in late 1993 after the commission deadlocked 2-2 over bringing an enforcement action. On July 27, 1994, the DoJ filed a complaint against Microsoft and a motion to approve a consent decree. In its complaint, the DoJ suggests that Microsoft's licensing practices erected or supported barriers to entry arising from the existence of network externalities and compatibility problems that disadvantaged potential rivals. Various contractual provisions Microsoft had with producers of hardware were challenged under the decree, including per-processor blanket licenses, lump-sum fees, minimum commitments, long-term contracts, tying, and restrictive nondisclosure agreements.[46]

However, the mere fact that a certain contractual device serves as a "barrier to entry" does not provide, in a more careful analysis, a reason to condemn the practice. The notion that entry barriers can improve welfare was recognized much earlier by von Weizsacker (1980), and by Demsetz (1982): "The [entry] barrier may reduce the severity of some externality or it may bring about improved levels of competition in activities other than that of direct concern."

Certainly, in the context of the model set out here, barriers to entry, in the form of some protection against free riding, are necessary to

---

[44] These antitrust actions are even more problematic when they are initiated by competitors who often have an incentive to subvert competition by interfering with their rivals' efficient contracting practices. See *Matsushita Electric Industrial Co., Ltd. v. Zenith Radio Corporation*, 475 U.S. 574 (1986). See also Baumol and Ordover (1985), and Baxter (1980).

[45] See *United States v. Microsoft*, 1995 U.S. Dist. LEXIS 1654 (D.D.C. 1995).

[46] See Levinson (1996a), and Warren-Boulton, Baseman, and Woroch (1995) for analyses of the Microsoft consent decree. Judge Sporkin initially refused to enter the decree as final. See 1995 WL 59480 (D.D.C 1995). The D.C. Circuit reversed and instructed entry of the consent order as final. See Docket nos. 95-5037 and 95-5039, U.S. Court of Appeals (D.C. Cir., June 16, 1995).

provide incentives for the development of original software programs. If the weakening of copyright protection for computer software prevents original authors from adequately appropriating a return to their investments, erection of "barriers" through use of blanket licenses, long-term contracts, and restrictions on disclosure by independent software vendors may be a necessary condition for the protection of information not adequately protected by software of patent law. Indeed, the use of restrictive nondisclosure agreements may be a prerequisite to the successful protection of information under trade secrecy law. A decree that prevents use and/or enforcement of such contractual restrictions under these circumstances may serve to eliminate the original software developer's only method of protecting his investment. This can reduce economic welfare by reducing incentives to produce original software.[47]

In contrast, the government characterized Microsoft's nondisclosure agreements with independent software developers (ISV) in the following way:[48] "[They] not only legitimately protect against the disclosure of confidential information to competing developers of operating systems but also discourage ISVs from developing their own competing systems and/or from developing applications for competing software systems."

That is, instead of viewing nondisclosure agreements as a way to reduce the negative externality caused by free riding and improve the level of competition, as well as the level of welfare, by stimulating the development of original software, they are instead characterized as "overly restrictive and anticompetitive" because they *prevent* free riding by ISVs and rival operating systems.

---

[47] While much of the *Microsoft* case centered around the supposedly anticompetitive effect of contractual restrictions on imitation operating systems (shown to be efficient in the model set out in the second section if such contracts limit free riding), these contracts can, separate from their function as a substitute for intellectual property protection, be defended on efficiency-enhancing transactions and information-cost grounds. The use of blanket or package licenses in other contexts have often been viewed as efficient contracts. For example, the use of blanket licenses by the performing-rights organizations, BMI and ASCAP, are viewed as an efficient mechanism that decreases the transactions costs of collecting royalties for the public performance of copyrighted works; see *BMI v. CBS*, 441 U.S. 1 (1979), Landes and Posner (1989: 358), Kobayashi and Yu (1995), and Kobayashi (1998). Likewise, see *United States v. Paramount Pictures, Inc.*, 334 U.S. 131 (1948) (block sales condemned), and the economic analysis of block sales (Kinney and Klein 1983; Stigler 1968; and Bernstein 1992). See also Marvel (1984) and Marvel and McCafferty (1984) suggesting the efficiency of resale price maintenance and exclusive territories, Klein and Saft (1985) suggesting the efficiency of tie-in sales and a movement toward a rational treatment of tie-ins. But see *Eastman Kodak v. Image Technical Services*, 112 S. Ct. 2072 (1992), and Klein (1993).

[48] *United States v. Microsoft*, 159 F.R.D. 318 (1995), 56 F.3d. 1448 (1995).

Less noticed at the time of the 1995 decree, the antibundling provisions contained in section IV(E)(I), which prohibited the tying of the sale of the operating system to the sale of other products, became the focus of later DoJ actions. In 1997 the DoJ sought to have Microsoft held in contempt for violating this section of the 1995 decree by tying Windows 95 and Microsoft's web browser, Internet Explorer (IE). Microsoft contended that it had not violated the decree, which explicitly allowed it to offer "integrated products." The district court held that Microsoft's practices did not constitute contempt. However, Judge Jackson held that further proceedings were required to determine if the decree had been violated. In addition, Judge Jackson, on his own motion, entered a preliminary injunction against conditioning the sale of Windows 95 with the Internet Explorer. In January 1998 the preliminary injunction was reversed by the D.C. Circuit, which held that, within the meaning of the decree, Windows 95 and IE were integrated products.

The DoJ, along with numerous states, also filed a separate but related monopolization case based on Microsoft's bundling of Windows 95/98 and the Internet Explorer, and on Microsoft's restrictive contracts with Internet service providers (ISP) and Internet content providers (ICP). The recent acquisition of Netscape by America Online, the largest ICP, illustrates the availability of a competitive counterstrategy to Microsoft's challenged contractual restrictions with ISP and ICP, and has been used by Microsoft as a basis for a Schumpeterian argument for why the current action will become irrelevant over the long run.

At the center of the government's antitying claim is a novel "predation of potential competition" theory. According to this theory, Microsoft, by controlling the browser market, is attempting to perpetuate a monopoly in the operating systems market.[49] If non-Microsoft browsers such as Netscape Navigator are not marginalized or otherwise controlled, they will inevitably spread the use of cross-platform languages such as "Java." If Java becomes widely disseminated, programmers would then find it more attractive to write Java-based programs, and Microsoft's operating system (OS) dominance would be threatened.

A necessary condition for this predation strategy to work is that Microsoft's browser, the Internet Explorer, cannot facilitate the dissemination of Java. Although Microsoft licenses Java, the version of Java contained in IE is a modified, Windows-specific, version that Sun Microsystems, Java's copyright holder, claims does not pass the compatibility tests set out as a condition of its license to Microsoft. In response

---

[49] See Lopatka and Page (1999). This novel theory is distinct from the standard monopoly leveraging theory of tying, or from standard predation theories in which future monopoly profits from the sale of browsers is the goal.

to this, Sun sued Microsoft for copyright infringement and unfair competition, and the district court entered a preliminary injunction that enjoined Microsoft from further distributing noncompatible versions of Java. This injunction was subsequently vacated by the Ninth Circuit Court of Appeals. Resolution of this private case in Sun's favor would de facto moot this portion of the DoJ's antitrust case against Microsoft.[50] Resolution in favor of Microsoft would highlight the inconsistency between the intellectual property laws and the DoJ's approach to antitrust law.

Without this novel theory, the tying case simply degenerates into a standard predation case (where Microsoft seeks future monopoly profits from a browser monopoly) or a standard leveraging case where the two products are sold in fixed proportions (Lopatka and Page 1999). The first seems implausible given that the source code for the rival Netscape browser has been released into the public domain, and the second is implausible as a matter of economics.[51] Thus, the public action against Microsoft relating to predation via tying seems unnecessary once the private intellectual property litigation is considered.

Although not part of the government's current case, some commentators have argued that Microsoft's Windows operating system has attained the status of an essential facility. One suggested remedy is that Microsoft should be required to predisclose the content of the application programming interfaces (APIs) to ISVs at the same time this confidential information is disclosed to Microsoft's application programmers. As the court noted in its decision in *Berkey Photo v. Eastman Kodak*, the "inherent uncertainties" associated with such a duty to disclose such confidential information "would have an inevitable chilling effect on innovation. They go far, we believe, towards explaining why no court has ever imposed the duty [to disclose] Berkey seeks to create here."[52]

While not part of the current *Microsoft* case, the essential facilities doctrine and mandated disclosure is at the center of the *Intergraph v. Intel* litigation.[53] In this case, Intel, in response to patent infringement claims by Intergraph, terminated its disclosure of confidential informa-

---

[50] The judge in the *Sun* case noted that the injunctive relief on the copyright infringement issue would eliminate the basis for the unfair competition claims. *Sun Microsystems v. Microsoft Corp.*, 21 F.Supp.2d 1109 (November 17, 1998), *vacated* 188 F.3d. 1115 (9th Cir. 1999).

[51] Other possibilities exist. One possibility is that the DoJ is using the antitrust laws to force Microsoft to satisfy those who demand the operating system unbundled from the browser. However, such a duty has been rejected in previous instances. See *BMI*.

[52] 603 F.2d 263 (1979).   [53] 3 F.Supp.2d 1255 (1998).

tion provided in existing license contract with Intergraph. Intergraph then added antitrust and state law contract claims to its lawsuit.

The Intel litigation starkly illustrates the perceived conflict between the intellectual property and antitrust laws (McGowan 1998). The district court held that Intel was an essential facility, had a duty to disclose confidential information, and entered a preliminary injunction requiring Intel to provide Intergraph with the confidential information covered by the terminated license contract. The district court also condemned Intel's own intellectual property suits as "retaliatory" and a restraint of trade. In doing so, this district court ignored the Supreme Court's holdings that define the "sham" litigation exception to antitrust immunity[54] and instead strikes at the ability of intellectual property owners to enforce their rights. The court instead condemns Intel's attempts to enforce their intellectual property rights, noting that "[a] monopolist cannot use the pretext of protecting intellectual property in order to violate the antitrust laws." This preliminary injunction was subsequently vacated by the Court of Appeals for the Federal Circuit.[55] Intel's conduct in the private case was also the basis for the Federal Trade Commission's (FTC) antitrust action against Intel (Papciak 1999). Given the litigation in the private antitrust case, it is unclear what marginal value is provided by the public antitrust case.

The DoJ's evaluation of horizontal mergers in software markets also provides an illustration of the use of an ex post analysis that minimizes intellectual property concerns.[56] In their evaluation of nonintellectual property horizontal mergers, the antitrust authorities have largely adopted the static approach and explicitly consider market structure and

[54] Those who petition government for redress are generally immune from antitrust liability, unless litigation "is a mere sham to cover . . . an attempt to interfere directly with the business relationships of a competitor. *Eastern R. Presidents Conference v. Noerr Motor Freight, Inc.*, 365 U.S. 127. In *Professional Real Estate v. Columbia Pictures*, 113 S.Ct. 1920 (1993), the Court held that litigation cannot be deprived of immunity as a sham unless it is objectively baseless. Whether this was the case in the present case was not addressed.

[55] 1999 WL 1000717 (November 5, 1999).

[56] As scholars of the theory of the firm have pointed out, contractual restrictions and mergers are simply alternative forms of contract. See Bittlingmayer (1982), Williamson (1985), and Klein, Crawford and Alchian (1978). Our analysis also would apply equally to Microsoft's use of blanket licenses with hardware manufacturers, challenged by the Antitrust Division as an anticompetitive practice, and Apple's long-standing use of vertical integration and proprietary operating systems. Certainly, the comparison between the treatment of Microsoft's relationship with independent hardware manufacturers, and the treatment of Apple, which, until recently, was completely vertically integrated into software and hardware, illustrates this point. Thus, concerns over the use-creation tradeoff should extend into the area of both horizontal and vertical mergers.

barriers to entry as a primary factor in determining the competitive conditions of an industry and in determining whether the proposed merger should be allowed under the federal antitrust laws.[57]

Similarly, the DoJ and the FTC have adopted specialized guidelines in evaluating licensing and other contractual arrangements between firms in intellectual property industries.[58] Like the analysis of mergers in nonintellectual property markets, the intellectual property guidelines find the potential for competitive harm depends on structural and static characteristics of the market such as concentration and barriers to entry into innovation markets.[59] While the introduction of the specialized intellectual property guidelines suggests an awareness that some special attention should be given to the use-creation tradeoff, nowhere in the set of examples that make up the guidelines are any indications that enforcement under these guidelines will do so in a serious fashion.

These market structure and innovation inquiries are often linked to Joseph Schumpeter. However, such analyses seem to stand Schumpeter's writing on its head. Indeed, Schumpeter explicitly rejected the static structuralist approach:

Economists who, ex-visu of a point of time, look for example at the behavior of an oligopolist industry – an industry which consists of a few big firms – and observe the well-known moves and countermoves within it that seem to aim at nothing but high prices are restrictions of output are making precisely [the mistaken hypothesis that there is a perennial lull].

One example of the federal antitrust agencies' reliance on the structural and static analysis is the acquisition of Ashton-Tate Corporation ("Ashton-Tate") by Borland International ("Borland"). The DoJ con-

---

[57] Typically, the analysis begins by calculating market shares and concentration indices in markets defined as "relevant." Based on these statistics, the agencies make a determination of whether the industry is concentrated and the extent to which the merger will increase the level of concentration. If the market is determined to be concentrated, the agencies consider whether entry by a new firm would be "timely, likely and sufficient" to counteract what they perceive would be anticompetitive effects of the proposed merger. If entry does not meet these criteria, or if the agencies believe that particular barriers to entry exist, it is likely they will oppose the merger or require the parties to restructure the transaction that would alleviate their concerns.

[58] See *Antitrust Guidelines for the Licensing of Intellectual Property*, issued by the U.S. Department of Justice and the Federal Trade Commission, April 6, 1995. The guidelines provide a nonexhaustive list of typical practices that could raise antitrust concerns, including licenses between horizontal competitors (5.1), resale price maintenance (5.2), tying (5.3), exclusive dealing (5.4), cross-licensing and pooling arrangements (5.5), grantbacks (5.6), and acquisition of intellectual property rights (5.7).

[59] Ibid., 4.1. See also Arrow (1962), Kamien and Schwartz (1982), Loury (1979), and Dasgupta and Stiglitz (1980). For a critique of the static market structure approach, see Demsetz (1969) and Nelson and Winter (1982).

cluded that the market for relational database management software systems (RDBMS), which included both Ashton-Tate's dBASE and Borland's Paradox, was concentrated, that the proposed merger would significantly increase the level of concentration, and that entry into the antitrust market was difficult and time consuming. Based on this analysis, the DoJ filed an antitrust complaint alleging that the acquisition would lessen competition in an antitrust market for RDBMS.

In both its competitive analysis of the industry and in the conditions included in the final judgment, the government took the position that the imitator firms, the producers of xBASE clone software, were important and valuable competitors in the market.

In evaluating the competitive effects likely to result from the acquisition, it was particularly relevant that several of the smaller competitors in the RDBMS software market offer compatibility with the dBASE standard by using some of the command names, menu command hierarchies, command languages and other features of the dBASE programming language. As a result, dBASE customers can switch to those products (known as "xBASE clones") at lower cost than to other products.

Subsequently, a consent was entered into whereby the government would allow the transaction to proceed if the parties agreed to certain conditions.[60] In the decree, the government required Borland to dismiss Ashton-Tate's copyright infringement claims against Fox Software Inc., the largest producer of the xBASE clone software, and enjoined Borland from asserting claims of copyright infringement related to the dBASE family of products.[61]

In effect, by eliminating the ability of the copyright holder to enforce its intellectual property rights, the DoJ's consent encourages imitation through the creation of an open standard and achieves the same result as the *Lotus v. Borland* case (Levinson 1996b). Through its endorsement of the imitators, the government clearly failed to consider the potential implications of its actions on the incentives of Ashton-Tate as well as other software firms for the future development of new products in the future. The government's intent was explicit: "the essence of this Final Judgment is prompt and certain remedial action to ensure that, ... Defendants' ability to exercise market power and restrain competition in the sale of relational database management system software is *not*

---

[60] See Final Judgement, *United States v. Borland International, Inc., and Ashton-Tate Corporation*, Civil Action no. C 91-3666 MHP (October 22, 1991).

[61] According to the DoJ, the dBASE family of programs had become an industry standard with other companies in the industry marketing "xBASE clone" imitation programs. Paradox was seen to be the major competitor of dBASE and the xBASE clones.

enhanced by an attempt to enforce claims to certain alleged intellectual property rights" (emphasis added).[62]

CONCLUSIONS

In a consistent framework, both the antitrust and intellectual property laws should point toward the same goal: the maximization of social welfare. The attainment of such a compatible goal suggests that both sets of laws should be harmonized to attain this common goal and come to a joint solution with respect to the use-creation tradeoff.

However, an examination of the state of antitrust and intellectual property right protection for software does not suggest movement toward the goal of maximizing welfare. There is little evidence that the antitrust enforcement agencies consider seriously the unique appropriability and free-riding problems facing intellectual property owners. As a result, the history of antitrust enforcement has been hostile to intellectual property contracting and intellectual property industries. Further, ex post competition arguments are now being used in support of weakening copyright protection. The outcome of this two-pronged attack is unlikely to yield a rational solution to the use-creation tradeoff.

APPENDIX

In this appendix, we set out the model and specific assumption used to generate the simulation results listed in Table 8.1. At the time the decision to invest in producing an original or imitation version of the source code, the profit functions for each type of inventor equal:

$$\Pi_O = [P(Q) - a_O]q_O - F_O \tag{1}$$

$$\Pi_I = [P(Q) - a_I]q_I - F_I, \tag{2}$$

where Q is the total quantity of software units produced and sold, and $P(Q)$ is the market demand function.

The first order conditions for profit maximization equal

$$[P(Q) - a_O] + q_O \, \partial P(Q)/\partial q_O = 0 \tag{3}$$

$$[P(Q) - a_I] + q_I \, \partial P(Q)/\partial q_I = 0. \tag{4}$$

Solving these equations for q_O and q_I yields the individual firms' reaction functions.

Under the further assumptions of linear market demand, we can derive the Cournot quantities and profits for each type of firm for a given period. Let there be N_O original and N_I imitation versions of the source code. Imposing symmetry restrictions across firms of the same type, and

---

[62] Final Judgement, *Borland.*

assuming that market demand $P(Q) = 1 - N_O q_O - N_I q_I$, the first-order conditions become

$$q_O = (1-(N_O-1)q_O - N_I q_I)/2 \qquad (5)$$

$$q_I = (1-N_O q_O -(N_I-1)q_I)/2. \qquad (6)$$

Solving for q_O in (5) and q_I in (6) yields the following reaction functions:

$$q_O = (1-a_O - N_I q_I)/(1+N_O) \qquad (7)$$

$$q_I = (1-a_I - N_O q_O)/(1+N_I). \qquad (8)$$

Simultaneously solving this system of equations yields the equilibrium Cournot quantities for each type of firm in any given period:

$$q_O{}^* = (1-a_O(1+N_I)+N_I a_I)/(1+N_I+N_O) \qquad (9)$$

$$q_I{}^* = (1-a_I(1+N_O)+N_O a_O)/(1+N_I+N_O). \qquad (10)$$

If we assume that the static per-period profits are collected in perpetuity, the present value of Cournot profits net of the costs of authorship or imitation equal

$$\Pi_O{}^* = [(1-a_O(1+N_I)+N_I a_I)/(1+N_I+N_O)]^2/r - F_O \qquad (11)$$

$$\Pi_I{}^* = [(1-a_I(1+N_O)+N_O a_O)/(1+N_I+N_O)]^2/r - F_I, \qquad (12)$$

where r is the appropriate discount rate. This assumption is made for expositional convenience and is not crucial to the analysis. Nor is the assumption that original and imitator versions of the software are sold in all periods crucial to the analysis. A more realistic assumption would be that the original inventor obtains a first-mover advantage, in which he and the other original inventors obtain higher profits for a short time period prior to the onset of imitation entry. It is sufficient to note at this point that the effect of a first-mover advantage is analytically identical to decreasing the difference between F_O and F_I. Thus, that inclusion of these considerations at this point in the analysis would unnecessarily complicate the analysis without changing the implications of the analysis.

The equilibrium market price is given by

$$P^*(Q^*) = 1 - N_O q_O{}^* - N_I q_I{}^*. \qquad (13)$$

The equilibrium present value of total welfare equals

$$TW^* = (1 - P^*(Q^*))(N_O q_O{}^* - N_I q_I{}^*)/2r + \Pi_O{}^* + \Pi_I{}^*. \qquad (14)$$

Whereas traditional antitrust models based on the Cournot model treat the number of firms as exogenously determined, the number of firms in our model is endogenously determined. Thus, our analysis now turns to the determination of the equilibrium number and distribution of firms. We assume that, given the existence of at least one version of the original source code, the marginal firm can choose to enter either with its own original version of the source code or with an imitation version of the source code. Thus, a distribution of firms (N_O^*, N_I^*) is an equilibrium if the following set of conditions are met. First, given the requirement that imitation versions cannot exist in the absence of at least one *original* version of the source code, the existence of an equilibrium requires that

$$N_O^* \geq 1. \tag{15}$$

Second, further entry by either an original or imitation firm cannot be profitable, that is,

$$\Pi_O(N_O^* + 1, N_I^*) < 0 \tag{16}$$

$$\Pi_I(N_O^*, N_I^* + 1) < 0. \tag{17}$$

Third, no existing firm of one type can make higher profits by changing its decision on whether to produce an original or imitation version, so that

$$\Pi_O(N_O^*, N_I^*) > \Pi_I(N_O^* - 1, N_I^* + 1) \tag{18}$$

$$\Pi_I(N_O^*, N_I^*) > \Pi_O(N_O^* + 1, N_I^* - 1). \tag{19}$$

Finally, all existing firms must expect that the present value of their investment in producing an original or imitation version of the software program must be profitable, so that

$$\Pi_O(N_O^*, N_I^*) > 0 \tag{20}$$

$$\Pi_I(N_O^*, N_I^*) > 0. \tag{21}$$

In order to generate the simulation results reported in Table 8.1, we made specific assumptions about the relationship between the level of copyright protection z and the cost of producing an original and imitation version of the source code. Absent copyright protection, the cost of imitation is assumed to be less than the cost of producing an original, that is, $F_O(0) > F_I(0)$. In addition, we assume that both $F_O(z)$ and $F_I(z)$ are assumed to be increasing in z, and that increases in z disproportionately affect the cost of imitation, that is, $F'_O(z) < F'_I(z)$.

Finally, we assume that the level of contractual restrictiveness affects the marginal costs of distributing software. We assume that $a_O(0) = a_I(0)$, and that $a'_O(k) < 0$ and $a'_I(k) > 0$. Specifically, we assume that

$$F_O(z) = .4 + .05z \tag{22}$$

$$F_I(z) = .1 + .10z \tag{23}$$

$$a_O(k) = .01 - .001k \tag{24}$$

$$a_I(0) = .01 + .01k. \tag{25}$$

REFERENCES

Arrow, Kenneth J. 1962. Economic Welfare and the Allocation of Resources for Invention. In R. R. Nelson, ed., *The Rate and Direction of Inventive Activity*, 609–26. Princeton: Princeton University Press.

Baird, Douglas G. 1983. Common Law Intellectual Property and the Legacy of *International News Service v. Associated Press*. *University of Chicago Law Review* 50: 411–29.

1984. Changing Technology and Unchanging Doctrine: *Sony Corporation v. Universal Studios, Inc. Supreme Court Review* 25: 237–53.

Bakos, Yannis, Erik Brynjolfsson, and Douglas Lichtman. 1999. Shared Information Goods. *Journal of Law and Economics* 42: 117–55.

Baumol, William J., and Janusz A. Ordover. 1985. Use of Antitrust to Subvert Competition. *Journal of Law and Economics* 28: 247–65.

Baxter, William. 1980. The Political Economy of Antitrust: Principal Paper by William Boxter. In R. D. Tollison, ed., *The Political Economy of Antitrust*, 3–49. Lexinton, MA: D. C. Heath.

Bernstein, Lisa. 1992. Opting Out of the Legal System: Extralegal Contractual Relations in the Diamond Industry. *Journal of Legal Studies* 21: 115–57.

Besen, Stanley M., and Shelia N. Kirby. 1989. Private Copying, Appropriability, and Optimal Copyright Royalties. *Journal of Law and Economics* 32: 255–80.

Bittlingmayer, George. 1982. Decreasing Average Cost and Competition: A New Look at the Addyston Pipe Case. *Journal of Law and Economics* 25: 201–29.

1988. Property Rights, Progress, and the Aircraft Patent Agreement. *Journal of Law and Economics* 31: 227–48.

Bowman, Ward S., Jr. 1973. *Patent and Antitrust Law: A Legal and Economic Appraisal*. Chicago: University of Chicago Press.

Dam, Kenneth W. 1994. The Economic Underpinnings of Patent Law. *Journal of Legal Studies* 23: 247–71.

1995. Some Economic Considerations in the Intellectual Property Protection of Software. *Journal of Legal Studies* 24: 321–77.

Dasgupta, Partha, and Joseph E. Stiglitz. 1980. Uncertainty, Industrial Structure and the Speed of R&D. *Bell Journal of Economics* 11: 1–28.

Demsetz, Harold. 1969. Information and Efficiency: Another Viewpoint. *Journal of Law and Economics* 12: 1–22.

1982. Barriers to Entry. *American Economic Review* 72: 47–57.

Easterbrook, Frank H. 1982. Insider Trading, Secret Agents, Evidentiary Privileges, and the Production of Information. *Supreme Court Review* 1981: 309–65.

Epstein, Richard A. 1992. *International News Service v. Associated Press*: Custom and Law as Sources of Property Rights in News. *Virginia Law Review* 78: 85-128.

Fisher, Franklin, John J. McGowan, and Joen E. Greenwood. 1983. *Folded, Spindled, and Mutilated: Economic Analysis of* U.S. vs. IBM. Cambridge, MA: MIT Press.

Friedman, David D., William M. Landes, and Richard A. Posner. 1991. Some Economics of Trade Secret Law. *Journal of Economic Perspectives* 5: 61–72.

Galler, Bernard A. 1995. *Software and Intellectual Property Protection: Copyright and Patent Issues for Computer and Legal Professionals.* Westport, CT: Quorum Books.

Gilbert, R. J., and D. M. G. Newbery. 1982. Preemptive Patenting and the Persistence of Monopoly. *American Economic Review* 72: 514–26.

Ginsburg, Jane C. 1997. Copyright, Common Law, and *Sui Generis* Protection of Databases in the United States and Abroad. *University of Cincinnati Law Review* 86: 151–76.

Hall, Christopher D. 1986. Patents, Licensing, and Antitrust. *Research in Law and Economics* 8: 59–86.

Hausman, Jerry A., and Jeffrey K. Mackie-Mason. 1988. Price Discrimination and Patent Policy. *Rand Journal of Economics* 19: 253–65.

Kamien, Morton I., and Nancy Schwartz. 1982. *Market Structure and Innovation.* Cambridge: Cambridge University Press.

Karjala, Dennis S. 1994. Misappropriation as a Third Intellectual Property Paradigm. *Columbia Law Review* 94: 2594–609.

Kinney, Roy W., and Benjamin Klein. 1983. The Economics of Block Booking. *Journal of Law and Economics* 26: 497–540.

Kitch, Edmund W. 1980. The Law and Economics of Rights in Valuable Information. *Journal of Legal Studies* 9: 683–723.

Klein, Benjamin. 1993. Market Power in Antitrust: Economic Analysis after *Kodak*. *Supreme Court Economic Review* 3: 43–92.

Klein, Benjamin, Robert G. Crawford, and Armen A. Alchian. 1978. Vertical Integration, Appropriable Rents, and the Competitive Contracting Process. *Journal of Law and Economics* 21: 297–326.

Klein, Benjamin, and Lester F. Saft. 1985. The Law and Economics of Franchise Tying Contracts. *Journal of Law and Economics* 28: 345–61.

Kobayashi, Bruce H. 1998. Performance Rights. In P. Newman, ed., *New Palgrave Dictionary of Economics and the Law*, 27–30. New York: Stockton Press.

Kobayashi, Bruce H., and Larry E. Ribstein. 1999. Uniformity, Choice of Law, and Software Sales. *George Mason Law Review* 8: 261–306.

Kobayashi, Bruce H., and Ben T. Yu. 1995. An Economic Analysis of Performance Rights: Some Implications of the Copyright Act of 1976. *Research in Law and Economics* 17: 237–70.

Krouse, Clement G. 1984. Brand Name as a Barrier to Entry: The ReaLemon Case. *Southern Economic Journal* 51: 495–502.

Kwoka, John E., Jr. 1979. The Effect of Market Share Distribution on Industry Performance. *Review of Economics and Statistics* 61: 101–9.

Landes, William M. 1992. Copyright Protection of Letters, Diaries, and Other Unpublished Works: An Economic Approach. *Journal of Legal Studies* 21: 79–113.

Landes, William M., and Richard A. Posner. 1989. An Economic Analysis of Copyright Law. *Journal of Legal Studies* 18: 325–63.

Lemley, Mark A. 1995. Intellectual Property and Shrinkwrap Licenses. *Southern California Law Review* 68: 1239–94.

1999. Beyond Preemption: The Law and Policy of Intellectual Property Licensing. *California Law Review* 87: 111–72.

Levinson, Robert J. 1996a. Efficiency Lost? The *Microsoft* Consent Decree. In A. Kleit and M. Coate, eds., *The Economics of the Antitrust Process*, 175–94. Boston: Kluwer.

1996b. Concerns Raised by Recent Software-Related Antitrust Cases. *Antitrust Bulletin* 41: 43–60.

Lichtman, Douglas Gary. 1997. The Economics of Innovation: Protecting Unpatentable Goods. *Minnesota Law Review* 81: 693–734.

Liebowitz, S. J. 1985. Copying and Indirect Appropriability: Photocopying of Journals. *Journal of Political Economy* 93: 945–57.

Liebowitz, S. J., and Stephen E. Margolis. 1990. The Fable of the Keys. *Journal of Law and Economics* 33: 1–26.

1994. Network Externality, an Uncommon Tragedy. *Journal of Economic Perspectives* 8: 133–50.

1995a. Path Dependence, Lock In, and History. *Journal of Law, Economics and Organization* 11: 205–26.

1995b. Are Network Externalities a New Source of Market Failure? *Research in Law and Economics* 17: 1–31.

1999. *Winners, Losers and Microsoft: Competition and Antitrust in High Technology*. Oakland, CA: Independent Institute.

Lopatka, John E., and William H. Page. 1999. Antitrust on Internet Time: Microsoft and the Law and Economics of Exclusion. *Supreme Court Economic Review* 7: 157–232.

Loury, Glenn C. 1979. Market Structure and Innovation. *Quarterly Journal of Economics* 93: 395–410.

Marvel, Howard P. 1984. Exclusive Dealing. *Journal of Law and Economics* 25: 1–25.

Marvel, Howard P., and Stephen McCafferty. 1982. Resale Price Maintenance and Quality Certification. *Rand Journal of Economics* 15: 246–359.

McGee, John S. 1966. Patent Exploitation: Some Economic and Legal Problems. *Journal of Law and Economics* 9: 135–62.

McGowan, David. 1998. Free Contracting, Fair Competition, and Article 2B: Some Reflections on Federal Competition Policy, Information Transactions, and "Aggressive Neutrality." *Berkeley Technology Law Journal* 13: 1173–1238.

1999. Networks and Intention in Antitrust and Intellectual Property. *Journal of Corporation Law* 24: 485–525.

Menell, Peter S. 1987. Tailoring Legal Protection for Computer Software. *Stanford Law Review* 39: 1329–72.

Merges, Robert P., Peter S. Menell, Mark A. Lemley, and Thomas M. Jorde. 1997. *Intellectual Property in the New Technological Age.* Aspen Law and Business.

Meurer, Michael J. 1997. Price Discrimination, Personal Use, and Piracy: Copyright Protection of Digital Works. *Buffalo Law Review* 45: 845–98.

Nelson, Richard R., and Sidney G. Winter. 1982. *An Evolutionary of Economic Change.* Cambridge, MA: Harvard University Press.

Nimmer, Raymond T. 1998. Breaking Barriers: The Relation between Contract and Intellectual Property Law. *Berkeley Technology Law Journal* 13: 827–90.

Nimmer, Raymond T., and Patricia A. Krauthaus. 1995. Software Copyright: Sliding Scales and Abstracted Expression. *Houston Law Review* 32: 317–83.

Paepke, C. Owen. 1987. An Economic Interpretation of the Misappropriation Doctrine: Common Law, Protection for Invention and Innovation. *High Technology Law Journal* 2: 55–89.

Palmer, John P. 1986. Copyright and Computer Software. *Research in Law and Economics* 8: 205–25.

Papciak, W. Greg. 1999. *Intergraph v. Intel Corporation. Berkeley Technology Law Journal* 14: 323–43.

Posner, Richard A. 1970. A Statistical Study of Antitrust Enforcement. *Journal of Law and Economics* 13: 365–419.

        1992. When Is Parody Fair Use? *Journal of Legal Studies* 21: 67–77.

Priest, George L. 1977. Cartels and Patent License Arrangements. *Journal of Law and Economics* 20: 309–77.

Salop, Steven C., and David T. Scheffman. 1987. Cost Raising Strategies. *Journal of Industrial Economics* 36: 19–34.

Schumpeter, Joseph A. 1942. *Capitalism, Socialism, and Democracy.* New York: Harper and Row.

Shapiro, Carl. 1989. Theories of Oligopoly Behavior. In R. Schmalensee and R. D. Willig, eds., *Handbook of Industrial Organization*, ch. 6. New York: Elsevier.

Stigler, George S. 1968. A Note on Block Booking. Reprinted in George S. Stigler, *The Organization of Industry*, 165–70. Chicago: University of Chicago Press.

Tirole, Jean. 1988. *The Theory of Industrial Organization.* Cambridge, MA: MIT Press.

von Weizsacker, C. C. 1980. A Welfare Analysis of Barriers to Entry. *Bell Journal of Economics* 11: 399–420.

Warren-Boulton, Frederick R., Kenneth C. Baseman, and Glenn A. Woroch. 1995. Economics of Intellectual Property Protection for Software: The Proper Role for Copyright. *Standard View* 3: 1–11.

Wiley, John Shepard, Jr. 1989. Bonito Boats: Uninformed by Mandatory Innovation Policy. *Supreme Court Review* 283–309.

Williamson, Oliver E. 1985. *The Economic Institutions of Capitalism.* New York: Free Press.

Willig, Robert D. Industrial Organization Theory, Merger Analysis, and Merger Guidelines. In C. Winston, ed., *Brookings Papers on Economic Activity: Microeconomics,* 281–312. Washington, DC: Brookings Institution.

Yu, Ben T. 1981. Potential Competition and Contracting in Innovation. *Journal of Law and Economics* 24: 215–38.

9

Conclusion

Dynamic competition research offers a plethora of new insights that could change antitrust policy and antitrust enforcement. However, it is not clear whether consistent application of dynamic insights would lead to greater or less antitrust activity. Some scholars see concepts like path dependence and unique corporate capabilities as additional sources of market imperfections that could be corrected by government action. Others view the potential for entrepreneurial innovation as a sign that monopolistic exploitation carries the seeds of its own demise; monopoly profits create attractive opportunities for alert firms who can dethrone the monopolist. For the former group, dynamic competition is something to be nurtured by careful intervention; for the latter group, dynamic competition means that unhampered markets are even more resilient than previously thought.

Before proceeding from research to policy, it would be helpful to clarify precisely what role dynamic considerations could take in antitrust proceedings. Is dynamic competition simply an additional factor that should be considered, along with more traditional static efficiency, or should analysis of dynamic competition completely displace static considerations? Here are some tentative thoughts on each option.

DYNAMIC COMPETITION AS AN ADDITIONAL FACTOR

If dynamic competition analysis supplements static efficiency analysis, the principal effect might be to create an additional "safe harbor" for firms that appear to have significant market power. Dynamic analysis would probably do little to alter antitrust decisions in markets that already appear competitive in a traditional, static sense, because the structure of such markets – the presence of numerous actual competitors or low barriers to entry – already makes antitrust action unlikely to improve consumer welfare. But as Table 9.1 shows, dynamic concerns give antitrust officials some additional categories of decisions.

Table 9.1. Dynamic Competition as a "Safe Harbor"

	Potential for Innovation	
	High	**Low**
Static Market Power		
High	No intervention	Intervene carefully
Low	No intervention	No intervention

Where substantial market power exists but the potential for innovation is high, there is a strong argument for refraining from antitrust action. The various "high-tech" industries, as well as telecommunications, may provide paradigmatic examples of this kind of situation. Some monopolistic exploitation may exist in the short run, but its existence virtually guarantees a substantial reward to the innovative entrepreneur who finds a way of rescuing consumers from the monopolist. Barriers to entry may be substantial, but potential competitors can innovate around them. Where a high degree of innovation is possible, natural market forces are likely to erode market power more surely and quickly than antitrust prosecution.

The decision is trickier in those markets where a high degree of market power may be accompanied by a low potential for innovation. Older industries like local gas and water distribution might be the best examples of this category. In these kinds of cases, innovation could be slow and marginal, if it comes at all, offering consumers little hope of a market-based solution to the monopoly problem. Antitrust action or regulation may offer a swifter and surer option.

Of course, borderline cases may require more complicated tradeoffs. For example, a dominant firm might possess a high degree of market power in an industry where there is modest potential for innovation. There is no guarantee that marketplace entrepreneurs would erode the monopoly more quickly than antitrust action. At the same time, antitrust action could subvert incentives for innovation by reducing the supernormal profits that successful innovators could expect in the future. Government action could thus stunt innovation by the dominant firm, as well as discourage potential competitors who would otherwise contest the dominant position. But failure to act could leave customers exposed to monopolistic exploitation for a long period of time.

DYNAMIC COMPETITION AS THE ONLY FACTOR

Another approach would dispense with static efficiency considerations entirely and base antitrust solely on dynamic competition. This approach represents a significant break from current practice, but it is worth considering if only to clarify our thinking about the nature and significance of dynamic competition.

An exclusively dynamic approach would not concern itself with preventing firms from exploiting conventionally defined market power. There are two reasons for this. First, in a dynamic market, a great deal of market power results from successful innovation. Supernormal profits are the reward that elicits innovative effort, and open-ended profit potential may be necessary to draw entrepreneurial attention to the most significant opportunities. Second, even if some market power could be curbed without reducing innovation, a principal reason for adopting an exclusively dynamic approach is the judgment that innovation and change contribute much more to human welfare than the elimination of conventional monopoly power. A decision to focus solely on dynamic competition implicitly assumes that the gains from elimination of static market power are relatively small. Under that assumption, the benefits of curbing static market power are unlikely to be worth the cost.

If static efficiency is no longer the Holy Grail of antitrust, what takes its place? In a dynamic world, the ideal public-policy goal would presumably be a rate and direction of innovative activity that maximizes consumer welfare. Given this goal, dynamic competition research simultaneously provides a degree of policy guidance and a degree of policy skepticism.

The policy guidance stems from the stylized fact that more and better innovation seems to occur when there are multiple sources of innovation. This generalization is consistent with evolutionary theory, which posits that evolution is the product of variation and selection. Multiple sources of innovation encourage variation, and the profit-and-loss system performs the job of selection. The type of monopoly that poses a threat to consumer welfare is a monopoly over the capability to innovate.

These simple insights offer policy guidance in several situations commonly faced by antitrust enforcers:

- Mergers threaten consumer welfare if they give the merged firms a monopoly over the capability to innovate in a given area. However, not even a merger to monopoly in a product market threatens dynamic competition if other firms possess innovative capabilities similar or superior to those of the monopolist.
- A dominant firm's actions can threaten dynamic competition if it monopolizes and restricts access to a critical resource that other firms need in order to innovate. The source of the dynamic problem is not the fact that the firm can earn monopoly rents but that it can

restrict access, and so the appropriate remedy should focus on ensuring access.

- A cartel may stunt innovation if it includes all firms with the capabilities necessary to innovate in a particular market, but there is little threat to dynamic competition if some firms with the requisite capabilities remain outside the cartel.

Such insights could guide a new generation of antitrust activism, but they also provide grounds for skepticism. Intellectually, dynamic competition makes antitrust enforcement even more difficult than it already was. Instead of simply defining product markets and hunting for evidence of market power, antitrust officials must assess which firms are capable of innovating in various areas. To avoid artificially restricting the breadth of the innovation market, officials must assess the innovative capabilities of firms that may not even compete with each other in a product market.

A skeptic would be justified in asking why and how enforcement officials would have the knowledge to make such assessments. The task is no longer one of collecting "objective" price and quantity data and computing demand elasticities, but the even less exact art of judging which firms are best equipped to succeed in future rounds of innovative competition. Antitrust officials offering such judgments would be perpetually subject to the damning query, If you're so smart, why aren't you rich? Indeed, in the absence of radical civil-service reform, the people with the best ability to assess firms' innovative capabilities will likely be bid away from government service by venture capital firms and Wall Street investment banks. In short, there is little reason to believe that antitrust officials can predict the future course of innovative activity any better than anyone else, and some reason to think they will do worse. While dynamic competition highlights some new antitrust problems, it also places roadblocks in the way of policy solutions.

For these reasons, dynamic competition research offers paradoxical contributions to antitrust practice. In some situations, it suggests that monopoly is less likely to be a problem than previously thought. But the research also highlights some new directions for antitrust enforcement – while simultaneously suggesting that officials should proceed with great humility and caution, if at all.

Index

269